Writing Is Hard: A Collection of Over 100 Essays
by Jim LaBate

Published by
Mohawk River Press
57 Carriage Road – P.O. Box 4095
Clifton Park, New York 12065
518-383-2254
www.MohawkRiverPress.com

If any teacher or educational institution wishes to make copies of one or more of these essays to use in a classroom for instructional purposes, that teacher or institution may do so by sending a check for $100 to Mohawk River Press, P.O. Box 4095, Clifton Park, NY 12065. That $100 fee allows the purchaser to make copies of essays for one academic year. If the purchaser decides to use the essays again in the future, that would require another $100 check for each academic year. Questions may be sent via e-mail to jimlabate@hotmail.com.

Photograph on the back cover by Anthony Salamone

Copyright (Text and Illustrations) © 2018 by Jim LaBate
First Printing 2018
Printed in the United States of America
Library of Congress Catalog Card Number: 2018902178
ISBN 9780966210033

10 9 8 7 6 5 4 3 2 1

This book is dedicated to everyone at Hudson Valley Community College in Troy, New York. I have been working there for over 25 years now, and everyone at HVCC has contributed to this book in some way. My students have always pushed me to make my ideas clearer and more concise. My fellow teachers and librarians have always been kind and considerate and generous with their time and suggestions when I pestered them with questions and requests for help. And the other employees on campus have always been helpful and encouraging, no matter what crazy idea or project I wanted to explore. I am sincerely grateful and blessed to have been placed in such a nurturing environment. Thank you.

Other Works by Jim LaBate

Let's Go, Gaels – A Novella

Mickey Mantle Day in Amsterdam – Another Novella

Things I Threw in the River: The Story of One Man's Life

My Teacher's Password – A Contemporary Novel

Popeye Cantfield – A Full-Length Play

To Writers Everywhere:

Have you ever read a writing and grammar textbook? Most likely, you haven't. Or if you have, you probably read it only because some teacher forced you. With that in mind, I wrote the following essays in an attempt to teach writing and grammar in a nontraditional and nonthreatening way.

These essays appeared initially in *The Hudsonian,* the student newspaper at Hudson Valley Community College in Troy, New York. As one of the writing specialists in The Writing and Research Center at HVCC, I have observed that many students are intimidated by formal textbooks that attempt to explain the entire writing process or to address all areas of punctuation, grammar, and usage. Thus, I tried to make these essays somewhat informal, and I purposely focused on only a small portion of the writing process or on one small part of the mechanics of writing.

My hope was that students might take a few moments to read the student newspaper, find the essay, and learn something that would stay with them for years. After publication in the newspaper, I reformatted the essays, and now, I use them as supplemental handouts for students who are struggling with commas or fragments or term papers or any other aspect of writing. As you read through the essays, I sure hope you find them a bit more interesting than your grammar textbook.

Table of Contents
Writing Is Hard: A Collection of Over 100 Essays

Chapter 4

The Writing Process

Chapter 5

The Key Parts of an Essay

Chapter 6

Ten Steps to Writing a Research Paper

Chapter 7

Six Essays on Proofreading

Chapter 8

Eight Articles on Plagiarism

Chapter 9

Literary Techniques

Chapter 10

Specific Writing Tasks

Chapter 11

Authors on Writing

Chapter 12

The Reading-Writing Connection

Chapter 13

Miscellaneous

Works Cited

Chapter 1
The Ten Commandments of Writing

1. Since Thou Art a Creative Writer, Thou Shalt Not Use Clichés

In the Bible's Old Testament, God speaks directly to Moses and gives him the Ten Commandments. Through the years, these commandments about honoring God and parents and avoiding mistakes such as lying, stealing, adultery, and murder, among others, have provided a basic code of human behavior for both believers and nonbelievers. Fortunately, a similar code exists for writers. The first commandment of writing follows.

Since Thou Art a Creative Writer, Thou Shalt Not Use Clichés.

A cliché is, basically, an overused phrase or expression such as, "I'm hungry as a horse," or "We'll cross that bridge when we come to it," or "They're selling like hotcakes." The first time you hear a cliché, you may think, "Wow, that's a neat little phrase," and you may be tempted to use it yourself. After you've heard the same phrase a few hundred times, however, you realize the phrase has

lost its vitality and its effectiveness. That's when you need to come up with a new way to express an old idea or, at the least, tweak the cliché just a bit to give it an added twist. After all, you don't want your words to sound like everyone else's words.

Imagine, for a second, the following scenario. You're a young man, and you've finally secured a date with the most beautiful girl on campus. When you pick her up, you notice that she has a fancy, new dress for the occasion and a new hairdo, and she looks even more beautiful than before. You look at her in amazement and say, "You are as pretty as a picture."

When you use a weak cliché like that, one of three things might happen: she will laugh at you, she will slap you, or she will ask you to leave. Obviously, then, you can avoid those unpleasant possibilities by being a bit more creative. You need to put as much effort and energy into the words of your compliment as she put into her preparation for that special first date.

You need to say something like, "You are more beautiful that the aurora borealis on a summer's night in the Canadian Rockies," or "You look like a cover model for *Mademoiselle* magazine." Whatever you come up with in that situation, you need to make sure that it's original.

For example, when I ask my Composition classes to rewrite the cliché "pretty as a picture," most students come up with some variation on one of the following two phrases: "pretty as a flower" or "pretty as a sunset." These two phrases are a little better than "pretty as a picture," but they're not much better. The similarity among the responses occurs because the first new phrase that pops into one person's head may also pop into someone else's head.

Thus, you may need to write down – and throw out – four or five new phrases before you come up with something that is unique and effective.

For instance, I had one student, a football fan, write the following line: "pretty as a Super Bowl touchdown pass from Tom Brady to Randy Moss." Another student – a fashionable, but frugal, young woman – wrote, "pretty as a 70% sale in the ladies' department at Macy's." These lines are effective because they are original and because they reveal something about the authors and what's important to them.

One of the funniest scenes in the 1988 baseball movie *Bull Durham* occurs when Crash Davis (Kevin Costner) teaches Nuke LaLoosh (Tim Robbins) how to use clichés. LaLoosh is a young pitcher who will freely say exactly what's on his mind. Davis, however, the veteran catcher, tells LaLoosh that as a professional athlete, it's usually better to use clichés to say nothing whatsoever. Professional athletes, after all, don't want to say anything that might give the opposition inside information or added motivation. As a writer, however, you need to take the opposite approach. You need to avoid clichés and definitely say something of value in your essays and your term papers.

2. *Thou Shalt Not Use General Words When Thou Can Be Specific*

In the Bible's Old Testament, God speaks directly to Moses and gives him the Ten Commandments. Fortunately, a similar code exists for writers. The second commandment of writing follows.

Thou Shalt Not Use General Words When Thou Can Be Specific.

Can you identify the problem in the following sentence? *"The boy and girl ran down the street and into the building."*

No, it's not a sentence fragment or a run-on sentence. The sentence has no spelling errors or punctuation mistakes either. Technically, in fact, the sentence is fine because it has a subject ("boy and girl") and a predicate ("ran") followed by two prepositional phrases ("down the street and into the building"). The problem with this sentence is that it has no life. This sentence has no passion or emotion or feeling. The sentence is lifeless because the writer has used no adjectives and has used a general verb rather than a

specific verb. Your writing may also be lifeless unless you concentrate on using specific adjectives and verbs.

Adjectives. Adjectives are used to describe nouns and pronouns. This particular sentence has four nouns: boy, girl, street, and building. Yet, the reader knows nothing about the nouns.

How old, for example, are the boy and the girl? What do they look like? What are they wearing? Why are they running? Where are they going?

As a writer, you can use specific adjectives to answer some of these questions. Consider this revision: *"The smiling, freckled-faced boy and the laughing, pony-tailed girl ran down the cobble-stoned street and into the refurbished building."* This revision is a little better than the original because the reader can visualize two young children playing in an old neighborhood that is apparently being restored.

Another revision might present a different picture altogether: *"The scarred and tattooed boy and the crying and disheveled girl ran down the dark street and into the abandoned building."* While the first revision portrays young children having fun, the second revision presents older individuals who may be in some kind of trouble. With just a few specific adjectives, the lifeless sentence could actually become the first line of an intriguing short story.

In addition to using adjectives, you can also use specific nouns rather than general nouns to give life to a sentence. For instance, you could use real people and real places in the sentence rather than the general nouns "boy, girl, street, and building." You might write the following: *"George Clooney and Julia Roberts ran down Broadway and into the Ed Sullivan Theater."*

Verbs. Verbs are action words or words that help to make a statement. Not all verbs are equal, however; some are more powerful than others. The verb "run," for instance, in the original sentence is an adequate general verb, but it's not very descriptive.

If a whole class of students were to line up on the football field, for example, and begin to run from one end zone to the other, a variety of running styles would be obvious. Some runners would "sprint," some would "jog," some would "lope," some would "gallop," and some would "fly."

Note, too, how certain verbs can set up metaphors (direct comparisons). When you write "runners gallop," you're comparing those runners to horses, and when you use the verb "fly," you're comparing those runners to birds or airplanes. These specific verbs are much more evocative and much more interesting than the general verb "run."

Going back to the original sentence, you might say the young boy and girl "skipped down the street" to create an air of playfulness. By contrast, you might say the older boy and girl "escaped down the street" to create a more sinister air.

As a writer, you want to draw readers into your stories and essays; you don't want to put them to sleep. So the next time you sit down to compose, instead of using general nouns, adjectives, and verbs, make sure you use strong, specific words to give life to your writing.

3. Remember to Keep Your Point of View Consistent

In the Bible's Old Testament, God speaks directly to Moses and gives him the Ten Commandments. Fortunately, a similar code exists for writers. The third commandment of writing follows.

Remember to Keep Your Point of View Consistent.

Consider the following sentence: "If you really want to learn how to write, a good writer should practice like I do."

Did you find that sentence confusing? You probably did because the sentence includes three different points of view rather than one consistent point of view. Under those circumstances, confusion is inevitable. As a writer, therefore, you want to make sure that you don't confuse your readers. Before you begin any writing task, you should decide upon your point of view, and you should stick to it.

Point of view is generally defined as the way in which you tell a story. The three general options are referred to as first person, second person, and third person. Here's an overview of each.

First Person. The first-person point of view is the one you use most often in normal conversation or in most autobiographical essays. When you get home at the end of the day, for instance, and you begin to tell others about your experiences, or you begin to write in your journal, you're using the first-person point of view. When you write in the first person, you will use the following pronouns: I and we, me and us, my and our, and mine and ours. Here's an example: "I got pulled over for speeding on my way to school. We all failed our quiz in math class. Then, my friends and I shared a pizza for lunch."

This point of view is appropriate whenever you are speaking or writing about your life. If an instructor asks you to introduce yourself in writing, or if you must describe an emotional moment that you will never forget, the first-person point of view is perfect.

Pulitzer Prize-winning author Russell Baker uses the first person in his essay called "Learning to Write." In this essay, Baker describes a turning point in his life when a high-school English teacher read Baker's essay aloud to the class: "I did my best to avoid showing pleasure, but what I was feeling was pure ecstasy at this startling demonstration that my words had the power to make people laugh. In the eleventh grade, at the eleventh hour, as it were, I had discovered a calling. It was the happiest moment of my entire school career" (188-89).

Second Person. Of the three points of view, the second person is used least often. However, that doesn't mean it's any less important. The second-person point of view is generally used when you want to teach someone how to do something (this essay is written in second person) or when you want to give directions to a specific location. With the second-person point of view, you will use the pronouns "you, your, and yours."

If you're having a party at your house, for instance, and you want to tell your friends how to get there, you might say or write the following: "You should drive north on 87, and get off at Exit 8. Then, you should turn left onto Crescent Road, and look for Lapp Road on your right. Turn right on Lapp, and go to the third house on the right."

With this point of view, you can sometimes leave out the pronoun "you" and go straight to the verbs because the word "you" is understood. You can see this in the last sentence in the example above: "Turn right on Lapp, and go to the third house on the right."

Author Garrison Keillor uses the second person in his teaching essay entitled "How to Write a Personal Letter": "Sit for a few minutes with the blank sheet of paper in front of you, and meditate on the person you will write to; let your friend come to mind until you can almost see her or him in the room with you. Remember the last time you saw each other and how your friend looked and what you said and what perhaps was unsaid between you, and when your friend becomes real to you, start to write" (226).

Third Person. You typically use the third-person point of view when you speak or write about others. When you write in the third person, you will use some of the following pronouns: he, she, it, they, him, her, them, his, her, its, and their. You might describe your instructor, for instance, in this way: "He's pretty tall, he wears glasses, his hair is gray, and his jokes are bad."

Generally speaking, you will use the third person in formal writing – such as term papers – or whenever you want to focus more on the subject of the essay and less on your own thoughts or opinions concerning the subject.

In his essay entitled "Grant and Lee: A Study in Contrasts," Civil War historian Bruce Catton uses the third person to describe generals Ulysses S. Grant and Robert E. Lee: "They were two strong men, these oddly different generals, and they represented the strengths of two conflicting currents that, through them, had come into final collision" (535).

Is it possible to state your personal opinion while writing in the third person? Yes. Just don't make the mistake of changing your point of view. After writing an entire essay in third person, for example, you might be tempted to switch to the first person in your conclusion and write, "I definitely think we should dredge the Hudson River." However, you should really stick with the third-person point of view by writing "The Hudson River should be dredged" or "The government should dredge the Hudson River."

Do the three points of view ever overlap? Yes, they do, especially when you're writing about yourself (first) and about others (third) or when you're trying to teach someone (second), but you're also drawing on your own experience (first) in the teaching process. When those overlaps occur, just make sure they do so because you want them to occur and not because you weren't paying attention to your point of view.

4. *Honor Your Readers with Appropriate Tone and Language*

In the Bible's Old Testament, God speaks directly to Moses and gives him the Ten Commandments. Fortunately, a similar code exists for writers. The fourth commandment of writing follows.

Honor Your Readers with Appropriate Tone and Language.

Did your high school sponsor dances for students? If so, you probably know that not all dances are the same. Some are simple, *informal*, Friday-night get-togethers. Others are somewhat special, *semiformal* parties. Still others are much more special and extremely *formal* affairs. Your college writing, generally speaking, falls into the same three categories: informal, semiformal, and formal.

Informal Writing. Informal writing is basically writing without rules. You don't have to worry too much about tone, language, spelling, grammar, and punctuation because your readers are more concerned with content than they are with correctness. In your personal life, informal writing is the type of writing you use to communicate with family members, friends, and neighbors. For instance, you might take a phone message for your sister, you might write directions to your house for a friend, or you might send an instant message or an e-mail to your significant other. As long as these people can understand your message, they probably won't worry too much about your tone, your language, your mechanics, or your point of view. Thus, anything goes.

While most of your college instructors will not want to see informal writing, some may allow it in certain circumstances. For example, some instructors may require you to keep a diary of your actions or a journal of your thoughts. Some instructors may ask you to write your reactions to a piece of literature. Some may even ask you to do some free writing or brainstorming to prepare you for another writing task. In these situations, the instructors are using the informal writing not to judge your ability to write but to get you to think about a topic for discussion or to move you closer to a more formal writing assignment.

Semiformal Writing. Semiformal writing is much more structured than informal writing, and most of your college writing will be semiformal. When you're writing for college instructors, you need to use a conversational tone, you need to spell your words correctly, you need to use correct punctuation, and you need to follow all grammar rules. This is especially true for all your English courses.

In addition, you should probably be a bit more creative with your language. Most instructors don't want you to use slang terms, street language, offensive words, or clichés (overused expressions). Instead, you may want to use a thesaurus to expand your vocabulary. For instance, rather than use a simple phrase like "he said," you may want to use a verb that is much more precise and provides a better description of the speaker's situation: he whispered, he grunted, he chattered, he argued, or he screamed. You may even want to use similes (comparisons using the words "like" or "as") and metaphors (direct comparisons) to give your writing more life and vitality.

Formal Writing. Typically, you will use formal writing for your college research papers. When you write a research paper, you must use a more polite tone and proper language, and you must use correct spelling, punctuation, and grammar. In addition, you must obey certain rules about contractions, names, and point of view.

In formal writing, you can't use contractions. So, instead of writing the contraction "can't," you must use the longer form of those words: "can not."

Regarding names, you should spell out a person's full name the first time you use it, and use only the last name in later references. Thus, if you're writing about Stephen King, after you mention his full name early in the paper, you always refer to him later as "King" and not "Stephen" or "Steve."

Finally, formal writing requires you to use the third-person point of view. That means you can't use the first-person pronouns (I, we, me, us, etc.) or the second-person pronouns (you and your). Some students struggle with this rule because they may want to conclude their papers with statements such as "I think abortion is wrong," or "You should vote in the presidential election." Fortunately, you can still express the same ideas by using the third-person point of view: "Abortion is wrong," and "All American citizens should vote in the presidential election."

Now that you understand the different types of writing, can you tell if this essay is informal, semiformal, or formal? Obviously, this essay can't be informal because the spelling, grammar, and punctuation are correct, and the language is proper. But, the essay can't be formal because it includes contractions, and it's written in the second-person point of view. Thus, this essay on informal, semiformal, and formal writing is semiformal.

5. *Thou Shalt Not Start a Sentence with the Words "It" or "There" Unless the Antecedent Is Clear, Appropriate, and Nearby*

In the Bible's Old Testament, God speaks directly to Moses and gives him the Ten Commandments. Fortunately, a similar code exists for writers. The fifth commandment of writing follows.

Thou Shalt Not Start a Sentence with the Words "It" or "There" Unless the Antecedent Is Clear, Appropriate, and Nearby.

There is nothing more annoying than an essay that begins with the word "there." It drives me crazy. It's really irritating, too, when students begin their essays with the word "it." There has to be a better way. Generally speaking, when you write, you should avoid using the words "there" and "it" as the first word of an essay, a paragraph, or a sentence.

Using "there" and "it" to begin an essay can be troublesome because those two words are used primarily as pronouns, words that take the place of nouns. (A noun is a person, place, thing, or idea.) Typically, "there" is used to refer to places or locations, and "it" is used to refer to objects or experiences. Here are some examples of the correct use of these pronouns.

"I grew up in Amsterdam. There, I played baseball, delivered newspapers, and fell in love with Noreen. I took Noreen to the Sophomore Soiree on my first date. It was a night to remember."

In the preceding paragraph, the word "there" refers to Amsterdam, and the word "it" refers to "my first date." The connections are clear because the noun "Amsterdam" directly precedes the pronoun "there," and the noun "date" directly precedes the pronoun "it." Unfortunately, when you use the pronouns "there" and "it" at the beginning of an essay, your reader has no previous nouns to refer to. These nouns that precede the pronouns are called "antecedents," and if your opening sentence does not have an antecedent, that sentence is not as strong or as clear as it could be.

For example, one student began his term paper in this way: *"There are four main arguments against legalized gambling."* Another student approached the same assignment with this sentence: *"It is almost impossible to win the Lottery."* Obviously, the first student is not using the pronoun "there" to refer to a place or a location, and the second student is not using the pronoun "it" to refer to an object but to an experience that has not yet been mentioned. Thus, these sentences could say the same things and be so much stronger if they were rewritten as follows: *"Four main arguments against legalized gambling stand out,"* and *"Winning the Lottery is almost impossible."*

Other mistakes involving the pronouns "there" and "it" generally have to do with the placement of the nouns that precede them. Look at the following sentence: *"I visited California and Kansas this summer, and the ocean views there were tremendous."* Obviously, this writer is referring to the ocean views in California, but that's not what the sentence says. The way the sentence is set up, the pronoun "there" refers back to the previous location: Kansas. Readers who are unfamiliar with American geography might assume incorrectly that Kansas has ocean views. The sentence should read as follows: *"I visited Kansas and California this summer, and the ocean views there were tremendous."*

Look at the next sentence for a similar error. *"I left my wallet in the library, and I haven't seen it since."* Most readers would understand that the writer lost his wallet, but technically speaking, either the library has disappeared or the writer hasn't returned to the library since he left his wallet there. Again, the way the sentence is set up, the pronoun "it" refers back to the previous noun: library. The sentence should read as follows: *"I haven't seen my wallet since I left it in the library."*

Finally, when you use the pronouns "there" and "it" in your sentences, you should also make sure that the nouns you're referring to are nearby. Consider this long sentence: *"I brought my guitar, my laptop, and my camera with me, and we visited numerous county fairs and craft shows during the summer months when the crowds were really big, and I think it was stolen in Idaho."* By the time you got to the end of the sentence, did you know what had been stolen? Most likely, you had to go back and re-read the sentence to determine that the pronoun "it" referred to the camera.

The sentence was written correctly, but if the reader has to re-read a portion of the sentence to figure out the correct meaning, the sentence is not as clear as it should be. In this case, the writer should have repeated the word "camera": *"I brought my guitar, my laptop, and my camera with me, and we visited numerous county fairs and craft shows during the summer months when the crowds were really big, and I think my camera was stolen in Idaho."*

In normal conversation, you probably use the pronouns "there" and "it" often at the beginning of your sentences, especially when you're surprised. For instance, you may say, *"There's a rat down there,"* or *"It's freezing outside."* When you're writing, however, you generally have more time to choose your words, and you may want to be more precise and less emotional: *"A rat is living in the basement,"* or *"The temperature is 10 degrees below zero."* So as you review your essays and term papers, ask yourself these three questions:

Do I really want to start my essay – or my paragraph or my sentence – with the pronouns "there" or "it"?

Do the pronouns "there" and "it" refer correctly to previously mentioned nouns?

Are the previously mentioned nouns nearby, so the reader will know exactly what I'm writing about without having to back up and re-read a particular sentence?

6. *Thou Shalt Not Use Personal Pronouns Unless the Meaning of the Sentence Is Clear*

In the Bible's Old Testament, God speaks directly to Moses and gives him the Ten Commandments. Fortunately, a similar code exists for writers. The sixth commandment of writing follows.

Thou Shalt Not Use Personal Pronouns Unless the Meaning of the Sentence Is Clear.

A personal pronoun is a word that refers to a person previously mentioned. For example, if you were writing an essay about singer Taylor Swift, you could write the following: "Taylor Swift was born on December 13, 1989, in Wyomissing, Pennsylvania, but Taylor Swift moved to Nashville, Tennessee, fourteen years later to follow Taylor Swift's dream of becoming a country singer."

Obviously, that sentence sounds silly because of the repetition of Swift's full name. Thus, to avoid the repetition and to simplify the sentence, you can use personal pronouns such as "she" and "her": "Taylor Swift was born on December 13, 1989, in Wyomissing, Pennsylvania, but she moved to Nashville, Tennessee,

fourteen years later to follow her dream of becoming a country singer."

The previous sentence is still clear because only one person is involved in the sentence. As soon as you add a second person, however, the possibility for confusion exists. Consider this sentence: "Tommy's dad said he couldn't go to the party."

At first glance, you might assume that Tommy can't go to the party because dads are generally in the position of saying whether a child can go to a party or not. In this example, though, notice that the pronoun "he" is closer to the noun "dad" than it is to the noun "Tommy." Thus, you have to assume that it's Tommy's dad who can't go to the party for some reason. If it were Tommy who couldn't attend, you should avoid using the pronoun "he" and write the following instead: "Tommy's dad said Tommy couldn't go to the party."

Another pronoun problem occurs if you use the pronoun prior to using the noun that it refers to. The noun that precedes the pronoun is called an "antecedent," and if your sentence does not have an antecedent, that sentence is not as clear as it should be.

For instance, consider the following sentence: "If you see her at the party, please tell Susie to call me." In this case the pronoun "her" precedes the noun "Susie." Thus, the reader or listener will be temporarily confused. Who is the person referred to as "her"? Sure, the reader or listener will know soon enough when "Susie" is mentioned specifically by name later in the sentence. However, that temporary confusion disappears if you use the noun before the pronoun: "If you see Susie at the party, please tell her to call me."

Finally, make sure you always include a noun to go along with your pronoun(s). Here's an example of a problem sentence: "They drive me crazy when they visit our house." In this sentence, the writer has used the pronoun "they" twice, but neither one refers to a specific noun, so the reader or listener doesn't know the identity of "They." To correct that sentence, you could write "My in-laws drive me crazy when they visit our house."

The original sentence is not too problematic when speaking because your listener could easily ask you, "Who drives you crazy?" However, if you use that same sentence in a written document, the reader will be lost or confused.

Thus, when using personal pronouns, you are always straddling a fine line between too few and too many. If you use too few pronouns, your sentences may sound wordy and redundant (like the original sentence about Taylor Swift above), but if you use too many, your writing may not be as clear and as precise as it should be.

7. *Thou Shalt Not Write Passive Sentences*

In the Bible's Old Testament, God speaks directly to Moses and gives him the Ten Commandments. Fortunately, a similar code exists for writers. The seventh commandment of writing follows.

Thou Shalt Not Write Passive Sentences.

The Philadelphia Phillies were defeated by the New York Yankees.

Is the previous sentence written correctly? Yes and no. On one hand, the sentence is correct grammatically because it has both a subject Phillies) and a predicate (were defeated). However, the sentence is not stylistically correct because it's written in the passive voice. In fact, when I wrote that sentence, my word processing program underlined the sentence in green and suggested that I change it to the following: "The New York Yankees defeated the Philadelphia Phillies."

Obviously, both sentences say the same thing, so does anyone really care about the structure of the sentence? Yes,

as a matter of fact. Millions of Yankee fans care. This triumph over the Phillies in 2009 was the Yankees' 27th World Series victory, and these fans would much rather see their beloved Yankees at the front of the sentence instead of the Phillies. In other words, they'd rather see the sentence written in the active voice than in the passive voice.

An active sentence puts the key performer of the sentence up front where he or she can stand out and really get credit for his or her actions. A passive sentence, however, puts the performer at the end of the sentence where he or she does not stand out as much. Look at the following two sentences; the first is active, and the second is passive:

Andy Pettitte struck out Ryan Howard.

Ryan Howard was struck out by Andy Pettitte.

Not only is the first sentence shorter, more direct and more powerful, but its structure also highlights the pitcher who caused the strike out rather than the batter who was struck out. Thus, as much as possible, you should strive to usc the active voice rather than the passive voice.

Is the passive voice ever acceptable? Yes, but only in certain situations. If you want to focus more on the action itself than on the person who performed the action, you may use the passive voice. For example, if you're hosting a party and you're waiting for the pizza to arrive, you probably don't care who delivers the pizza as long as it arrives on time. In that case, you might use the passive voice to say to your guests, *"The pizza was delivered"* rather than the active voice, *"The guy from Domino's delivered the pizza."*

You can also use the passive voice if you don't know who performed the action or if the identity of the performer is unimportant. Let's say you have to check an entire building to make sure all the lights are out. In that case, you might say to your supervisor,

"When I got to the third floor, the lights were already turned out."

Finally, you may want to use – or be required to use – the passive voice in certain scientific situations. If you're reporting on an experiment, for instance, and you want your actions to be viewed as purely objective, you may want to remove yourself from the report. So, instead of writing, *"I filled the beaker with water,"* you might write, *"The beaker was filled with water."* Regarding scientific assignments, you should always check with your instructors to see which voice or point of view they prefer.

So now that you understand the difference between active and passive sentences, you know that most writing should be in the active voice. Thus, the conclusion of this essay could say the following: *"Passive sentences should not be written by you."* Obviously, however, a better alternative follows: *"You should not write passive sentences."*

8. *Thou Shalt Not Add Long Suffixes to Create Even Longer Words*

In the Bible's Old Testament, God speaks directly to Moses and gives him the Ten Commandments. Fortunately, a similar code exists for writers. The eighth commandment of writing follows.

Thou Shalt Not Add Long Suffixes to Create Even Longer Words.

When you put your thoughts on paper, you probably use the first words that pop into your head. That's fine for a first draft. However, when you begin to revise, you should look carefully at each word, especially if you have a long word with a long suffix.

A suffix, as you may remember, is a word ending. One of the most common examples is the suffix "-er" which transforms the action verb "teach" into the noun "teacher" (one who teaches). The same suffix changes "build" to "builder"; "walk" to "walker"; and "fight" to fighter."

That simple two-letter and one-syllable suffix doesn't drastically affect your writing because the suffix "-er" merely changes a one-syllable word (such as "speak") into a two-syllable word ("speaker"). Adding longer suffixes to even longer words, however, can dilute the strength of your writing.

At the other end of the suffix rainbow is the five-letter and two-syllable suffix "-ation." This suffix can present problems because it changes a strong verb such as "recommend" into the weaker noun "recommendation." Similarly, "consider" becomes "consideration"; "consult" becomes "consultation"; and "inform" becomes "information."

Long suffixes, like "-ation," weaken your writing because they make your sentences longer, with more words and more syllables. For instance, the sentence *"I gave him a recommendation"* has five words and nine syllables. By contrast, the sentence *"I recommended him"* has only three words and six syllables. The shorter version is stronger and more direct.

Other long suffixes have these same negative effects.

-ment. *"Bill will take over management of the project."* You can save three words and five syllables if you simplify this sentence to *"Bill will manage the project."* When you turn a verb into a noun, you must then supply a verb or verb phrase, and, generally, the longer sentence isn't as good as the shorter version.

-ance. *"Please make sure you are in attendance for the meeting."* Using strong verbs is especially important when you are directing others. Strong verbs give your writing an air of authority and expertise. *"Please attend the meeting"* is so much better than the sentence at the beginning of this paragraph.

-sion. With words like "decide" and "conclude," you have to alter the spelling a bit before you can add the suffix "-sion." The effect, however, is still negative. You've turned strong verbs ("decide" and "conclude") into weaker and longer nouns ("decision" and "conclusion"), and your writing becomes less crisp.

Some people might say that saving a few words or syllables in a sentence isn't a big deal, but if you save them throughout your essay, your overall writing becomes tighter and clearer. Would you rather wear a blazer that has long sleeves and is too big in the shoulders, or would you prefer to wear a blazer that is perfectly tailored to your individual measurements? Naturally, you'll look better in the blazer that has the better fit, and an essay that is tightly written will look just as good.

In her essay entitled *On The Art of Fiction* (1920), American novelist Willa Cather wrote, "Art, it seems to me, should simplify" (7-8). Oftentimes, college students get themselves into trouble because they fail to simplify. They have the mistaken impression that they need to use long words and long sentences to impress their teachers. Don't fall into that trap. Don't turn your strong verbs into weak nouns, and don't write sentences that are unnecessarily long.

Yes, you could make a decision to use the organization of your thoughts for an explanation of your conclusion. However, both you and your readers will be much better off if you decide to organize your thoughts, explain yourself, and conclude.

9. *Thou Shalt Not Covet Another Writer's Style*

In the Bible's Old Testament, God speaks directly to Moses and gives him the Ten Commandments. Fortunately, a similar code exists for writers. The ninth commandment of writing follows.

Thou Shalt Not Covet Another Writer's Style.

A while back, a computer hacker tried to use my e-mail account to convince my friends to send him money. Fortunately, I found out about the attack quickly, and I was able to change my account password before anyone was ripped off. The details of that experience, however, also reinforced a lesson that I have often preached to my students: your writing style should be as distinctive as your fingerprints or your personality.

If you've read any of the previous articles in this series, or any of my essays for that matter, you are already aware of my writing style. Typically, I like to use a relaxed, conversational style. When possible, I also try to inject a bit of humor, and I often use personal stories to make my point. That style has become familiar to those who read

my work, and a friend's wife, Maria, actually alerted me to the e-mail scam. She realized something was wrong because although the e-mail message came from my account, the hacker wasn't using my style of writing.

The following is what the hacker wrote: "Sorry to bother you with this, I travel to Spain (Barcelona). To visit my ill cousin, She has a severe diabetes and extensive heart complications. she is undergoing testing to determine if she is eligible to receive a heart pump (L-VAD); she is in the final stages of congestive heart failure. If she passes the tests, surgery will be next. It would be open heart and very risky; but the benefits of the procedure would be life-changing and life-extending for someone in the last staes of congestive heart failure. I am deeply sorry for not writing or calling you before leaving, the news of her illness arrived to me as an emergency and that she needs family support to keep her going, I hope you understand my plight and pardon me. Left Ventricular Assist Device (L-VAD) is very expensive here in Spain, So I've decided to transfer her back for her to have the surgery implemented. Please I'm wondering if you could be of help to me. Please I need about 3,500 USD to make out all necessary arrangement; I'll gladly appreciate whatever amount you can assist with. I'll reimburse you at my return."

As soon as Maria read the message, she knew it wasn't mine. After all, she knows I'm an English teacher, and I would never use so many run-on sentences. She also told me the writing was too stiff and stilted, and she assumed the hacker was a foreigner who was using English as a second language. Thus, she called me immediately and let me know what was going on.

Obviously, the content of the e-mail (Emergency – Send me money) also would have been a red flag to many, but if the hacker had used my style of writing, he might have convinced someone to contact him.

In an essay entitled "How to Write with Style," American novelist Kurt Vonnegut Jr., writes, "The writing style which is most natural for you is bound to echo speech you heard when a child" (22). Then, Vonnegut adds, "I myself grew up in Indianapolis, Indiana, where common speech sounds like a band saw cutting galvanized tin and employs a vocabulary as ornamental as a monkey wrench" (22).

At the beginning of each semester, when I first begin to talk about having a distinctive style of writing, my Composition students seem skeptical. They assume their own writing is pretty much like that of their classmates. Since we use peer-writing groups every week, however, they gradually begin to catch on. In fact, by week fifteen, if a student forgets to put his or her name on the paper, a classmate will read it and typically say to the writer, "Even without your name, I knew it was yours."

Thus, when you are trying to develop your own unique writing style, you may want to recall the words of William Shakespeare in the story of *Hamlet*: "To thine own self be true" (219). In other words, don't mimic the words or style of another writer; instead, develop your own.

10. Thou Shalt Not Covet Another Writer's Ideas

In the Bible's Old Testament, God speaks directly to Moses and gives him the Ten Commandments. Fortunately, a similar code exists for writers. The tenth commandment of writing follows.

Thou Shalt Not Covet Another Writer's Ideas.

I can remember vividly the first time I became aware of the word "plagiarism." I was in junior high at the time, and I was reading an article in the sports' pages about a local athlete who had earned a scholarship to play basketball at a major university. Unfortunately for this particular athlete, the article stated that he would be unable to play during the upcoming semester not because he was injured physically but because he had injured his academic reputation and had been found guilty of plagiarism. I was stunned, and I knew at that precise moment that plagiarism must be a serious offense.

"So what is plagiarism?" I said to my English instructor when I went to school the next day.

"Plagiarism is a lot like stealing," she said, "but instead of stealing something solid like a wallet or a purse, you are stealing someone's ideas. You are pretending that those ideas are your own, and you are trying to get credit for them" ("Plagiarism," *The Newbury House Dictionary* 654). Then, like any good teacher, she took that opportunity to explain plagiarism in more detail to the entire class later that afternoon. Over 50 years later, obviously, that lesson still stays with me.

So does Hudson Valley Community College have a policy on plagiarism? Yes. According to the HVCC Plagiarism Policy, "A student is guilty of plagiarism any time s/he attempts to obtain academic credit by presenting someone else's ideas as her/his own without appropriately documenting the original source."

Most colleges today have a similar policy regarding plagiarism, but, interestingly enough, plagiarism hasn't always been considered such a serious offense. In the long ago past, for example, students and writers were actually encouraged to take the wisdom of their elders and predecessors, and no one was expected to cite their sources. According to Brian Hansen, author of "Combatting Plagiarism," the ancient Greeks called this "mimesis," or imitation, and the absence of citations "was grounded in the belief that knowledge of the human condition should be shared by everyone, not owned or hoarded. The notion of individual ownership was much less important than it is today" (782).

So when did ownership of ideas become so much more important? Hansen goes on to say that two factors contributed to the change in thinking; the invention of the printing press and the introduction of copyright laws "advanced the notion that individual authorship was good and that mimesis was bad" (784). Thomas Mallon agrees with this view. In his book entitled *Stolen Words: Forays into the Origins and Ravages of Plagiarism*, Mallon writes, "plagiarism didn't become a truly sore point with writers until they thought of writing as their trade" (3-4). Thus, as a student, you should be aware that plagiarism is not only a college issue that professors worry about but also a real world issue that involves professional writers and concerns everyone.

Unfortunately, since the invention of the printing press in 1440 spurred the ownership of creativity, another recent invention has threatened

to undermine the corresponding individual ownership of ideas. Hansen writes that "The advent of the Internet makes committing plagiarism easier than ever" (783). This is especially true for a generation of students who grew up with computers and for a while became accustomed to the free file sharing of music. In other words, some students assume that if it's on the Internet, it's free for the taking, and these students may simply "copy" text from the Internet and "paste" it into their term papers. That could be a problem.

The problem isn't necessarily the using of the information. After all, the Internet always has the most current information, and teachers definitely want you to have up-to-date information in your research. The problem occurs when you fail to cite the source of your information. Just as composers and musicians demanded to be compensated when their music was shared on the Internet, writers and researchers demand to be acknowledged and recognized for their work, and teachers expect their students to cite their sources.

So as you begin working on your term papers for this semester, make sure you take meticulous notes and document your sources properly. Then, you will, most likely, avoid the consequence of damaging your own academic reputation by being accused of plagiarism.

Chapter 2
Articles on Punctuation and Grammar

The Ten Basic Comma Rules

Hundreds of years ago, British playwright William Shakespeare came down from Mount Everest with two huge, stone tablets engraved with the ten basic rules about commas. Okay, that's not even close to being true, but just as Moses had his ten commandments to live by, writers have ten basic comma rules that they need to know if they want their writing to be clear and precise.

One. Commas are used to separate the parts of complete dates and addresses. This is probably the easiest rule of all because most people know that they need to separate the date from the year and the city from the state when they write about their birthdays or their homes. ("I was born on May 17, 1951. I grew up in Amsterdam, New York.")

Two. Commas are used to separate items in a list of three or more. If you have only two items – like "peanut butter and jelly" – you don't need a comma, but once you add a third item, you need commas. ("Please go to the store and buy peanut butter, jelly, and bread.") The comma before the word "and" is called the "serial comma" (for items in a series), and some people feel this comma is not necessary because the word "and" separates the second and third items. However, without that serial comma, a misreading of your sentence might occur, so most instructors will always insist on that comma before the word "and."

Three. Commas are used to separate the introductory part of a sentence from the main idea of the sentence. If you introduce your main idea with a short phrase, you should insert a comma after that phrase to tell the reader to pause before the main idea. ("After class, I will eat lunch.") A minor controversy exists regarding this rule as well. Some people feel the comma is not necessary after a short introductory phrase because the reader doesn't really need to pause after two words in a six-word sentence. Again, however, to avoid a possible misreading of the sentence, and also for the sake of consistency, your instructors will generally expect you to insert a comma after your introductory phrase, no matter how long or short it may be.

Four. Commas are used after a dependent phrase (one that can't stand on its own) at the beginning of a sentence but not if the dependent phrase occurs at the end of the sentence. The first half of this rule is obviously similar to the previous rule. ("If it rains, the game will be canceled.") The phrase "If it rains" is dependent because it does not express a complete thought, so you need to use a comma to separate that phrase from the main idea: "the game will be canceled." However, if you start with the main idea and end with the dependent phrase, you do not need the comma separating them. ("The game will be canceled if it rains.")

Five. Commas are also used to show contrast, especially when you add a contradictory thought to your main idea by using the words "not, never, or unlike." Here are three examples: (1) "I like the Mets, not the Yankees." (2) "He is so cool, never anxious at all." (3) "Young children can be brutally honest, unlike most adults."

Six. Commas are used to separate two independent thoughts which are connected by one of the seven coordinating conjunctions: "for, and, nor, but, or, yet, so." Thus, you may want to remember the acronym "FANBOYS" to remember these coordinating conjunctions. ("I am tired, but I can't fall asleep.") However, once some students grasp the idea of connecting two independent thoughts, these students often put a comma before the word "because." ("I can't sleep, because I've had too much coffee.") In this example, though, the comma is unnecessary because the word "because" is not one of the FANBOYS. While exceptions to the general rule may exist, typically, you don't need a comma before the word "because."

Seven. Commas are used to introduce quotations, essentially to separate a direct quote from the rest of the sentence. (President John F. Kennedy said, "Ask not what your country can do for you – ask what you can do for your country.") The comma usually precedes the quoted words in most essays, but it often follows the quotation when a writer is using dialogue. ("I can't trust you," Pamela said to her boyfriend.)

Eight. Commas are used whenever you speak directly to someone, in your writing. ("Bill, may I borrow your car tonight?") This is called "direct address." Usually, the comma will follow the person's name, but the comma could precede the person's name if the name is used at the end of the sentence. ("Can you give me a ride, Bill?") Also, you would need two commas if the person's name is in the middle of the sentence. ("Please, Bill, give me a ride.")

Nine. Commas are used whenever you include "extra" information in your sentence. Extra information typically includes details that are not essential but helpful. For example, if you wrote "Tina complimented me at work today," that sentence is not quite as strong or as informative as "Tina, my boss, complimented me at work today." Other types of extra information include transitional words or phrases that make your writing easier to follow. ("First, Mr. Smith should be elected because he has budgetary experience, and, second, because he is, as you may be aware, committed to reducing the national deficit.")

Ten. Commas are used when you have more than one adjective to describe a noun. ("He drives a sleek, red Mustang.") These adjectives are called "coordinate" adjectives because they are working together to describe the Mustang; the Mustang is sleek and red. If your adjectives build on one another, however ("cumulative adjectives"), you do not need commas. ("He drives a bright red Mustang.") In the second example, the word "bright" describes "red" and red describes the Mustang.

Typically, struggling writers use either too many commas or too few, and as a result, their sentences are often choppy or hard to follow. Now that you know the ten commandments of commas, however, you can write more clearly and more confidently. Who knows? You may become the next William Shakespeare.

Joe Comma and the FANBOYS – Coming Soon to a Class Near You

Do you mean to tell me you've never heard of Joe Comma and the FANBOYS? Why they've been around longer than Tom Petty and the Heartbreakers. They're more popular than Gladys Knight and the Pips. And they're much more useful than Country Joe and the Fish. In fact, if you become a big fan of Joe Comma and the FANBOYS, you may be surprised at what happens to your grades this semester.

Joe Comma and the FANBOYS have been around for about 1,500 years, ever since people began writing and punctuating in English. No, they're not a musical group. FANBOYS is an acronym to help you remember the seven coordinating conjunctions:

> For
> And
> Nor
> But
> Or
> Yet
> So

A coordinating conjunction is used to connect words, phrases, and clauses of equal weight. If you're connecting two items that are not complete thoughts, you don't need a comma before the coordinating conjunction, which in the following example is separating the lead singer from the rest of the group: "I enjoy the music of Country Joe and the Fish."

However, if you want to connect two complete thoughts, you do need a comma before the coordinating conjunction separating the first complete thought from the second: "I enjoy the music of Country Joe and the Fish, but I don't understand the fascination with Joe Comma and the FANBOYS."

When I present this rule in class, most students nod and say they understand. (Note, no comma is needed before the word "and" because "nod" and "say" are not complete thoughts.) When these same students turn in their papers, however, I find three common mistakes.

First, some students make the mistake of putting a comma before the word "because" in their sentences.

However, this comma is unnecessary because the word "because" is not one of the FANBOYS. While exceptions to the general rule may exist, typically, you don't need a comma before the word "because."

Secondly, some students also put a comma in the second half of a sentence that reads like this: "Jack and Jill went up the hill, and fetched a pail of water." Unfortunately, the comma after the word "hill" is incorrect because the phrase "fetched a pail of water" is not a complete thought by itself. That phrase is missing its subject: "Jack and Jill," or a pronoun such as "they." Thus, the sentence "Jack and Jill went up the hill, and they fetched a pail of water" does

need the comma, but that same sentence without the word "they" does not.

Finally, some students simply leave the comma out of their sentences so I have to put it in when I correct their papers. The previous sentence, for example, should have a comma before the word "so" because both halves of the sentence can stand alone as complete thoughts.

Naturally, this short essay can't cover everything you need to know about using commas correctly. However, if you can remember what the FANBOYS are and if you can remember to use commas before them when connecting two complete thought, you've mastered one aspect of commas that often causes problems for student writers.

Semicolons Are Awesome; You Should Use Them

My three favorite places in the world are Amsterdam, New York, London, and Paris.

If you were counting as you read that sentence, you probably noticed that I mentioned four cities even though I introduced my list with the phrase "My three favorite places." So, either I should change "three" to "four," or I should correct my punctuation; I should have used a semicolon.

The semicolon is located to the right of the letter "L" on your keyboard and is made up of a period above a comma. Generally, the comma alone tells the reader to pause, and the period alone tells the reader to stop. The semicolon is the perfect combination of the two because the semicolon is more than a pause but less than a stop. Let's call the semicolon a temporary halt. Typically, semicolons are used in two situations: to break up a series of items that includes commas and to indicate a close relationship between two complete thoughts.

To break up a series of items that includes commas. In the sentence above about my three favorite places, I should have used a semicolon after "New York" because I was referring to the Amsterdam in upstate New York, my hometown, rather than the Amsterdam in Holland. Using a semicolon in that spot eliminates the confusion and makes it easier for readers to understand. "My three favorite places are Amsterdam, New York; London, and Paris."

Notice where the commas and the semicolons appear in the following example to tell readers where to pause and where to halt temporarily. "My favorite baseball teams are the 1961 Yankees with Whitey Ford, Mickey Mantle, and Roger Maris; the 1969 Mets with Tom Seaver, Cleon Jones, and Tommie Agee; and the 1986 Mets with Doc Gooden, Darryl Strawberry, and Gary Carter."

To indicate a close relationship between two complete thoughts. Generally, when you have a close relationship with someone, you want a special symbol to demonstrate that special relationship to the world.

The engagement ring that I gave to my wife, Barbara, for example, lets the world know that she and I have a special connection to each other. The semicolon serves the same purpose between two ideas. For example, to separate the following two thoughts, you could use either a period or a semicolon, but the difference in punctuation would also present a subtle difference in meaning.

"I met Maria recently. I'm in love." The period indicates a separation between the two thoughts and may mean the speaker is in love with someone other than Maria.

"I met Maria recently; I'm in love." The semicolon, however, lets the reader know for sure that the two thoughts are closely related and that the speaker is definitely in love with Maria.

If you wanted to make that connection even more obvious, you could also add a conjunctive adverb or a transitional phrase after the semicolon. Here are two examples, the first with a conjunctive adverb and the second with a transitional phrase.

"I met Maria recently; consequently, I'm in love."

"I met Maria recently; as result, I'm in love."

The chart below shows some other conjunctive adverbs and transitional phrases that you can use after semicolons to indicate certain relationships.

If you're like most student writers, you've probably never used semicolons before because you weren't sure how or where to use them. Now, however, you have no excuse. You know how to use semicolons; you should use them in your writing.

Relationship	Conjunctive Adverbs	Transitional Phrases
Addition	furthermore besides	in addition, the next
Comparison	similarly likewise	by comparison another similarity
Contrast	however otherwise	on the contrary on the other hand
Summary	therefore accordingly	after all in conclusion
Time	subsequently finally	in the beginning after a while
Emphasis	certainly	indeed without a doubt as a matter of fact

Colons Do Two Things:
They Separate, and They Indicate

If you've ever played a round of golf, you know that you have a full bag of clubs available to you. You have a driver and two or three woods to give you power when you tee off. You also have numerous irons to help you make those delicate approach shots to the green. You may even have a pitching wedge in case your ball ends up in the sand trap. Finally, of course, you must have a putter so you can gently tap your ball into the hole. Just as a golfer needs a full bag of clubs to score well, as a writer, you need to use a full bag of punctuation marks to communicate effectively.

From my experience as a Composition teacher, I've noticed that many student writers use only two basic punctuation marks: the comma and the period. Students often ignore other punctuation marks – such as the dash, the colon, and the semicolon – primarily because these students don't know how to use the punctuation marks correctly. As a result, students don't score as well on their essays as they might because they're not using all the tools available to them.

This essay will focus on the colon.

The colon looks like one period placed on top of another period and is located to the right of the letter "L" on your keyboard, on the same key as the semicolon. The colon can be used in various situations, but it is used primarily for two tasks: (1) to separate and (2) to indicate what will follow. The first use is pretty easy; the second is a bit more complicated.

Colons Separate

You may have already used a colon in one of the following situations:

• To separate the salutation of a business letter from the body of that letter

 – Dear Mr. Kennedy:

• To separate the hours from the minutes in a reference to time

 – I'll meet you at 9:30 a.m.

• To separate the chapter from the verse in a Bible reference

 – John 3:16.

• To separate the numbers in a proportion

– The ratio of students to teachers is 15:1.

• To separate a long quotation from the main text of your term paper

– Shakespeare's Hamlet once said the following: "To be or not to be; that is the question . . . ."

Colons Indicate What Will Follow

A colon is also used to indicate that something will follow, and usually that something is a list. For example, "I enjoy the music of three musicians: Bob Dylan, Billy Joel, and Bruce Springsteen."

Note that you must have a complete independent clause before the colon. Thus, you shouldn't write, "My three favorite musicians are: Bob Dylan, Billy Joel, and Bruce Springsteen." The colon in this example is not necessary because the phrase "My three favorite musicians are" is not a complete independent clause. Generally speaking, the colon follows phrases like "as follows" or "include the following."

In other situations, however, you may want to use a colon not for a list of items but to emphasize one item or one idea.

"When you come to class, make sure you bring one thing with you: your brain."

"I want you to always remember one thing: I love you."

Finally, you may also use a colon between independent ideas when the first idea introduces a subject and arouses the reader's curiosity, and the second idea illustrates the subject and satisfies the reader's curiosity. For example, Joe Namath – the Hall of Fame quarterback for the New York Jets – is well known for the line, "I can't wait until tomorrow: I get better looking every day."

Believe it or not, your writing will get better every day if you're willing to use all the punctuation marks that are available to you. After all, limiting yourself is like playing a round of golf with only one or two clubs. A better way to score well – both on the golf course and on your essays – is to use all the tools and to use them correctly.

The 800-Word Dash to Better Punctuation

Tony: Have you ever thought about using dashes in your writing?

Frank: Wh — Wh — What did you say?

Tony: Have you ever thought about using dashes in your writing?

Frank: I don't give a — about writing.

Tony: Well, you should. You're smart — smart enough to use proper punctuation.

Frank: I hate —

Tony: Don't tell me what you hate.

Are you one of those people, like Frank in the conversation above, who hates punctuation and couldn't care less about writing? I doubt it. If you were, you wouldn't have read this far already. Since you obviously do care about writing and punctuation, perhaps you'd like to know how to use the dash correctly in your essays and term papers.

The first thing you should know is that the dash is different from the hyphen. The hyphen is the key to the right of the number zero on most keyboards, and the hyphen is typically used in compound words such as mother-in-law or in phrases like "part-time student," where two or three words describe another word. The dash, however, is made up of two hyphens.

Generally speaking, the dash is used in eight different situations, and four of those situations are demonstrated in the conversation above. The dash is used in the first situation to demonstrate a stutter or hesitant speech as Frank struggles with his first line. Second, a dash is used to show where an offensive word has been omitted like when Frank expresses his thoughts about writing. A dash is also used to separate a repeated word like when Tony tries to emphasize how smart Frank really is. And, finally, a dash is used to show an interruption before a sentence is complete. At the end of the conversation above, for example, Tony interrupted Frank before Frank had a chance to say what he hated, so a dash is used to indicate that interruption.

Typically, these first four uses of the dash occur when authors are writing dialogue for plays or movies. Student writers, however, are more likely to use dashes for the following purposes: to

Define

Accentuate

Separate

Hinterrupt.

Define. Sometimes in your writing, you may want to use a word that may be unfamiliar to your readers. If that should happen, you should also include the definition of that word within a pair of dashes. Here's an example: "As your instructor, I'd like to accentuate — highlight — your accomplishments."

Accentuate. At other times, you may want to highlight someone's accomplishments or special characteristics when you write about that person: "William Kennedy — the Pulitzer Prize-winning author — will be on campus next week." Obviously, too, you can use dashes in a similar way to accentuate information pertaining to places, things, or ideas in addition to people.

Separate. Can you name the starting five for the New York Knicks when they last won the Championship in 1973? If so, you may want to include those names between dashes when you write about that team or whenever you want to separate the individual parts from the whole unit: "The starting five for the 1973 Knicks — Willis Reed, Walt Frazier, Dave DeBusschere, Bill Bradley, and Earl Monroe — are all in the Basketball Hall of Fame."

Hinterrupt. Obviously, I'm misspelling the word "interrupt" here to make this acronym work and to make it easier for you to remember when to use dashes. This last use may occur when you want to lead your reader in one direction and, then, jolt the reader with a surprise or a twist or an added emphasis: "I think you will like — no, I'm sure you will adore — my cousin from Schenectady."

As you read through the last four examples, you probably noticed that I always put the dashes and the information between them in the middle of the sentence. Do you always have to do it that way? No. You can put a single dash at the beginning or end of a sentence. Here are two examples:

"Moe, Larry, and Curly — these Three Stooges are my role models."

"I'll never forget my first date with Barbara — or my last."

Here are three final points to keep in mind regarding dashes. Yes, you may use parentheses in the same way that dashes are used, but remember that parentheses tend to de-emphasize your information while dashes make it stand out. Second, you should be able to remove the dashes and the information between them from your sentences and still have complete thoughts. And, finally, don't overuse dashes in your writing. Use dashes sparingly — for effect.

To Hyphenate or Not to Hyphenate?

When our two daughters, Maria and Katrina, were about nine and seven years old, they took gymnastics classes at a studio about 20 minutes from our home. As we drove to that studio each week, we passed a large, metal building with a sign out front that read "Hot Tub Factory." As we passed the sign, I always asked the girls the same question: "Is that a '*Hot,* Tub Factory?' or is it a '*Hot-Tub* Factory?'"

Initially, the girls showed some interest in the distinction between the two options, but after a while, they tired of my question and simply said, "Whatever." As a writing instructor, however, I am always evaluating not only the way in which people arrange words but also how they punctuate those words. In this case, the answer to my question centered on whether that sign needed a comma or a hyphen.

A hyphen is a short horizontal line that is located on the top row of the keyboard between the zero and the equal sign. Most people use the hyphen without even thinking when they write words such as "fifty-one"

or "mother-in-law." Generally, you need to hyphenate all the numbers from "twenty-one" to "ninety-nine" and all fractions such as "one-fourth" or "two-thirds." Similarly, some words such as "good-bye, vice-president, and merry-go-round" always require a hyphen, and you should check your dictionary if you're unsure whether a hyphen is needed.

In other cases, though, the use of a hyphen is determined by what you're trying to express. For instance, if you're using two or more words to describe an additional word, you typically need a hyphen. Let's say you're looking to buy a car that doesn't have much mileage on it; in that case, you might post a request for a "little-used car." If, however, you want to buy a small car, such as a Volkswagen, but you don't want the latest model, you need a comma rather than a hyphen to advertise for a "little, used car."

Looking at the two choices, you have to ask yourself if you need a hyphenated, compound adjective ("little-used" car) or two separate adjectives separated by a comma ("little, used" car). As you do so, though, keep in mind the following rules:

• If one of the words in question is the word "very" or an adverb that ends in the letters "-ly," you do not need a hyphen ("very old car" or "lightly used car").

• If your adjectives follow the noun, you also do not need a hyphen ("I'm seeking a car (noun) that is little used").

So returning to our original example, did the owners of that metal building need a hyphen on their sign out front? Most likely, they did. After all, if they were merely making tubs, why would they want to advertise to the world that the building was hot inside ("Hot, Tub Factory")? On the other hand, if they specialized in making hot tubs, the hyphen would make that piece of knowledge more obvious ("Hot-Tub Factory").

Or, as my two daughters might say, "Whatever."

Apostrophes: Needed Or Not Needed?

Recently, my wife and I attended a community festival, and we enjoyed sampling the food at the various booths. One vendor in particular caught my attention because his main sign read, "Tom's Snack Shack," and below that professional sign, Tom had handwritten the following small sign for that particular event: "Today were selling deep fried cookie's."

That big, printed sign and that small, scribbled sign both intrigued me because they highlighted the basic thought to keep in mind as you decide when to use apostrophes in your writing; sometimes, you need them, and sometimes, you don't.

Apostrophes Needed. Basically, you need apostrophes in only two situations: first, when you want to show possession, and, second, when you want to indicate that certain letters have been omitted when you use contractions.

1. **Possession**. The main sign at this food booth was punctuated properly, and that sign indicated clearly that the "Snack Shack" belonged to Tom. Most people use apostrophes correctly in similar situations when they want to indicate that one person owns one particular item: "Mary's car, Steve's dog, or Susie's computer." These same people, however, sometimes get confused when the owner's name ends in the letter "s" or when they want to indicate multiple owners of the item or items.

The owner's name ends in the letter "s." Most names don't end in the letter "s," but when they do, the regular possessive form sounds odd: "Jesus's mother" or "Moses's robe." As a result, many grammar handbooks suggest you omit the final "s" and simply write "Jesus' mother" or "Moses' robe."

Multiple owners. If Jack and Jill drive up a hill in one car, you would only need one apostrophe to write "Jack and Jill's car." However, if both of them drive their own cars up the hill, you would need two apostrophes to write "Jack's and Jill's cars." Also, the number of owners of one item will indicate where the apostrophe needs to be located. If one girl owns one car, you would write "the girl's car" (with the apostrophe before the letter "s"), but if two girls jointly own one car, you would write "the girls' car" (with the apostrophe after the letter "s").

Again, you could eliminate the letter "s" after the apostrophe because it would sound odd. Finally, if multiple girls own multiple cars, you would simply make the word "car" plural and write "the girls' cars."

2. Letters have been omitted.
As Tom was writing his last-minute sign, he decided to use the contraction "we're" instead of "we are." In his haste, unfortunately, he forgot to use the apostrophe to indicate the missing letter "a." Again, most people understand this rule, and they correctly punctuate the common contractions: "I'm" for "I am"; "You've" for "You have"; "They're" for "They are"; "it's" for "it is"; and "didn't" for "did not."

Apostrophes Not Needed.
Some people are tempted to add the apostrophe whenever they add the letter "s" to a singular word, but the apostrophe is never needed to indicate the plural form. Thus, Tom did not need to insert an apostrophe to highlight the fact that he had more than one cookie to sell.

In addition, the apostrophe is not needed when you are adding the letter "s" to a verb. Thus, the verbs in the following sentence do not need an apostrophe: "He *runs*, she *follows*, and it *looks* like love."

So, you're (apostrophe to indicate a contraction) probably wondering if I enjoyed Tom's (apostrophe to indicate possession) deep fried cookies. No, I did not. When Tom fries (no apostrophe with the verb) his cookies (no apostrophe with the plural form), they get too soft for my liking. And since no one likes writing that is punctuated improperly, when it comes to using apostrophes, make sure you take your time to determine when they are needed and when they are not needed.

Sentence Fragments. Not a Good Idea.

If you watch a lot of television or if you often read newspapers and magazines, you have been bombarded with sentence fragments. These fragments are typically used in television and print advertising – or in article headlines – because they are short, direct, catchy, and powerful. As a result, you may be tempted to use that same fragmented style in your writing. If you do, however, you should know that most college instructors don't want to see fragments and are more interested in complete sentences that are grammatically correct.

A sentence fragment is, essentially, a group of words that looks like a complete sentence but is really only part of a sentence. By contrast, a complete sentence is made up of three parts: (1) a noun (a person, a place, a thing, or an idea); (2) a verb (an action word or a word (or words) that helps to make a statement); and (3) an independent idea.

Here's an example: "Michael Phelps swims." In this particular sentence, "Michael Phelps" is the noun (a person), and "swims" is the verb (an action word). Here's a second example: "Athens is the capital of Greece." In this example, "Athens" is the noun (a place) and "is" is the verb that helps to make the statement an independent idea. If you find yourself writing fragments, you have probably made one of the following three mistakes.

Common Mistakes

1. You begin an introductory thought with a subordinate conjunction but never follow through with the main idea. A subordinate conjunction is a connecting word that introduces a clause to indicate time, place, reason, or contrast. The following list shows examples of these subordinate conjunctions and examples of fragments (in italics).

• Time: before, during, after, when, whenever, until, while. *Until the day I die.*

• Place: where, wherever. *Wherever you see water.*

• Reason: if, since, because, unless, in order to, so that. *In order to succeed in business.*

• Contrast: though, even though, although. *Even though math is difficult for me.*

In order to turn these fragments into complete sentences, all you have to do is replace the period with a comma, and, then, supply the main idea after the introductory phrase.

Until the day I die, I will always love you.

Wherever you see water, you should go swimming.

In order to succeed in business, you must learn from your mistakes.

Even though math is difficult for me, I am determined to succeed.

2. You use a gerund (a verb form ending in the letters "ing") without a helping word or phrase. Look at the following fragments:

Walking to the store.

Dancing in Denver.

At first glance, these two fragments look like complete sentences because they both have a noun ("store" in the first example and "Denver" in the second), and they both have a verb form (the action words "walking" and "dancing"). However, neither fragment has the third part mentioned in the second paragraph: an independent idea.

To turn these fragments into complete sentences, you can again replace the period with a comma, and, then, supply the main thought ("Walking to the store, I found a five-dollar bill"). Or, you can add words to make the initial phrase an independent idea ("Dancing in Denver is delightful"). A third option is to add another noun to the gerund ("Willie

was walking to the store" and "Dorothy is dancing in Denver"). In each case, the revisions are complete sentences because they contain all three key parts.

3. You end your sentences too soon. Some students make the mistake of inserting a period where it's not needed or where another punctuation mark should be used. For instance, they describe one action, end the sentence, and, then, add another action. Here's an example: "I built the shed. And painted it too." In this case, both actions should be included in the same sentence. Thus, the period after the word "shed" isn't necessary, and the letter "a" in the word "and" should be lower case: "I built the shed and painted it too."

Some students also insert a period before a list or an example. Look at the following two sentences: "He likes all sports. Baseball, basketball, football, and hockey. He has one favorite, though. Football." In this situation, you should really use colons rather than periods after the word "sports" and after the word "though." The first colon tells the reader that a list of sports will follow, and the second colon indicates that the name of the favorite sport will follow.

"He likes all sports: baseball, basketball, football, and hockey. He has one favorite, though: football."

So, if sentence fragments are such a serious writing offense, why does this article's headline include two fragments? As mentioned earlier, fragments are effective if you're trying to grab the reader's attention. Fragments may also be acceptable when you're trying to be creative or when you're writing informally in a brainstorming session or a journal. Overall, though, for most formal college writing assignments, sentence fragments are not a good idea.

Don't Let Your Sentences Run On and On and On

My Aunt Susan is one of the sweetest people I know. She's extremely loving, caring, and helpful. However, when she talks, she has a tendency to ramble on and on and on until her listeners can't take her any more, and they begin to tune her out. When you write, your readers will also begin to tune you out if your sentences run on and on and on. Here's what you can do to avoid run-on sentences.

First, you need to know the definition of a run-on sentence. Basically, a run-on sentence contains two complete thoughts that are not properly punctuated. Here's an example: "I have a term paper due next week I'll never finish it on time."

This run-on sentence, often called a fused sentence, has two complete thoughts and no punctuation between those thoughts. This example needs the proper punctuation after the word "week" to separate the first complete thought from the second.

When I point out this lack of punctuation, most students suggest a comma, but a comma alone doesn't solve the problem. Adding only a comma merely creates another type of run-on sentence called a "comma splice." To properly punctuate the sentence, you may choose one of the following five options. The proper choice will depend on how you view the relationship between the two thoughts.

1. Semicolon – "I have a term paper due next week; I'll never finish it on time."

First, you can fix the run-on sentence by placing a semicolon after the word "week." You should use the semicolon to let the reader know that a subtle connection exists between the two thoughts. A semicolon in this case creates a pensive feel, as if you're thinking about the possibility of meeting the term-paper deadline. After a bit of thought, however, you realize you're not going to make it.

2. Semicolon and a Conjunctive Adverb – "I have a term paper due next week; however, I'll never finish it on time."

A second option involves a semicolon and a conjunctive adverb. A conjunctive adverb serves as a stronger transition between the two thoughts. The conjunctive adverb "however" gives the reader a more obvious indication that you're not going to make the deadline even before your second thought expresses it. Other conjunctive adverbs include words such as "accordingly, consequently, incidentally, subsequently, and therefore," among others.

3. Comma and a Coordinating Conjunction – "I have a term paper due next week, but I'll never finish it on time."

The third option uses a comma and a coordinating conjunction. The seven coordinating conjunctions are "for, and, nor, but, or, yet, and so." (You may want to use the acronym "FANBOYS" to remember them.) Use this option if you want your thoughts to flow together in a more matter-of-fact way. This option lets your reader know that you've already thought about the task and the time remaining, and you've concluded that the two will never meet.

4. Period – "I have a term paper due next week. I'll never finish it on time."

The fourth option – the period – creates two distinct sentences. This is the proper punctuation if you want to be blunt and emphasize the separation between the two thoughts. In other words, you know there's no way in the world you'll ever finish the term paper on schedule.

5. Subordinating Conjunction at the beginning of the sentence and a Comma after the word "week" – "While I have a term paper due next week, I'll never finish it on time."

This final option uses the subordinating conjunction "while" to make the first idea less important than the second. In this case, you want to de-emphasize the fact that you have a term paper due and highlight that fact that you won't be able to complete it on schedule.

When reviewing your essays for run-on sentences, look for individual, complete thoughts. Then, make sure that you don't have two thoughts running together unless they have the proper punctuation.

My Aunt Susan is almost 70 years old now and has a lot of stories to tell most people don't want to hear those stories though they can't wait to get away from her once she gets going.

Can you see now why run-on sentences are so difficult to follow? Don't let your writing sound like a rambling monologue from Aunt Susan. Make sure you use proper punctuation to separate your ideas.

I Feel Bad
When You Speak or Write Badly

On Friday nights, after I've watched the local television news, I usually sit in my recliner and flip between the late-night talk shows. What drives me crazy about these shows, however, is the guests who don't know the difference between an adjective and an adverb.

For example, I once heard a famous singer say that his voice sounded "poorly." I also heard a Hollywood actress say she felt "badly" when her cat died. I even heard an ice-cream manufacturer say that he often had to sample his product to make sure that it tasted "well." In each case, the speakers used adverbs when they should have used adjectives.

The basic difference between an adjective and an adverb is that an adjective describes a noun (a person, a place, a thing, or an idea) while an adverb describes a verb (an action word), an adjective, or another adverb.

To see the difference between the two, look at the following sentences:

"The careful woman tiptoed through the tulips."

"The woman walked carefully through the rose bushes."

In the first sentence, the word "careful" is an adjective that describes the woman, and in the second sentence, the word "carefully" is an adverb that describes how the woman walked.

In these examples – and in most sentences – the adjectives precede the nouns they describe ("careful" precedes and describes "woman"), and the adverbs follow the words they describe ("carefully" follows and describes "walked"). In addition, adverbs often end in the letters "ly," but adjectives generally do not. Unfortunately, as a speaker or as a writer, you may get confused when you form sentences that don't follow the normal patterns. Fortunately, you can avoid mistakes if you remember these two rules.

1. If the verb you're using pertains to one of the five senses (I feel, I look, I sound, I smell, or it tastes), you should use an adjective instead of an adverb.

2. If the verb you're using refers to a state of being (I am, you were, he will be), then, you should also use an adjective

rather than an adverb. These verbs pertaining to the five senses and to a state of being are called "linking verbs" because they typically connect nouns and adjectives. Other linking verbs include words such as the following: seem, become, appear, and remain. Example: Adam seemed calm (not calmly), and Eve appeared nervous (not nervously).

Thus, the famous singer referred to earlier should have said his voice sounded "poor" (an adjective) rather than "poorly" (an adverb) because he was describing his voice, which is a noun. The Hollywood actress should have said she felt "bad" instead of "badly" because she was describing her emotional state and not her sense of touch. (If she really "felt badly," she might reach for her drink and spill it all over herself.) And the ice-cream manufacturer should have said his ice cream tasted "good"

or "delicious" or even "horrible." He, too, needed an adjective.

Actually, the ice-cream manufacturer was closer to being correct than either the singer or the actress because the word "well" can be used as both an adjective and an adverb. However, as an adjective, the word "well" usually refers to one's health. Thus, the ice-cream manufacturer was mistakenly describing the health of the ice cream when he wanted to describe the ice cream's taste.

Why do I care about the language problems of the rich and famous? I care because many students listen to these celebrities, assume the superstars know what they're talking about, and, then, repeat the mistakes as they speak and write. Don't fall into that trap. You now know the difference between an adjective and an adverb. And if you forget, just remember the title of this article.

Eight-Word Sentence, Using All Eight Parts of Speech

"Good Morning Mr. Phelps, . . . Your mission, should you decide to accept it . . . As always, should you or any of your IM Force be caught or killed, the Secretary will disavow any knowledge of your actions . . . this tape will self-destruct in five seconds."

If you've ever watched *Mission Impossible*, either the old television show or one of the movies, you know that Mr. Phelps and the rest of the Impossible Mission Force usually accomplished the task, no matter how difficult or dangerous. However, I believe the following task is, indeed, impossible. Try to write an eight-word sentence using all eight parts of speech.

Obviously, before you attempt this task, you need to know the eight parts of speech and how they fit into a sentence, so here is a quick review.

Verb – A verb is either an action word or a word that helps to make a statement. For example, words such as "run, swim, dance, and fly" are all verbs that demonstrate action. At times, however, our sentences are not filled with action;

they merely make statements. For example, in the statement "The Jets are awesome," the verb is the word "are," and most verbs that help to make statements are connected to the verb form "to be": am, is, was, were, has been, have been, will be, etc.

Noun – A noun is a person, place, thing, or idea. The first three are relatively easy: "Joe" is a person, "Troy," is a place, and "computer" is a thing. The "idea" is more difficult to grasp because ideas are not tangible; they can't be touched or handled. Thus, subjects such as "love, peace, and democracy" are all ideas that are nouns.

Adjective – An adjective is a word that describes or modifies a noun. For instance, if we said "Big Joe lives in beautiful Troy with an old computer, the words "big, beautiful, and old" are adjectives that describe the nouns "Joe, Troy, and computer." Similarly, we could say "Joe was seeking a permanent peace," and "permanent" is the adjective modifying the noun "peace."

Pronoun – A pronoun is a word that takes the place of a noun. When writing about Joe, for instance, we wouldn't want to use his name every time because that would be monotonous. So, instead, we might use the pronouns "he" or "him" to refer to Joe. Other common personal pronouns include the following: "I, we, us, our, you, she, it, her, his, they, and their."

Adverb – An adverb is a word that can describe a verb, an adjective, or another adverb. Usually when people think of adverbs, they think of words that describe verbs and also end in the letters "-ly." When we write "Beautiful Mary dances smoothly," or "Big Joe runs quickly," for instance, the adverbs "smoothly" and "quickly" describe how Mary dances and how Joe runs.

However, adverbs can also describe the adjectives "beautiful" and "big" or the adverbs, "smoothly" and "quickly." We might write "Extremely beautiful Mary dances smoothly," or "Big Joe runs very quickly." In those cases, the words "extremely" and "very" are adverbs that describe the adjective "beautiful" and the adverb "quickly."

Conjunction – A conjunction is a connecting word that shows the relationship between words, phrases, or clauses. If we wrote "Mary and Joe love each other, but they will never get married," the conjunctions are the words "and" and "but." Other common conjunctions are "for, nor, or, yet, and so."

Preposition – A preposition is a word that connects a noun or pronoun to the rest of the sentence or shows the position of a noun or a pronoun. Using our previous example – "Big Joe lives in beautiful Troy with an old computer" – the prepositions in that sentence are "in" and "with." Those words tell the reader where Joe lives and connect the word "computer" to that same location. Other frequently used prepositions include the following: "over, under, around, through, to, and into."

Interjection – An interjection is a word, or a group of words, used to express a person's strong emotion, and interjections are usually followed by an exclamation point. Some familiar examples follow: "Wow! Holy cow! Yippee!" These words or phrases by themselves don't make up a complete sentence and are usually considered part of the sentence that follows: "Wow! The Jets beat the mighty Patriots recently."

As this essay ends, notice that the previous sentence includes eight words. However, the sentence does not include all eight parts of speech. So now that you know and understand all eight parts of speech, try to do the impossible: include all eight parts of speech in one eight-word sentence. If you succeed, please send your sentence to me at the following e-mail address: jimlabate@ hotmail.com. Please note, too, that this article will self-destruct in five seconds.

The Architecture of a Sentence: Diagramming Sentences

When I was in grade school during the early 1960s, we learned a skill that is not used very often today. We learned how to "diagram a sentence." If you've never heard that phrase before, diagramming basically allows you to see how the words of a sentence work together to express an idea. I call it the architecture of a sentence. And just as a blueprint can help an architect or an engineer construct a beautiful building, knowing how to a diagram a sentence can help you craft your ideas into essays that are clear and precise.

The basic structure of a sentence diagram is a horizontal line bisected by a vertical line, and you place the verb (the action word) to the right of the vertical line and the noun (the person, place, thing, or idea) to the left. The noun is called the Subject of the sentence, and the verb is called the Predicate. Thus, the simple sentence "Maggie dances" would look like this.

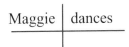

Since we typically use more than two words in our sentences, we also need to include adjectives and adverbs, the words that describe nouns and verbs. However, since the adjectives and adverbs are secondary to the main idea of the sentence, they are placed on slanted lines below the corresponding nouns and verbs. So, if we want to diagram the sentence "Beautiful Maggie dances gracefully," the picture would look like this.

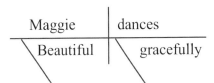

Two other parts of speech that may be present in a sentence are prepositions and conjunctions. Prepositions – words such as "to, from, over, and under" – often show where the action of a sentence takes place, and they connect these locations (nouns) to the rest of the sentence but on a level below the main horizontal line. The preposition and the noun that follows are called a prepositional phrase. Conjunctions, meanwhile, are joining words, and they are usually placed on a dotted line between the connected words. Three of the most common conjunctions are "and, but, and or." So, if we extend our sentence, we see that "Beautiful Maggie dances gracefully at home and at work."

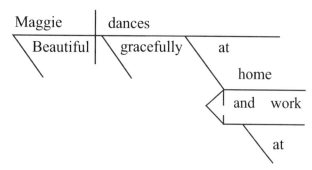

Finally, the last two parts of speech are pronouns and interjections. Pronouns are words like "I, you, he, she, it, we, and they," and these words take the place of nouns. As a result, pronouns usually show up on the horizontal lines that usually contain nouns. Similarly, interjections are also placed on horizontal lines, but these words – words that typically express strong emotion – are placed on a separate line above the sentence. Thus, the sentence "Wow! She dances gracefully" would be diagrammed in this way.

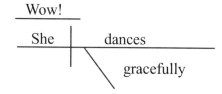

In addition to the previously mentioned Subject and Predicate, some sentences also have a Direct Object which receives the action of the verb. If we wrote "Maggie bought the gift," the Direct Object would be the word "gift" because it answers the question "What did Maggie buy?" On the diagram, the Direct Object is

added on the main horizontal line to the right of the verb, and a short vertical line separates the verb from the Direct Object. We could also add an Indirect Object which receives the noun of the Direct Object. In other words, it lets the reader know that Jim is the recipient of the gift, and the Indirect Object is placed on a horizontal line below the verb: "Maggie bought Jim the gift." (If that same sentence also included the preposition "for," then what was considered an Indirect Object would be converted to a prepositional phrase.)

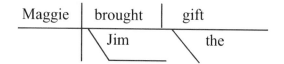

Finally, some sentences also have a Subject Complement. The Subject Complement is an adjective that describes the subject, and this adjective is placed to the right of the verb on the main horizontal line. This is a rare case where an adjective is placed on a horizontal line, but this adjective is placed after a short, slanted, vertical line that points back to the subject. Thus, "Maggie is beautiful "would be diagrammed in this way.

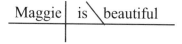

Obviously, this short article does not cover every possible combination of words, but the six diagrams provided should give you a basic picture of how the eight parts of speech are used in the most common formats. Thus, even if you never become an architect or an engineer, at least you now know how to construct a sentence properly.

Chapter 3
Types of Writing

Three Ways to Tell Your Story

Once upon a time, there was only one way to tell a story. The story began in the beginning where the readers (or listeners or viewers) met the main character. Then, a problem arose, and the main character had to figure out a solution. Finally, after the problem had been solved, everyone lived happily ever after. Obviously, this three-part summary is an oversimplification, but it does present one basic approach to telling a story while hinting at two others.

The traditional three-part story is called the chronological approach. With this approach, the narrator, or storyteller, describes the events in the order in which they occurred. Thus, a story that covered only one full day would begin in the morning, continue through the afternoon and early evening, and conclude at night.

A classic example of the chronological approach is evident in the movie *The Wizard of Oz*, based on the book by L. Frank Baum. When the tornado hits Kansas, Dorothy and Toto are transported to the Land of Oz.

There, the Munchkins tell Dorothy that in order to go home, she must follow the Yellow Brick Road to The Wizard who will help her. During her journey, of course, she meets The Scarecrow, The Tin Man, and The Cowardly Lion, and she helps all of them overcome their problems before she confronts The Wizard, clicks her heels, and discovers that "There is no place like home."

This method of telling a story works pretty well because most people are familiar with the format, they are accustomed to the pace, and they know what to expect: a character, a problem that involves some tension or excitement, and a solution that typically includes a moral or a lesson. The weakness of this method is that it's sometimes too predictable.

As a result, some storytellers go to the other extreme. Rather than begin at the beginning, they begin at the end. In other words, they start at the end, go back to the beginning, and, then, move forward. One of my favorite movies begins with the narrator saying, "All true stories end in death; this is a true story." Thus, the audience knows immediately that the main character will die. Still, I watch the movie intently, not because I am curious about the ending, but because I am curious about how the character will face his death and how others will react to it. This method is often used for well-known, true stories, and the movie I am referring to is *Brian's Song* (1971), the story of Brian Piccolo, a professional football player who died of cancer at age 27.

A variation on this start-at-the-end method of storytelling is common in police dramas like *CSI, Cold Case,* and *Without a Trace.* These shows usually begin with the crime scene of a murder, a kidnapping, or a theft. When the police arrive, their task is to determine who committed the crime; thus, the detectives work their way back to the beginning by interviewing those who owned the stolen property or who knew the victim. After a series of false leads or incorrect guesses, the detectives eventually find the criminal, determine the motivation, secure a confession, and send the offender off to jail. While this approach has the advantage of keeping the audience members guessing, it can backfire if the outcome becomes obvious too early or too easily.

The third approach to telling a story is to start in the middle. Some storytellers refer to this method as "in medias res," a Latin phrase for "in the middle of things." This may actually be the most entertaining method because the story begins at a point of high excitement and, if done well, maintains that high excitement throughout the work. The storyteller will go both forward and backward to advance the plot and fill in the details. Naturally, this balance between past and future is difficult to achieve, and the danger is that the audience may become lost or confused. However, when this method is successful, excited readers will often say, "I couldn't put the book down" while viewers might say, "I was on the edge of my seat the entire time."

In the 1993 movie *The Fugitive*, for example, prisoner Richard Kimble's story begins when he has an opportunity to escape from the authorities. The viewers don't know why Kimble is a prisoner or if he can really escape, but the chase is exciting. Then, the chase becomes even more exciting when the story flashes backward periodically to gradually reveal that Kimble is innocent. Thus, as the story moves forward, viewers run with Kimble as he tries to prove his innocence before he's locked up all over again.

At various times during your college career, your teachers may ask you to write a story. In your first Composition class, for instance, you may have to tell your own story. Later, in a history class, you may have to relate the story of an important leader, a major scientist, or a significant humanitarian. Even your science or business teachers may ask you to explain how a major discovery or event changed the way people lived or communicated. Obviously, your teachers' expectations and your subject matter may well determine the approach you use. If, however, you have the freedom to choose, try to at least consider all three options before you choose the one that will be the most interesting to your readers.

Showing Versus Telling in Your Writing

In ancient Israel, a king by the name of David was guilty of two terrible crimes. First, he committed adultery with a woman named Bathsheba, and, then, he had Bathsheba's husband, Uriah, murdered, so that Bathsheba would be free to marry David. When Nathan, a common man, found out what happened, he wanted to confront David, but Nathan knew it might be dangerous to accuse the king. Thus, Nathan did what more writers should consider doing. He didn't tell David what was wrong; instead, Nathan showed David what was wrong.

To illustrate his point, Nathan used a story about two men, one rich and one poor. The rich man had numerous sheep and cattle, but the poor man owned only one small lamb, a lamb he cherished and treated like his own child. Unfortunately, when the rich man needed a meal for a guest, the rich man stole the poor man's lamb, killed it, and served it to the guest. After David heard Nathan's story, David erupted in anger: "The man who did this deserves to die." At that point, of course, Nathan said that David was the rich man who had committed the crime against the poor man. When confronted in this way, David admitted his guilt (*The NIV Study Bible*: 2 Samuel 11-12).

Nathan's story was more effective than a direct accusation in this case because Nathan wanted David to think about what had occurred and come to his own conclusion. As a writer, you can involve your readers and let them draw their own conclusions in a similar way. For example, if you wanted to describe a tall person, you could tell what he looked like and write, "He was six feet, seven inches tall." That's an extremely precise description, and it might be appropriate for a police report. However, if you want to be a bit more creative and involve your readers, you might show the same information by writing the following: "He ducked as he entered the room." That second sentence is not as precise as the first but does require the readers to visualize the scene and figure out the approximate height of this character.

As another example, you could tell the reader about a certain female character and write, "She was drunk." Or you could show the readers certain details and let them figure the situation out for themselves. You could write the following: "She stumbled down the street, burped twice, and threw up in the gutter." Again, if you're simply providing information in your writing, you can tell, but if you really want to engage your reader, you should show.

Throughout history, various authors have used fables, parables, and allegories to make their points. One familiar fable involves the tortoise and the hare. Rather than simply tell readers that "perseverance is important," the anonymous writer of this fable showed how the slow but steady tortoise was able to beat the quick but lazy hare in a long race.

Similarly, Jesus Christ used various parables to teach His followers. He could have told them to build their lives on a firm foundation. Instead, Christ showed them how a house that is built on sand – instead of rock – will be washed away when the rains and storms of life hit.

Finally, George Orwell used an allegory in his novel *Animal Farm*. Obviously, Orwell could have written a political essay to tell his readers about the political process and how people secure power and hold onto it. However, he decided to write a story about animals to show his readers what happens when one party is overthrown, and another party takes over.

Does that mean you should always show rather than tell in your writing? No. What you should do is think seriously about the purpose of your writing and your intended audience. If you're writing an informative essay on a technical subject, you should probably tell your readers what they need to know. If, on the other hand, you're writing a more persuasive work about a personal experience or passion and you want to involve your readers as much as possible, you may want to show rather than tell.

Transport Your Readers with Sensory Details

When I was a 10-year-old boy, we used to spend our summers playing baseball on the asphalt playground of the Academy Street School in Amsterdam, New York. Afterwards, we would go to Mac's, the local soda shop, to order a 10-cent Coke with a squirt of cherry syrup.

Today, as a 65-year-old homeowner, I spend my summer Saturdays cutting the lawn and relaxing afterwards with a cool drink. Despite the disparity between baseball and mowing the grass and despite the 55-year difference, these two experiences are linked together in my mind because of the sensory details.

Sensory details are the specific words you use as a writer to describe sights, sounds, tastes, smells, and feelings. For instance, if you wanted to describe Mrs. Jones, your Composition I teacher, you might write the following: "She is short and thin, she has red hair, she wears long, flowery dresses, and she walks with a slight limp."

That particular description gives a pretty good picture of what this woman looks like, but the description isn't as strong as it could be because it refers to only one of the five senses: sight. Thus, the reader has only a visual impression of this woman. A much stronger description might go beyond the visual to include the following details: "Mrs. Jones smells much too sweet because of her excessive perfume and hairspray, and her high, nasally voice reminds me of long fingernails on a blackboard."

The preceding sentence describes what Mrs. Jones smells like when she enters the room and what she sounds like when she speaks. A description using two or three senses is much more memorable than a description using only one sense. Personally, I think that's why music videos are popular; some people like pictures with their music.

Does that mean you should try to include all five senses in your descriptions? No, not necessarily. Too many sensory details may overwhelm the reader. What you may want to do, instead, is move beyond the visual, the most common, to describe another sense. Or you may want to focus on a dominant impression, the overwhelming feeling you get when you meet someone, when you taste a certain food, or when you experience a special moment.

For example, in his essay "Once More to the Lake," E. B. White recalls a thunderstorm, and he compares its sounds to the sounds of a symphony: "Then the kettle drum, then the snare, then the bass drum and cymbals, then crackling light against the dark, and the gods grinning and licking their chops in the hills" (199).

In an essay entitled "Feel No Pain," John Seabrook describes the pain rowers feel when they compete in a race: "Marathon runners talk about hitting the wall at the twenty-third mile of the race. What rowers confront isn't a wall; it's a hole – an abyss of pain, which opens up in the second minute of the race. Large needles are being driven into your thigh muscles, while your forearms seem to be splitting."

The personal examples I referred to in my introduction relate to the senses of sound and taste. After I mow my lawn, I always use a long, pressure-treated stick of wood to clean out the grass that accumulates in the mower. When I finish, I toss the stick on the driveway and the "thud" of this wood hitting asphalt reminds me of my baseball days. When I hear that thud, I see my old buddies – Larry, Bernie, and Kenny – and I remember how they would toss their wooden bats on the asphalt after they struck out to end the inning.

Similarly, when my grass cutting is complete, I like to reward myself with a bottle of cold, Cherry Coke. The sweet taste of the cherry syrup in the soda reminds me of Mac's and the fountain cokes with a squirt of cherry that I drank back in 1961. Today, the Academy Street School and Mac's no longer exist, so I can never return physically to play ball or drink soda. However, these certain sensory details bring me back mentally to a time and a place I like to visit once in a while. If you use strong sensory details in your writing, you may be able to transport your readers in a similar way.

How to Write the Example Essay

A while back, I read an article by a movie reviewer, and he tried to convince his readers that the best movies ever made were produced in the 1970s. At first, I didn't think he was serious. After all, the movie industry has experienced major improvements in technology during the last 40-45 years. Could the movies from that long-ago era really compare favorably to modern films? Yes, according to this author, and he provided five strong examples to make his case. Naturally, you can also use examples to support your persuasive arguments, but as you write the example essay, you should try to answer the following three questions.

How many examples should you have? For an example essay, the magic number is usually a minimum of three. If you have only one example, your argument might not be very convincing because that one example could be an aberration – an out-of-the-ordinary event that rarely occurs. For instance, if you tried to argue that people in the Capital District of upstate New York should build tornado shelters because a tornado hit

Mechanicville a few years back, most people probably wouldn't take you seriously. Tornadoes rarely occur in this area, so building shelters locally just doesn't make sense financially.

In addition, even two examples might not make a strong argument. For instance, as a big fan of the New York Mets, I might argue that they are the best team in the history of baseball, and, as evidence, I would point to their two World Championships. However, most New York Yankees fans would laugh at me and point out that my two examples are weak because those championships occurred in 1969 and 1986. Thus, the Mets have only won twice during their history (their first year was 1962), and their last championship occurred in 1986. Meanwhile, the Yankees have won eight times during that span. In fact, numerous teams have won more than the Mets during that time (through 2016), and even more teams have won twice, just like the Mets. Obviously my two examples do not make for a strong argument in this case.

Naturally, a third example could help my argument significantly. If the Mets win this year, then, I could soften my position a bit and convincingly point out that the Mets have been one of the best teams since the Mets began playing in 1962. So, as you write your example essays, try to have a minimum of three examples, and don't go much beyond five or six examples. At that point, your readers should get the message.

What's the proper order for your examples? When you put together an outline of your essay or write a first draft, you might just list your examples in a random order, most likely the order in which you thought of those examples. However, that random order might not be appropriate for the final draft, so you should give some thought to the order which is most effective. For instance, some writers like to start with their strongest argument and work down to their weakest argument. Other writers like to take the opposite approach – start weak and end strong for a more powerful conclusion. Either approach can work; the important point is to have a thoughtful organization of ideas rather than a random order.

Also, you might want to consider a chronological order, offering examples in the order in which they occurred. Historians often use this approach. As an example, some financial analysts might theorize that the stock market performs better during the year after a Republican presidential candidate is elected. To support that argument, they could go back to 1980, and analyze the stock-market returns for the first year after each presidential election. Since the Republicans have won six of the last ten presidential elections (through 2016), these analysts would be able to compare those six examples to the four examples available after Democratic victories.

What kinds of details should you include for each example? You've probably heard the following cliché: "Don't compare apples and oranges." That piece of wisdom applies to your example essay, as well. When you offer various examples to support your point, you should make sure that the details for each example are somewhat consistent. Thus, if you were writing about movies and you mentioned that one movie sold a certain amount of tickets and won a certain amount of Academy Awards, you should mention those same categories for the other examples. If a particular movie didn't win any Academy Awards, you should at least acknowledge that fact before moving on to other significant details. In this way, your readers will feel as if they are receiving a consistent and objective analysis.

Speaking of movies, the author mentioned in the first paragraph chose the following: *Star Wars, The Godfather, Jaws, The Deer Hunter, and Rocky.* While I may not agree that these five movies are the best ever, I can at least respect the author's argument because he backed it up with strong examples. Make sure that you also provide your readers with strong examples when you are using this particular technique to make a persuasive point.

Use the Compare-and-Contrast Essay to Make a Decision

One of my favorite weekly magazines is *Sports Illustrated*, and one of my favorite features in that magazine is the summer issue called "Where Are They Now?" Typically, the magazine highlights former athletes whose pictures once appeared in the magazine, and each article explains what those athletes are doing now. This "before-and-after" essay is a classic example of comparison and contrast, and you may want to use this format in your own writing.

Fortunately, you have already had some experience with this compare-and-contrast technique. For example, every time you open your wallet or your purse to spend money, you're evaluating all the similar options available to you. For instance, if you decide to buy lunch or dinner today, you can choose from among the following nearby establishments: Wendy's, Pizza Hut, Deli and Brew, Market 32, Chinese Wok Buffet, Alexi's Diner, or Moscatiello's Italian Restaurant.

As you make your decision, you are using both comparison (finding similarities) and contrast (finding differences). If you have only a few dollars and a short amount of time, you may choose one of the fast-food options. If you have $20 to spend and plenty of free time, however, you might be willing to wait for food that is prepared specifically for you at a much slower pace – and a much higher price.

Obviously, then, you can choose from among numerous options, but your instructor may ask you to write this type of essay using only two options. Thus, you may want to compare Wendy's and Pizza Hut. Once you've narrowed the scope of your compare-and-contrast essay, you must then choose between the "block" method or the "alternating" method. With the block method, you devote the first half of your essay to one option and the second half to the second option. With the alternating method (sometimes called the point-by-point method), you go back and forth between your two options.

Using the block method, you might have a four-paragraph essay. The first paragraph introduces the subjects (Wendy's and Pizza Hut); the second paragraph focuses exclusively on Wendy's (the type of food, the prices, and the service); the third paragraph focuses exclusively on Pizza Hut (again discussing the same three elements: the type of food, the prices, and the service); and the fourth paragraph summarizes your thoughts in your conclusion. Thus, the body of the essay consists of two blocks: one on Wendy's and one on Pizza Hut.

With the alternating method, however, you'll probably have a five-paragraph essay. Paragraphs one and five, of course, will be your introduction and conclusion, but your three middle paragraphs will focus on the three key elements mentioned earlier. Paragraph two discusses the types of food in both restaurants, paragraph three discusses the prices, and paragraph four discusses the service. Thus, as you're discussing the key elements, you're also alternating between the two restaurants.

At the end of this compare-and-contrast essay, do you have to recommend either Wendy's or Pizza Hut? That may depend on your instructor's expectations. If your instructor wants a purely informative essay, you simply present the similarities and differences and let the reader decide. If your instructor wants a persuasive essay, though, you should definitely make a decision and recommend one based on the information you provided. Typically, professional reviewers choose the persuasive approach.

Obviously, the compare-and-contrast technique can be used in numerous situations. In fact, writers often use this technique to measure the strengths and weaknesses of political candidates, to analyze the pros and cons of a new product, or to determine the likely outcome of an athletic contest. Thus, whenever you are faced with a choice of two or more options, you may want to write a compare-and-contrast essay to clarify your thoughts and make a decision.

Block Method		**Alternating Method**	
1. Introduction		1. Introduction	
2. Wendy's	Type of Food Prices Service	2. Type of Food	Wendy's Pizza Hut
		3. Prices	Wendy's Pizza Hut
3. Pizza Hut	Type of Food Prices Service	4. Service	Wendy's Pizza Hut
4. Conclusion		5. Conclusion	

How to Write the How-To Essay

Have you ever become frustrated while trying to assemble a 10-speed bike? Have you ever tried to learn a computer program by reading the manual or following online instructions? Or have you ever gotten lost because the driving directions you received were vague or missing key details? If you answered "Yes" to any of the above questions, you definitely know the importance of "how-to" writing.

How-to writing is generally referred to as "process analysis." With a process-analysis essay, you're basically teaching the reader to perform a particular task. This type of writing has become extremely popular in recent years as evidenced by the large how-to sections in most bookstores and by the proliferation of how-to articles in many popular magazines. In fact, how-to books have become so popular that *The New York Times*, in addition to its best-seller lists for fiction and nonfiction, also has a best-seller list for how-to books. If your instructor ever asks you to write a process-analysis essay, you should remember these six key guidelines.

First, choose a familiar task or a task you understand well. If given a choice, you should always write about something you know and love. The mistake some students make is they choose a task solely because they think it will impress the teacher. However, if you choose a subject that you don't really understand, your writing may sound strained and stilted. When you write about your field of expertise, though, your passion and your knowledge will provide added strength and power to your essay.

Next, use the second-person point of view. The second-person point of view requires extensive use of the pronoun "you." Since you're teaching the reader to perform a particular task, you should write directly to the reader with phrases like the following: "You should use a thesaurus to find synonyms for overused words, but make sure you also use a dictionary to understand the exact meanings of those synonyms." Note, too, that you don't have to repeat the word "you" every time you give a direction. The word "you" is implied and understood in direct phrases such as, "Eat healthy foods, and get plenty of sleep."

Third, find strong, specific verbs and precise nouns and adjectives. One of the biggest problems readers have with how-to writing is that the directions are not as clear as they should be. If, for example, the directions say, "move the part to adjust the water temperature," those directions are not that effective. A much better directive might say, "turn the red dial at the bottom of the hot-water heater to the right to increase the maximum water temperature and to the left to decrease the minimum water temperature." The more details you can give your readers, the more likely you are to communicate effectively.

Then, simplify or explain unusual words and technical terms. If you saw a technical manual that told you to "find the URL and check the suffix," would you know what to do? You might be confused if you didn't already know that the "URL" is the abbreviation for "Uniform Resource Locator" which is an Internet address, and the suffix is the ending to that address (such as .com; .edu; .org; or .gov). Obviously, if you're writing to a specialized audience of experienced computer users, they may understand your computer language, but if you're writing to a general audience of computer beginners, you should simplify the terminology or add an appropriate explanation.

Fifth, use appropriate transitions. What's wrong with the following directions? "Turn off your computer,

but only after saving your file." Obviously, an impulsive reader might quickly turn off his or her computer before reading the part about saving one's file. Thus, as you move your reader through the process you're teaching, make sure to use appropriate transitions such as "first, second, and third" or "before, next, and after" among others. Regarding the previous example, a better phrasing of the directions follows: "First, save your file, and, next, turn off your computer."

Finally, test your essay on another reader. Once you've finished writing your essay, you should give it to a classmate or friend to see if he or she can follow what you've written. Sometimes, writers of how-to essays know their subject so well that they skip over certain steps or details, or they assume too much knowledge on the reader's part. If your reader struggles with your text in any way, that struggle may be a sign that the essay needs to be revised.

Two of the more popular sets of how-to books have titles such as *Computers for Dummies* or *The Complete Idiot's Guide to Computers*. While those titles may sound somewhat offensive to the readers, the titles do reflect a key concept behind how-to writing: Good how-to writing should be understandable to anyone, even those with very little knowledge of the task being explained.

Writing the "How" Essay

When most people think of writing a process essay, they think of the more common "how-to" essay. The how-to essay is popular because readers love to educate themselves on everyday subjects such as how to cook, how to invest in the stock market, or how to find the perfect mate. However, the less popular form of the process essay, often called the "how" essay, is also useful in various situations.

The how essay typically explains how something happens, but the writer doesn't expect the reader to perform the task being described. For example, every autumn, numerous magazine and newspaper stories explain how the leaves on the trees gradually change colors and eventually die and fall to the ground.

According to Robert Strauss, a writer for *The New York Times*, the green leaves of spring and summer actually contain other colors; these colors remain hidden, however, because the strong green pigment of the chlorophyll, which uses sunlight to produce food for the tree, overwhelms the lighter colors

until late summer. At that point, when the temperatures begin to drop, the cool weather breaks down the chlorophyll, and the previously hidden colors – red, orange, and yellow – emerge.

So now that you know the basics of how that process works, could you take a green leaf from a tree and make it change colors? No, you could not. Thus, while the how-to essay is usually practical and possible to replicate, the how essay is written primarily for informative and educational purposes. Sometimes, too, authors will use the "how" essay to argue a position in a persuasive essay.

For instance, if you were writing against the death penalty, you might write a how essay to describe in gory and graphic detail what happens when a convicted murderer is electrocuted. Your purpose in that essay is not to teach your reader how to electrocute someone but, rather, to demonstrate how barbaric and inhumane the process is to a fellow human being.

By contrast, if you feel the death penalty is appropriate for a convicted murderer, you might use the how essay to describe the steps the criminal went through as he planned the murder, prepared for the murder, and executed the victim, again with gory and graphic details. Your purpose in that essay is not to teach the reader how to murder but to convince the reader that the convicted murderer deserved to receive the death penalty as punishment.

One other major difference between the how-to and the how essay involves the point of view. With the how-to essay, you will generally use the second-person point of view which means using the pronouns "you" and "your" in what is, essentially, a personal, teaching essay: "When you cook pasta, your cooking time will depend on the thickness of your pasta."

By contrast, when you write the how essay, you should avoid the second-person point of view because you're writing a more formal essay, perhaps even a research paper. Thus, you should use the third-person point of view and use pronouns such as "he, she, it, and they": "When the NASA scientists prepared the spaceship to go to the moon, they knew they would need a rocket strong enough to escape the earth's atmosphere."

One final detail to consider when writing either the how-to or the how essay involves the use of transitional words and phrases. Since most process essays include at least three steps, try to use words such as "first, second, and third," or "initially, later, and finally," to move your reader through the essay. Note, too, that you should include the number of steps in your title and/or thesis, so your readers know ahead of time what to expect. For example, you might call your essay "The Four Stages of a Butterfly's Life," or you might write a thesis similar to the following: "The new skyscraper was completed in five gradual stages."

So how do you decide between the how-to or the how essay? As mentioned earlier, if your instructor expects a personal, teaching type of essay, you can use the how-to essay. The how-to is perfect when you possess a special skill that you want to pass along to your readers. If, however, your instructor expects a more formal essay or a research paper about a person, a place, an event, or a completed process, you should use the how essay.

Inquiring Minds Want to Know – Cause and Effect

A few years ago, the clothes dryer in our home died. Since this dryer is more than 30 years old, and we've already fixed it three or four times, my wife and I assumed we'd finally have to buy a new one. We began by talking to friends who had recently purchased a new dryer of their own, and, then, we looked at *Consumer Reports* for the best models and prices. Once I looked at the prices of a new dryer, however, I decided to take the dryer apart one more time to see if I could determine the cause of the machine's malfunction. And taking something apart is exactly what you should do whenever you're trying to write a cause-and-effect essay.

With a cause-and-effect essay, you're essentially investigating an event or a subject or a question. One way to approach this type of essay is to sketch a timeline. If, for instance, you're writing about a car accident where a driver hit a telephone pole, you use the accident itself as the center point for your timeline. Then, since the causes had to precede the accident, you should list them to the left, and since the effects follow, you should

list them to the right. Next, you will want to order these causes and effects.

Assume, for example, that the accident occurred because the driver was speeding, the road was wet, and a child had run in front of the car. After examining each cause, you might decide that the primary cause was the speeding, the secondary cause was the child in the road, and the third cause was the wet road.

Next, you examine the effects and determine the following order: when the driver swerved to avoid the child, the car slid on the wet surface and hit the pole, and (1) the accident knocked out power to the neighborhood; (2) the driver totaled his car; and (3) he broke both legs.

At this point, you could write a short, basic cause-and-effect essay and concentrate solely on the immediate causes and/or effects, those closely connected to the accident. However, you could also explore further to determine the remote causes and/ or effects, those much further removed from the accident itself.

For instance, you might ask why was the driver speeding in the first place? Perhaps he was drunk, and he was drinking because his girlfriend broke up with him, and she did so because he watched too much football on television. Similarly, at the other end of the timeline, you might find out that because this driver broke both legs, he lost his job and income, which caused him to default on all his loan payments, so he turned to crime, and after being arrested for Internet fraud, he ended up in jail. While this particular example is fabricated and bizarre, the reader can at least see the connections on the timeline between the implied idea that too much football viewing can lead to jail time.

This cause-and-effect style of writing is extremely common in history courses. Your instructor, for example, may ask you to explain the causes of the Civil War or the effects of the Emancipation Proclamation. In some cases, too, you may have to write about both causes and effects, or you may have to examine a chain of events. You may even be asked to explain hypothetical questions such as the following: If Hillary Clinton were elected president, what effect would her election have on the national debt?

Finally, your inquiring mind is probably still wondering what effect that broken dryer had on our household chores and our budget. Fortunately, that story has a happy ending. When I took the dryer apart, I discovered that the problem was merely a broken fan belt, a part that I could easily replace for only $25, and I could install it myself. Thus, the final effect on our budget wasn't nearly as bad as I thought it might be, and this fact caused me to celebrate by taking my wife out to dinner.

Car Accident – Driver Hit a Telephone Pole	
Causes	**Effects**
1. Speeding	1. Neighborhood Lost Power
2. Child in the Road	2. Car Totaled
3. Wet Road	3. Driver Broke Both Legs

Definition Cannot Stand Alone

Usually when I tell my students that they're going to write a definition essay, they look at me as if I've lost my mind. They think I'm crazy because definitions are typically one sentence long, and these students can't imagine writing an entire essay on the meaning of a single word or phrase. And, quite frankly, they shouldn't be expected to do so. Definition is a writing technique that cannot stand alone; definition essays must include at least one other technique to be truly effective. Choosing the correct technique, then, is paramount.

Narration – For example, when Frank Deford decided to write a book about cystic fibrosis, he could have written a scientific textbook to explain the disease's causes and effects and treatments. Instead, however, Deford used narration to tell the story of his daughter Alexandra who suffered and died from this horrible disease (*Alex, the Life of a Child*). Personalizing the disease in this way allowed Deford to reach readers who may not have read the technical cause-and-effect approach.

Description – When Margaret Atwood wrote an essay on pornography, she, too, chose an alternate approach. She began by implying that most people associate pornography with "naked bodies and sex," but she explained that pornography today, unfortunately, is much more dangerous. She describes vivid scenes of pornography that involve not just sex but also violence, torture, rape, and death (20-26).

Example – Gilbert Highet wrote an essay about the word "kitsch." He begins by explaining that the word could be applied to "anything that took a lot of trouble to make and is quite hideous" (472). Then, he brings that word to life by quoting examples from fiction, from poetry, and from drama. Interestingly, Highet feels, in effect, that this type of literature is so bad that it is entertaining: "It is horrible, but I enjoy it" (472).

Comparison/Contrast – In her essay entitled "The Tapestry of Friendship," Ellen Goodman focuses, obviously, on friendship, but she does so by pointing out the similarities and differences in friendship between males and females. She begins by explaining that males don't really have friends; they have "sidekicks" or "partners" or "buddies" (238). Then, she makes her point by making observations such as the following: "buddies bonded, but friends loved"; "buddies hang tough together; friends hang onto each other"; and "buddies seek approval, but friends seek acceptance" (238-239).

Division and Classification – Gloria Naylor tackled one of the most racially charged words in the English language when she wrote her essay entitled "Mommy, What Does 'Nigger' Mean?" Then, rather than define the word from a negative, white perspective, she defines the word from a positive, black perspective, and she does so using division and classification. She explains that the word has one meaning when used in the singular form and an entirely different meaning when used in the plural form. In addition, the word has another meaning altogether when used by a woman as a possessive adjective (108-111).

Process Analysis – Humorist Suzanne Britt Jordan defines the word "fun" in her essay "Fun. Oh Boy. Fun. You Could Die from It." Jordan doesn't, however, tell her readers "how to" have fun; rather, she explains "how" fun happens: "It is a mystery. It cannot be caught like a virus. It cannot be trapped like an animal . . . When fun comes in on little dancing feet, you probably won't be expecting it. In fact, I bet it comes when you're doing your duty, your job, or your work" (267).

Cause and Effect – The word "Spanglish" is obviously a combination of the words "Spanish" and "English," and Janice Castro defines Spanglish as "common linguistic currency whenever concentrations of Hispanic Americans are found in the United States" (259-60). In addition, she explains both the cause and the effect of Spanglish. She writes that this "free-form blend" of languages is popular because certain English words or phrases are easier to use and better reflect the faster pace of American life. As a result, "Spanglish has become a widely accepted conversational mode."

Persuasion – A persuasive essay that uses definition also needs one of the techniques mentioned earlier to be effective. For instance, Bruno Bettelheim's essay "The Holocaust" defines that word, but he argues that the standard definition is insufficient. Thus, he also uses description to say that what the Germans did to the Jews during World War II was the "most callous, most brutal, most horrid, most heinous mass murder" (435).

If you've ever browsed through a dictionary, you know that it contains much more than just definitions. A good dictionary also contains the proper pronunciation of the word, the various forms of the word, the part – or parts – of speech, the alternate meanings, the stories behind the words, examples of usage, and, in some cases, illustrations and photographs. These added features, of course, bring the words to life. Your definition essays will also pulsate with life if you go beyond the dictionary definition to explain the meaning of a word or phrase in new and interesting ways.

Divide and Conquer

When my daughters were in grade school, they loved to use colored strings to weave friendship bracelets for their classmates. Typically, though, Maria and Katrina became frustrated early in the process because their colored strings had become a tangled mess, and the girls had a hard time picking out the four colors they wanted to use for their bracelets. Inevitably, they'd come to me and ask, "Daddy, can you help us untangle this ball of string?" Though my daughters didn't realize it, they were really asking, "Daddy, can you show us how to write a division/classification essay?"

When you write a division/ classification essay, you're really doing the same thing my daughters were trying to do. You're trying to bring some kind of order or logic or organization to a subject that has not yet been categorized. In my daughters' case, for instance, they solved the tangled-string problem by, first, separating all the different colors and, then, storing them in different compartments in a new, plastic divider they purchased solely for that purpose. The separation and

organization by color made it so much easier for them to choose their colors and to begin work on their bracelets.

Other examples of division/ classification are all around you. In your backpack, for instance, you probably have a collection of folders to divide your academic paperwork by courses. At home, you probably have a plastic divider in your silverware drawer to separate the knives, forks, and spoons. And when you walk to the grocery store across the street, you'll see that the aisles are divided according to various categories such as fruits and vegetables, dairy products, baked goods, frozen foods, etc. All these forms of division/ classification make the world easier to deal with and comprehend.

Technically, the difference between division and classification is a small one. When you divide, you take one big, general subject – such as literature – and carve it up into smaller parts such as novels, plays, short stories, poems, and essays. When you classify, however, you, essentially, reverse the process. You can take various literary works – such as *Romeo and Juliet* by William Shakespeare and "The Raven" by Edgar Allen Poe – and slot them into the appropriate categories (play and poem) from the same five categories mentioned above. With division, you start with one and separate according to differences, but with classification, you start with many and organize according to similarities.

When you are asked to write a division essay, your teacher probably wants you to choose a single subject and divide it into three or four key categories. For instance, one student wrote about a football team, and he divided the team into three units: offensive players, defensive players, and special-teams' players (those who play during kickoffs, punts, field goals, and extra points). Another student wrote about the Beatles, and she wrote about each of this musical group's four members: John, Paul, George, and Ringo. One classic professional example is the book *On Death and Dying* by Elisabeth Kübler-Ross. In this particular work, Kübler-Ross divided the dying process into five distinct stages: (1) denial and isolation, (2) anger, (3) bargaining, (4) depression, and (5) acceptance.

When you are asked to write a classification essay, your teacher probably wants you to choose a series of items and organize them by some logical process. For instance, one student listed her ten favorite television programs and then divides them into four categories: soap operas, comedies, dramas, and reality shows. Another student looked at the racial makeup of the nine wards in his hometown and labeled them as primarily white, black, Hispanic, or mixed. Finally, author E. B. White wrote an essay entitled "The Three New Yorks." In this essay – from his 1949 book *Here Is New York* – White looks at the millions of New York City people and fits them all into three groups: those who were born in New York City and continue to live there, those who work in New York City but live somewhere else, and those who were born elsewhere but came to New York City to settle.

The hardest parts about writing the division/classification essay may be choosing the subject and, then, dividing or classifying the various categories and components. Once you've completed those tasks, however, make sure you also explain the purpose of your essay, and think about using definitions, examples, and comparison and contrast to show similarities and differences.

Types of Literature

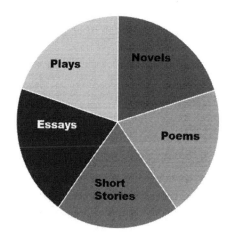

Persuasion Is All Around You

Writing a persuasive essay is at once the easiest and most difficult writing task of all. The persuasive essay is easy to write because you are surrounded by so many examples. For instance, most newspapers and news magazines include editorials that try to convince you to support a particular opinion, vote for a certain candidate, or take a particular action in your own life. In addition, those same newspapers and magazines are full of advertisements that are trying to persuade you to purchase various products or services. Finally, if you watch television, you are constantly bombarded by mini persuasive essays called commercials.

The difficult part, however, of writing a persuasive essay has to do with the approach. When you write a persuasive essay, you can't rely on persuasion alone; you must also choose one or more writing techniques to structure your argument. Generally, you will use one of the following eight techniques as your primary approach, and your choice will depend on what you're trying to accomplish.

Description – If you're trying to convince someone that a particular place is special, you may want to use description to vividly paint that particular setting: the sights, the sounds, the smells, etc. This technique is used often in autobiographical essays that describe the views from country homes, the sounds of city streets, or the smells of ethnic kitchens. You may even see this approach used in the promotional materials of four-year colleges as you consider your future educational options.

Narration – If you're trying to sell a product, a service, or an idea that has a long history of success and satisfied customers, you may want to use narration. For example, one local moving company tells the story of how the business began by shipping apples. Their key selling strategies are experience and great care for your valuable possessions. After all, if the company's employees can move apples without bruising them, those same employees can certainly transport your family treasures in the same way.

Examples – If I said that the best movies ever made came from the 1970s, you might think I'm crazy. After all, how can the cinematography of almost 40 years ago compete with today's technology? Yet, if I could provide you with three or four strong examples of classic films from that decade, I might be able to convince you. You, too, can use strong examples to support opinions that on the surface may appear hard to believe.

Compare and Contrast – With comparison, you point out similarities, and with contrast, you point out differences. This technique is useful when you are trying to choose between two (or more) options, whether they are political candidates, plans of action, or even choices of restaurants. As you use this technique, though, make sure you evaluate the same characteristics for each possible choice. For instance, if you're contrasting two products, you can't compare the cost, the features, and durability of one without also mentioning the cost, the features, and the durability of the other. *Consumer Reports* is a monthly magazine that uses this approach regularly to allow its readers to make educated decisions about their purchases.

Division and Classification – When you divide and classify, you're trying to bring order and organization to a topic that otherwise might appear disjointed and overwhelming. One modern example is *The Five Love Languages* by Gary Chapman. In this book, Chapman says, "there are five emotional love languages – five ways that people speak and understand emotional love" (15). Those languages include the following: "words of affirmation, quality time, receiving gifts, acts of service, and physical touch" (202). Chapman's main message is that for a successful relationship, each person needs to "identify and learn to speak" (16) the other person's primary love language.

Cause and Effect – This type of writing is used often in history courses when you're trying to explore the reasons why a certain event occurred, or you're trying to analyze the eventual consequences of that particular event. To write this type of essay,

you need a strong starting point or focus such as the attacks on the World Trade Center on September 11, 2001. To help you visualize this task, you might want to draw a timeline with the starting point in the center of your page; then, to the left, add the causes that preceded the event, and to the right, the effects that followed. For shorter assignments, you may want to focus solely on causes or effects, but if space permits, you may be able to cover both. Note, too, that you may want to argue that one cause or effect is more significant than the others, or you may want to highlight certain causes or effects that have been underreported or ignored altogether.

Definition – When you're expressing an opinion on an extremely complicated subject, such as global warming, or on a relatively new phenomenon, such as blogging, you may have to define the subject first before you can make your persuasive point. For example, Karen L. King, a lecturer at Harvard Divinity School, wrote a book called *What Is Gnosticism?* In the book, she uses recently discovered ancient writings to clarify the beliefs of this pre-Christian religious doctrine.

Process Analysis – This type of essay not only encourages you to perform a particular task but also shows you exactly how to do it. For example, you have probably seen numerous stories that emphasize the importance of regular exercise. These essays usually explain how to set up and maintain a regular routine – such as walking, swimming, or jogging – and also describe the benefits of adhering to the routine.

This particular essay is primarily an example essay because it features the eight techniques you can use with persuasion. However, the essay also uses process analysis and persuasion because the essay shows you how to write the persuasive essay, and the "how-to" advice is intended to convince you that you can write the persuasive essay. Now, all you have to do is get started.

Chapter 4
The Writing Process

Building a Bookcase Is a Lot Like Writing a Paper

When my wife and I became engaged on New Year's Day in 1984, I began to think about building a special wedding present for her. I figured I'd have plenty of time to get it ready before our July 28th wedding date. Unfortunately, the process took a lot longer than I thought, and I wasn't able to deliver this special gift until Thanksgiving, almost four months late. The extra time was necessary, though, if I wanted to do a good job. And as I look back at that building process, I see that the six steps I went through to craft this special gift are very similar to the six basic steps in the writing process.

First, I had to come up with a good idea. I knew I wanted to build a bookcase for her because when we met the previous summer, I was trying to sell *World Book* encyclopedias, and she was my boss. I didn't want just a normal bookcase, though; I wanted something special and unique. So I pulled out a pencil and some drawing paper and began sketching ideas until I found one that I liked, a design that included a spot for a world globe in the center with the *World Books*

surrounding it. As a writer, you should do something similar. Instead of sitting around merely thinking about ideas for papers, you should **write to get a good idea**. Brainstorming, free writing, and journaling are all excellent ways to get started.

My second step as an amateur carpenter was to gather the lumber and tools I needed to complete the project. I asked an architect friend to go with me to the lumberyard to pick out the best oak available, and, then, I brought it to my father's basement, so I could use all of his tools. As a writer, you, too, need two things. You need to **gather thoughts and information**, typically from your own personal experience and your research. The classic advice for writers is to "write what you know," and if you don't know, you should visit the library for the information you need.

My third step was to measure and cut the wood and put it together in the form I had designed. This step took much longer than I expected because I had never used a router before to make the cross cuts for the shelves, and, quite frankly, I didn't do a very good job. And just as you need to **write a rough draft** to move forward, I needed this sad-looking bookcase to make me realize that I needed to ask for help. I didn't want to give my bride a piece that was less than perfect any more than you want to be graded on your "sloppy copy."

Fortunately, my dad has some woodworking experience, and he showed me what I had done wrong and how to correct my mistakes. Basically, I needed to take the bookcase apart and put it all back together again in a much better way. My dad showed me all my errors, and that's exactly what readers can do for writers. After you've written an essay, you need to **gather comments from readers** to know the strengths and weaknesses of your work. Then, and only then, can you begin to improve on your work.

Naturally, my next step was to make the changes my dad had suggested. I was much more precise the second time around. My second attempt was much more successful than my first, and the result was a bookcase that actually looked good and was sturdy, too. And while you may have to write more than a second

draft before you feel good about your paper, at some point, you must **write a final draft**, one that you will be proud to hand in to your instructor.

The final step in my bookcase adventure involved sanding and staining. I used sandpaper to smooth out the rough spots, and I chose a clear oil to highlight the natural grain of the wood. As a writer, you must also go through a final step, a proofreading step to **gather mistakes and eliminate them**. Otherwise, your readers may be too distracted by all the minor errors to appreciate the overall paper.

Is it possible to skip over or eliminate any steps in the essay building process? Of course it is. But if you do, you may wind up with a weak and wobbly essay. So rather than finish with a work that is less than your best, remember the following formula for writing success: WG3.

Write to get a good idea.

Gather thoughts and information.

Write a rough draft.

Gather comments from readers.

Write a final draft.

Gather mistakes and eliminate them.

Helping Students to See Writing as a Process

Most of the students we will see in The Writing Center are a part of the "Millennials" generation. Thus, according to Neil Howe and William Strauss, who wrote the book *Millennials Rising*, some of these young people have never done any of the following: they've never had to roll up a car window, they've never had to walk across the room to change the channel on a television, and they've never had to press the carriage return on a typewriter (24). Consequently, as writing instructors, we may have to work extra hard to convince these students that writing – unlike many facets of modern life – is not a one-step process. Instead, we may have to convince them that writing is a multi-step process, and in The Writing Center, we typically break that process down into seven steps.

One: Pre-Writing. The first step occurs when students come to The Writing Center and admit that they have the assignment, but they are unsure about how to proceed. Under those circumstances, we typically start with a conversation about the instructor's expectations. For example, we help the students determine if the teacher wants a personal experience or an analysis of a reading assignment. In addition, we try to determine if the essay should be based on experience or on research and whether that essay should be informative or persuasive. Once the students have a pretty good idea of the teacher's expectations and a general idea of where they want to go, they can move forward.

Two: Gathering ideas or information. Rather than simply think about their general ideas, we encourage students to get their thoughts on paper with one or more of the following strategies: free writing, brainstorming, journaling, and answering the reporters' questions (who? what? where? when? why? and how?). In addition, we suggest that students also use visual organizing techniques such as diagramming, mapping, and clustering to help see the connections and the relationships among their ideas and their details and, perhaps, begin to put together an outline. Finally, if the students are working on a research paper, we show them how to use library databases or Internet search engines to find even more information related to their ideas and their topics.

Three: Writing a first draft.

Some students are so worried about the first sentence or first paragraph that they can't make any additional progress. When that happens, we tell students to temporarily forget about the introduction and focus exclusively on the main idea and the body of the paper. In doing so, they should also be able to figure out the main organizational technique. Finally, we also stress that the first draft is generally referred to as a "rough" draft, so students shouldn't worry too much about spelling, grammar, or punctuation until much later in the process.

Four: Asking for feedback.

Once students have finished their first drafts, they can usually benefit by having someone else read their papers for constructive criticism. Typically, when we read their papers, we check to see if the first draft has a solid introduction with a clear thesis, an organizational pattern, information that fits the pattern and supports the thesis, and a strong conclusion. In addition, we also talk to the students about point of view, transitions, and language (colloquial versus formal).

Five: Making revisions.

Quite honestly, most students don't want to make major revisions, either because a major revision means too much work or because the students don't have enough time. In either case, we try to show students what needs to be done, and we will emphasize how they will be more likely to receive a better grade if they take the time to

do the assignment correctly. For instance, we encourage students to write a few introductions and conclusions, so they can choose those that are most interesting, most powerful, and most memorable. In addition, we also ask lots of questions to help students eliminate material that doesn't belong and to add material to fill in gaps in the text.

Six: Proofreading.

Some students would like to use The Writing Center as a proofreading service. Obviously, we don't provide that kind of service in The Writing Center. Instead, we ask the student to sit with us as we read the paper, and as we read, we also try to explain why something is wrong and how that same error can be avoided in the future. In addition, we will show the student how to use the spell checker and the grammar checker on the computer, or we may refer a student to one or more of the various handouts that are available in The Writing Center. Ideally, each student walks away as both a better writer and a better proofreader.

Seven: Citing sources.

Students who have never written a research paper before will probably need guidance regarding both in-text citations and the list of sources at the end. With these students, we talk first about plagiarism and, then, about paraphrases, summaries, and direct quotes. Then, we show them sample papers and describe how everything fits together. Finally, we also explain the different ways to cite sources based on the type of source or the documentation style.

Author William Zinsser – who wrote the book *On Writing Well* – summarized his subject in four words: "Writing is hard work" ("Simplicity" 33). Most incoming freshmen know this because they've been writing essays for years, but in the midst of a new environment with lots of new responsibilities, these students may need a gentle reminder. When these students visit The Writing Center, we will provide them with that reminder.

To Outline or Not to Outline?

When you visit the grocery store, do you go with list in hand and methodically check off each item as you add it to your shopping cart? Or do you breeze in and simply cruise through the aisles grabbing whatever you think you need? Personally, I prefer the breeze-cruise-and-grab method, but I know I do a much better job of shopping if I go in with a plan. Writing, too, is easier if you have a plan or outline before you begin.

Now, I know what you're thinking. Just because I'm a writing instructor, you assume I have to be in favor of outlines. If I weren't, those in charge might kick me out of the English Department and take away my thesaurus. And while that might be true, I really learned the importance of outlines when I worked as a technical writer for over ten years.

From 1986 to 1997, I wrote tax and financial articles for bank newsletters. During that time, I dealt with two types of customers: one type allowed me to suggest article topics alone for each newsletter while the other type wanted both topics and outlines for each of the topics suggested. The second type wanted to have a better idea of how the topic was going to be handled before it was approved.

Naturally, I had to invest more time and energy up front for the customer who wanted both topics and outlines. Later, however, I found it so much easier to write the articles themselves when I had my outlines in front of me. If you've never used an outline before, you might want to consider the following four-step outline for writing an outline. (You may also want to look at the "Planning Sheet" on page 220.)

First, you have to choose a subject for your paper. Some instructors assign subjects, but if your instructor allows you to choose your own, you should choose a subject you truly know, love, or care about. Otherwise, the paper could become a painful exercise rather than an enjoyable adventure.

Next, you have to figure out the main idea or thesis of your paper. If your paper is purely informative, you may want to write about a topic such as rap music, computers, or instant replay in the National Football League. Note, however, that a topic is not a thesis. Your thesis should focus in on a specific aspect of your topic. For instance, you might write about the origins of rap music, how computers work, or famous touchdowns that involved the use of instant replay. In addition, if you must write a persuasive paper, your thrust may be that rap music is a unique American art form, that computers are the eighth wonder of the world, or that the instant replay ought to be abolished.

Once you've decided upon a topic and a thesis, you should have a good idea of the overall organizational pattern of your paper. You might use narration to chronicle the origins of rap, you might use process analysis to explain how computers work, or you might use examples to show how instant replay has positively or negatively affected the outcome of particular games. Then, you can fill in your outline with the key elements in your narration, the steps in the process, or the details of each example.

Finally, you should try to come up with tentative ideas for your introduction and your conclusion. You may use a quotation or a question, for example, to begin the paper, but you may want to use a summary or a call to action to conclude. The purpose of your introduction is to draw your reader in while your conclusion should remind the reader of your key point.

Home economists and budget experts say you shouldn't go into a grocery store without a list because you're likely to buy some things you don't need and forget some of the essentials. Similarly, when you write without an outline, you may include unnecessary information and neglect critical components. No, you don't always need an outline, especially if you're writing a creative piece and you're trying to explore your thoughts, feelings, and emotions. In most cases, though, a strong outline will make the writing process much more enjoyable than a trip to the grocery store.

Writers' Block –
Remove That Roadblock

A while back, two of the major highways in the Albany, New York area – the Northway (Interstate 87) and the Thruway (Interstate 90) – both endured heavy rains, flooding, and landslides that blocked those roads to traffic. As a driver, such a roadblock can be annoying, frustrating, and time-consuming. Unfortunately, you may also experience similar roadblocks as you try to complete a writing assignment, yet as a writer, you must remove that writer's block and get back on the highway to productivity.

The first thing you should do is make sure you are physically ready to write with a pen or pencil and paper or a computer. Once you are settled in and somewhat ready to go, you may want to try one or more of the following techniques.

Just start writing. This may sound counterintuitive, especially if you feel you have no ideas whatsoever. However, in the movie *Finding Forrester,* the main character, a writer played by Sean Connery, tells his young protégé, "the first key to writing is to write, not to think." In some ways,

thinking inhibits your writing because you edit yourself too soon. You may get so hung up on having the perfect first line or introductory paragraph that you can't progress any further. In this situation, you should force yourself to write continuously for three to five minutes without ever stopping to edit. In other words, your pen or pencil or computer keys should be moving constantly, and you shouldn't take time to think or go backwards. If at any time during the process, you can't think of anything to write, you should write, "I can't think of anything to write." Eventually, of course, you will think of something to write. In fact, you might even consider typing at a computer with the monitor turned off, so you can't see what you have written. The whole idea here is to go straight from brain to page or screen without worrying about spelling, grammar, punctuation, or any other distracting element. Quite honestly, most of what you write may not be useful, but if one good idea or thought surfaces, you will benefit. As William Forrester says later in the same scene mentioned previously, "Sometimes, the simple rhythm of typing gets us from page one to page two." Even later, Forrester adds, "Punch the keys, for God's sake."

Gather ideas. If actually stringing words together in sentences seems too difficult or complicated, you can simplify the process with brainstorming. Brainstorming is a simple listing of all ideas that come to mind regarding a certain subject. The listing may include words, phrases, whole sentences, or questions. The order does not have to be logical, nor do the items on the list have to be connected to one another. If you are writing about baseball, for instance, you may jot down the names of famous ballplayers or may include details about a baseball and a broken window that led to a fight. The first idea might lead to an example essay about Hall of Fame inductees while the second might inspire a narrative about a memorable experience.

Organize your ideas. A technique called mapping is similar to brainstorming except that mapping is much more visual and may help you to see connections among ideas. Start by writing the main topic in the center of a blank sheet of paper. Then, add ideas as they occur and place them according to similarities or differences. For instance, ideas about the history of baseball might go in one corner of the page while details about the game's rules might go in another. In addition, you may use lines to connect similar ideas or surround the ideas with circles, squares, or triangles to indicate certain similarities.

Ask yourself some questions. One way to dig up more information is to ask yourself the same six questions that journalists ask when they work on a newspaper or magazine story: Who? What? Where? When? Why? How? If for instance, you are writing about a turning point in your life, you can ask the following questions and write down the answers. Who was

involved? What happened? Where did it happen? When did it happen? Why is it important? How did it change you? The answers should provide plenty of information to start with, and those six basic questions should lead to additional questions and more extensive answers.

Talk to someone. You may sometimes struggle to write because you lack confidence in your ideas. You may, in fact, be reluctant to commit your ideas to paper, but if the ideas come out verbally first, you may be able to move forward. Thus, your classmate, your friend, or your family member may serve as a "sounding board" for you. If an idea sounds reasonable and workable for the assignment, you should proceed. If, however, the initial idea sounds weak or incomplete, you must keep talking and try to come up with more specific details.

Google your subject. One of the best ways to get ideas about a subject is to read about that subject. Thus, you might just type your topic into a search engine on the Internet such as Google (www.google.com) or Yahoo (www.yahoo.com). After perusing or reading the web pages that come up, you may be inspired to develop one of these ideas further, or the web pages may suggest another direction altogether. Just be sure to credit any source used in the final paper (just as this article mentions the film *Finding Forrester* in the third paragraph). Otherwise, you may be accused of intellectual theft or plagiarism.

Generally speaking, the actual act of writing does not require a lot of physical strength; the task is more mental and emotional. However, if you can remove a roadblock from your path, your achievement is just as significant as removing an immense boulder from the Northway or the Thruway.

The Benefits of Keeping a Journal

The first time I ever kept a journal occurred during my senior year of college when I was taking a course in Art Appreciation. The professor forced us to write in our notebooks every day because he wanted us to notice the beauty that surrounded us, and he wanted us to think about beauty and write about it. At the time, of course, I thought the journal was a stupid idea, but, gradually, I came to realize the benefits of free writing on a regular basis. Four major benefits come to mind.

Freedom to Express Yourself. One of the major benefits of writing in a personal journal is that no one has to read what you write (unless, of course, you want to show your journal to someone). When you don't have an intended reader, you can bc completely honest, and you don't have to worry about offending anyone. You can write exactly what's on your mind, and you can explore thoughts and feelings you didn't even know you had. To paraphrase a familiar quote by British author E. M. Forester about a benefit of writing, "How can you know what

you're thinking unless you put your thoughts down on paper?" (Troyka 2).

Freedom to Explore. You may have a hard time expressing yourself because you want to be perfect. You're so worried about misspellings and errors in grammar and punctuation that you stifle your own creativity. You're afraid to take chances with your writing. In a journal, of course, you don't have that problem. You can experiment with words, phrases, and ideas. You can break all the rules and not be penalized for it. A journal may be a liberating experience for you, one that allows you to express yourself more easily when you return to the confines of a standard essay.

Freedom to Edit. If you're not in the habit of writing, you may struggle to write 250-300 words for a one-page assignment. You may view a one-page essay as a monumental task. As a result, you probably turn in the first 250-300 words you write without editing any of them. If you are used to writing in a journal, however, you might fill up two or three pages rather easily. Consequently, you can edit out your weak writing and turn in your best 250-300 words. If you can discipline yourself to write regularly in a journal, you'll probably become both a better editor and a better writer.

Yes, keeping a journal requires discipline, and when you first start keeping a journal, you'll be tempted to skip a day here or there. Try to resist that temptation. Even if you only write one sentence in your journal each day, that's better than not writing at all. And what you'll probably find is that you can't write just one sentence. One sentence will lead to two which will lead to three and so on. The hardest part, obviously, is writing that first sentence. If you can write that first sentence every day, you're likely to fill up that journal in no time.

Freedom to Excel. Writing well – like playing a sport or playing a musical instrument – requires practice. Yet, if you practice writing only when your instructors request an essay or a term paper, you may never really excel. If, however, you write regularly in a journal or diary, your skills will naturally improve, and you'll become more comfortable with the whole writing process. "Practice" will, indeed, "make perfect."

Ever since I kept my first journal in college, I've used journals at various times in my life to record special moments or experiences. For instance, I kept a journal during my two years as a Peace Corps Volunteer in Costa Rica and during the first few years of our two daughters' lives. Though I don't go back and read these journals often, I know that they have helped to make me a better writer, and I know that they are priceless souvenirs of my life. My former art professor would be pleased to know that some of the beauty in my life has been captured in those journals.

Incubation Isn't Just for Baby Chicks

When my wife and I first bought our townhouse, we noticed that the living room had neither ceiling light fixtures nor any power outlets in the ceiling from which to connect lights. Since I'm not that comfortable working with electricity, I asked my handyman father if it would be possible to install some type of ceiling lights. "No, I don't think so," he said after a quick look, "but you can get by with some good floor lamps." However, I knew that his initial response wouldn't be his final answer.

Sure enough, about three weeks later, my dad stopped by the house again and said, "I think I figured out a solution to the lighting problem in your living room. I can take power from a wall outlet and run that power up through the wall and install ceiling track lights." Then, within a week, I was reading the newspaper by those newly installed fixtures. My father had solved the problem by allowing it to incubate in his mind for a time while he went about his daily activities. Fortunately, you, too, can use incubation to solve problems that occur in your writing or to discover options

that hadn't occurred to you previously.

Incubation is consciously letting go of a particular task for a period of time, so your unconscious mind can work on that same task for a while. You may have already experienced incubation in your own life. For instance, have you ever struggled to remember the title of a book or a movie? The more you think about the missing name, the less likely you are to come up with it; yet, as soon as you start doing something else, the name comes to you. This occurs because your unconscious mind keeps working while your conscious mind moves on to another task.

One example of incubation I remember well concerns a feature article I was writing for a Christian magazine. The article concerned a high-school wrestler, and this young man told me that his relationship with Jesus Christ had gone through three distinct phases: first, an initial introduction with a subsequent loss of interest; then, a follow-up meeting with renewed interest; and, finally, a third encounter with a firm commitment. As I struggled to write the story, I felt like I had the basic plot, but I didn't have a strong central focus or any effective figures of speech. Thus, I left that article for a day or so to work on other projects, and when I returned to the first piece, I found exactly what I was looking for.

I compared the three distinct phases in the young man's life to the three rounds of a typical wrestling match, and I compared his spiritual struggle to the Biblical character of Jacob who actually wrestled with God before submitting to Him (*NIV Study Bible*: Genesis 32:22-32). That particular feature article is one I'm particularly proud of and one that benefited the most from incubation.

How much time do you need for incubation? The answer may depend on the difficulty of the problem. If you're simply looking for the right word or phrase, a ten-minute walk might suffice, but if you're looking for a key idea or organizing principle as I was, you may need to let go of your writing overnight or even longer if your deadline permits.

Martin Moynihan, a former movie reviewer for the Albany *Times Union*, was typically working on tight schedules, but when possible, he always liked to let his first drafts rest overnight, so his unconscious mind could think about them and, perhaps, he could make them even better in the morning ("Martin Moynihan"). You may have heard other people say basically the same thing – "I think I need to sleep on it" – before they make a final decision about a major purchase, a job change, or a long-term commitment.

Usually, when people think of incubation, they think of the time spent by baby chicks or premature infants in special chambers called incubators. These chambers provide warmth and oxygen for the chicks or the babies until they are big enough and strong enough to survive without the assistance. If during the writing process, you feel that your ideas or early drafts aren't quite big enough or strong enough, you may want to leave them alone for a while. Writer and educator Peter Elbow calls this time of incubation "cooking" (48-69). So maybe if you allow your first draft of an essay to simmer for a while before you proceed, you, too, will be pleased by how you can improve upon that work when you return.

Dig for the Treasures in Your Writing

In the days before banks and safety deposit boxes, people who wanted to hide or protect their treasures often buried them. Unfortunately, some of these treasures were never recovered because their owners either died or were forced to leave their land before they had a chance to retrieve their buried items. As a result, modern archaeologists sometimes find these treasures when they dig near ancient cities or civilizations. As a writer, believe it or not, you, too, can dig up treasures in your writing if you're willing to burrow beneath the surface of your first draft.

Generally speaking, a first draft includes all the details that come immediately to mind when you begin writing on a certain subject. For instance, when I was in high school and college, I can remember being asked to write about topics such as "A Memorable Day" or "The Most Difficult Day of My Life" or "A Turning Point." In each case, I found myself writing about a particular day in sixth grade, the day my little sister Peggy died.

Yes, I probably could have used that same basic essay over and over, but, instead, I found myself exploring more and more the specifics of the day: my feelings at school when I first heard the bad news; the ride home from school with Mom, Dad, and my four sisters; my time alone, crying in my bedroom; our first family dinner without Peggy; and the wake and funeral that followed.

After I finished college, I still found myself thinking about Peggy and her premature death at age four (due to extensive medical problems). At one point, I wrote a long poem about her, and, even later, I turned the whole experience into a short novel. As I look back at the entire writing process, I realize that I was working like an archaeologist. First, I had to dig through the rough drafts and final versions of all the short essays to find the poem, and, then, I had to go below the surface of the poem to get to the novella. The writing helped me deal with my sister's death, and the novella keeps the memory of her alive.

American author John Steinbeck followed a somewhat similar process to create one of his most famous works. In an amazing display of creativity and discipline, Steinbeck wrote the first draft of his 500-page novel *Grapes of Wrath* during the summer and autumn of 1938. This Depression-era story describes the Joad family's migration from the Dust Bowl of Oklahoma to California to work as fruit pickers, and the book won the Pulitzer Prize in 1940. However, this is not a work that Steinbeck found in the topsoil of his writing. Rather, he, too, had to dig through other writings on the subject to get to his masterpiece.

According to Robert DeMott – who served as editor for Steinbeck's book entitled *Working Days: The Journals of "The Grapes of Wrath"* – Steinbeck went through three preliminary steps before he wrote his famous novel. First, in 1936, Steinbeck wrote a series of newspaper articles called "The Harvest Gypsies" to highlight the difficulties faced by the Oklahoma farmers who sought a better life in California.

Then, in 1937, Steinbeck began writing a novel called *The Oklahomans* about how these migrant workers would change California once they settled down. However, Steinbeck never finished writing *The Oklahomans*.

Instead, he began another long work, a satire called *L'Affaire Lettuceberg* about the battles that took place between the growers and the workers in Steinbeck's hometown of Salinas, California. Though Steinbeck actually finished this particular work, he wasn't happy with it, and he destroyed it. In fact, as Steinbeck was writing *L'Affaire Lettuceberg*, he described the work in this way: "it has a lot of poison in it that I have to get out of my system, and this is a good way to do it" (Steinbeck and DeMott xxxix).

Thus, the entire process was therapeutic for Steinbeck, and once he had moved through these three writing projects, he was finally ready to write *The Grapes of Wrath*.

As a college student facing numerous papers and tight deadlines, you may feel like you don't have the time or the energy to dig beneath the surface of your thoughts. Consequently, you may be tempted to take a short cut now and then. You may be tempted to hand in a rough draft instead of digging deeper for a more polished essay. You may be tempted to turn in the minimum five-page term paper when your teacher gives you the option of writing "five to ten pages." Or, you may be tempted to adapt an old paper to fit a new assignment.

Don't give in to these temptations. Instead, like Steinbeck, try to keep working, keep digging, and keep plowing through the layers of your life and your research to find the treasures that are buried there.

Don't Submit Your Sloppy Copy

When our two daughters were in grade school, their writing instructors used to refer to students' rough drafts as "sloppy copies." Those teachers probably used that phrase not only for its rhyming quality but also to emphasize that submitting such work was lazy, careless, or negligent. Thus, before you rush to submit the first draft of an essay, make sure you consider the following eight items on this list; when evaluating your research paper, make sure you consider all ten items.

Introduction

The first few sentences of your essay are critical because those sentences influence whether readers will continue to read the rest of the essay. To make the introduction more interesting, you may want to use one of the following techniques: a question, a joke or story, a quotation or bit of dialogue, a detailed description, a comparison, a vivid example, a startling statement or statistic or an unusual fact, a definition, or an allusion.

Point of View

Generally, personal essays call for the first-person point of view, and you should use pronouns such as "I, me, my, mine, we, us, our," and "ours." Instructional pieces call for the second-person point of view, and you should use pronouns such as "you and your." Finally, formal essays and research papers call for the third-person point of view, and you should use pronouns such as "he, she, it, they, him, his, her, them," and "their."

Thesis

Typically, the last sentence of the first paragraph contains the thesis or the main idea of your essay. However, a strong thesis will also provide a particular position and a specific direction for the reader. For example, instead of writing "Dredging the Hudson River is a major issue for upstate New York," you might write "Dredging the Hudson River is a necessity for upstate New York for three main reasons."

Transitions

Transitions are the words or phrases that move readers through your essay. For instance, if an essay has three strong arguments, you might use words like "first, second, and third"; however, if the essay is telling a story in chronological order, you might use some of the following words or phrases: "at first, next, later, afterwards, subsequently, finally, at last, etc."

Topic Sentences

Usually, the first sentence of each paragraph serves as the topic sentence for that paragraph and provides a general overview of that particular paragraph. For example, you might write the following: "Mickey Mantle played for the New York Yankees for 18 seasons, but his career can be broken down into three distinct phases."

Organizational Structure

While most writers use a variety of techniques within one essay or research paper, one primary technique should serve as the obvious framework for your paper. The nine basic techniques are as follows: narration, description, examples, compare and contrast, cause and effect, definition, process analysis (how to), division and classification, and persuasion.

Conclusion

The conclusion is extremely important because when readers finish the essay, the conclusion is what the readers remember. Thus, to make the last paragraph and the last sentence memorable, you should restate your main ideas and close with one of the following: a call to action, a quotation, a question with an obvious answer, an overall summary, or an echo of something mentioned earlier to serve as a unifying element.

Mechanics

Numerous mechanical errors in spelling, grammar, and/or

punctuation can seriously detract from your essay. Thus, you should use the spelling- and grammar-check functions in your word-processing program, or you should ask more experienced writers to help you find some of the common errors and correct them.

Parenthetical Citations

In a research paper, you must provide readers with basic information about sources used within the text of the paper. Thus, whenever you quote or paraphrase a source, you should also cite the author's last name within parentheses immediately after the quotation or paraphrase. In some cases, you may also need additional information.

Works Cited Page or Reference Page

For a research paper, you also need to provide a complete listing of author, title, and publication information for all of the sources at the end of your paper. This list of sources should be in alphabetical order (by the authors' last names) and should properly match the parenthetical citations. Since improper documentation of sources can lead to charges of plagiarism, you must make sure you use the proper format for your documentation.

Writing an essay or a research paper can be a long, painful process. As a result, when you finish that first draft, you may be tempted to print it, turn it in to your teacher, and be done with it forever. Unfortunately, turning in a sloppy copy often results in one of two outcomes: either you receive a poor grade for your effort, or your teacher asks you to revise your work, which you probably should have done in the first place.

Will You Proofread My Paper?

As a writing specialist in The Writing Center, this is one of the questions I hear most often. Unfortunately, the question can be hard to answer because students typically have different meanings for their questions. Four common meanings come to mind.

However, before I can attempt to answer the question, I have to ask some questions of my own. Typically, if you come to me for assistance, I will ask you for the name of the course and the name of the instructor. Then, I will ask you if you have an actual printed copy of the assignment, so I know exactly what the teacher wants. If you don't have a printed copy of the assignment, I will ask you to explain the assignment to me. Finally, I will also ask for the length of the assignment and the due date. Once I have the answers to all those questions, I can try to answer the proofreading question. As I mentioned above, proofreading means different things to different people.

First, the proofreading question sometimes means, **"Will you read my essay and let me know if that's what my teacher wants?"** This question usually occurs when a teacher asks for an essay that you, the student, have never written before. For example, the teacher might ask you for an analysis of a poem or a short story. Many students assume the teacher wants to know simply what the poem or story is about, so they write the essay just as if they were writing a high-school book report with all the facts: who, what, where, when, why, and how. When this happens, I'll read the essay and, then, explain that the teacher doesn't want a summary of the facts of the work. After all, the teacher is already familiar with the work; instead, what the teacher really wants, in most cases, is a review or critique of the work that explains its strengths and weaknesses. In other words, the teacher wants to see your thoughts or interpretation of the work

Next, the question sometimes means, **"I'm not feeling very confident about this essay, so will you please read it and tell me that it's okay?"** Freshman writers, in particular, are likely to ask this question. You may be a great writer, and you may understand the assignment perfectly, but you simply need a little boost of confidence. When this happens, I'll read and, then, explain that the assignment is in good shape, and the teacher will probably be pleased with your final outcome. If this happens to you, you should walk away feeling more confident about yourself and about your writing ability.

Third, the question sometimes means, **"I know I have major errors, but I don't even know what they are, so can you help me?"** When this happens, I'll read and, then, point out major problems such as a weak introduction, a lack of a thesis, an inconsistent point of view, or inappropriate language for the type of assignment. To solve these types of problems, I'll typically explain what's needed and why it's needed, and, then, I'll give you a handout on the subject discussed, so you can work further on the essay. Ideally, you will make revisions, but, then, you will probably ask the proofreading question again – this time with a different meaning (listed below).

Finally, the question often means, **"I know I have a lot of spelling, grammatical, and punctuation errors, so will you go through and find them and correct them for me?"** Obviously, I want to help you, but, obviously too, I can't do your work for you; I can't go through your paper and point out and correct every single error. My real goal is to help you

build confidence and independence by teaching you to become a better writer, a better editor, and a better proofreader. Thus, my typical answer to this question is, "I can read your essay and give you some feedback."

Then, if you are willing, I will begin teaching. For instance, I might explain that you have a problem with run-on sentences. Then, I'll explain what a run-on sentence is, I'll point out a few examples from the paper, and I'll show you different ways of correcting the errors. Once I feel you understand, I'll ask you to find and correct other run-on sentences in the paper, and I will encourage you to finish the task independently. Before you leave, I will also give you a handout on run-on sentences and show you the chapter on run-on sentences in your textbook, which is available in The Writing and Research Center.

So will I proofread your paper? In a general sense, yes, I will point out major problems that might be present, what English teachers call "global concerns," but, no, I don't go through and point out and correct every single error that exists, the so-called "local concerns." Overall, in The Writing and Research Center, we ask questions about the assignments, we read the essays, and we offer constructive criticism and instruction, but you do your own final editing and proofreading.

Chapter 5
The Key Parts of an Essay

An Introduction to Introductions

If you've ever attended a formal banquet, you probably noticed that the host doesn't automatically begin with the evening's primary purpose. Instead, he or she may start with a joke or a story to warm up the audience and to establish a rapport with those in attendance. In other words, the host wants to secure the audience's attention first before he or she proceeds with the main idea. When you write an essay, you should also use a strong introductory device to secure your reader's attention before you proceed.

Unfortunately, too many students begin their essays with bland, matter-of-fact statements such as, "This essay will discuss . . . ." or "I plan to write about . . . ." Those statements, obviously, are not very captivating or interesting. So if you want to capture your reader's attention, you have to do something different. You have to be creative. Here are nine introductory devices you may want to consider.

A Startling Statement. In his 1986 essay entitled "Just Walk On By," Brent Staples begins with this line: "My first victim was a woman" (75). That sentence intrigues most readers immediately because they assume the writer is a criminal about to reveal details about his crimes. While Staples is not a criminal, he is often mistaken for a criminal, and his startling introduction kidnaps his readers and allows him to explain how he deals with the unwanted attention. Note, too, that an unusual fact or statistic can also be part of a startling statement.

A Quotation. Sometimes, a direct quote about your subject may also intrigue a reader. To begin his essay entitled "How Do We Find the Student in a World of Academic Gymnasts and Worker Ants," James T. Baker uses the words of French novelist Anatole France: "The whole art of teaching is only the art of awakening the natural curiosity of young minds" (316). This quote not only attracts readers, but it also allows Baker to later make his point about how difficult it is to actually awaken that curiosity.

A Story. Doctor John Lantos writes about "Life and Death in Neonatal Intensive Care," and he begins that essay with a story: "It was while I was working in the neonatal intensive-care unit that I first achieved that dream of doctors everywhere: to actually save a patient's life" (350). That one sentence is obviously the beginning of his story, but because he also hints at the dramatic nature of the experience, the introduction is so much more powerful than a traditional – and bland – once-upon-a-time type introduction.

An Allusion. An allusion is an indirect reference to a well-known person, place, or event from history, from mythology, from literature, or from other works of art. Allusions attract readers because they have to think about the connection the author is trying to make. In his famous "I Have a Dream" speech, for instance, Martin Luther King Jr., uses three allusions in his very first line: "Five score years ago, a great American, in whose symbolic shadow we stand, signed the Emancipation Proclamation" (506). King is alluding to the Gettysburg Address, Abraham Lincoln, and the Lincoln Memorial in Washington, D.C. Though King's speech was originally intended for listeners rather than readers, an allusion as an attention-getting device works well in either realm.

A Comparison or Contrast. When former U.S. Open tennis champion Arthur Ashe began his letter to *The New York Times* in 1977, he began with a strong contrast: "Since my sophomore year at the University of California, Los Angeles, I have become convinced that we blacks spend too much time on the playing fields and too little time in the libraries" (qtd. In Funk, Day, and McMahan (1997) 286). Then, Ashe uses statistics and examples to show that blacks are over represented in the athletic professions and underrepresented in the fields of law, medicine, and engineering.

A Vivid Description. In "Wind," William Least Heat-Moon writes about a married couple that was literally lifted away by a tornado. He begins with this description: "Paul and Leola Evans are in their early seventies but appear a decade younger, their faces shaped by the prairie wind into strong and pleasing lines" (34).

A Definition. Before Judith Viorst divides and classifies her friends in an essay entitled "Friends, Good Friends, and Such Good Friends," she begins with a definition: "Women are friends, I once would have said, when they totally love and support and trust each other, and bare to each other the secrets of their souls, and run – no questions asked – to help each other, and tell harsh truths to each other (no, you can't wear that dress unless you lose ten pounds first) when harsh truths must be told" (143).

An Example. When William Zinsser began his essay about "College Pressures," he started with an example of a note from a student to a resident dean at Yale University: "Dear Carlos: I desperately need a dean's excuse from my chem. Midterm which will begin in about 1 hour. All I can say is that I totally blew it this week. I've fallen incredibly, inconceivably behind" (308).

A Question. Similarly, when Robert Heilbroner wrote "Don't Let Stereotypes Warp Your Judgments," he began with a question to provoke his readers to think: "Is a girl called Gloria apt to be better-looking than one called Bertha" (110)?

So now that you have a much better idea about various techniques you can use to begin an essay, you may be thinking, "When am I ever going to use this information once I finish this Composition course?" That's easy. You can also use any one of these techniques the next time you have to serve as the host of a formal banquet.

Don't Let Your Bus Take Off Without a Thesis

Should you use a question to begin a college essay? Yes. A rhetorical question is an excellent way to arouse the reader's curiosity. You might also consider other introductory devices – such as a quotation, a startling statistic, a vivid example, or even a joke – to stimulate the reader's interest. The most important part of the first paragraph, however, is the thesis, which is the main idea or "promise" of the essay, and your thesis belongs in the last sentence of the first paragraph.

The thesis should be located at the end of the first paragraph for two major reasons: direction for you the writer and direction for your readers.

When you write an essay, you don't want to be wandering all over a subject like a tourist exploring the countryside. Instead, you should have a clear destination in mind and precise directions on how you're going to get there. One way to keep you focused on your writing task is to imagine that you are a bus driver and that your essay is your bus. Your thesis, then, is the sign on your bus that lets both you and your passengers/readers know where you're going.

Keep in mind, too, that the more precise your thesis is, the more focused your essay is likely to be. A general idea about football, for example, may give you a start on your journey, but a specific thesis – such as "The three major problems facing the New York Giants" – is clearly superior. Similarly, a thesis like "What I learned this summer," is adequate, but "Why I will never again work at the county fair" is much more intriguing. A strong thesis allows you to see where you're going and reminds you of what you need to do to get there.

Directions are also helpful for your readers because most readers are like those who ride the bus. When they climb aboard, they want to know exactly where they're headed, and they want the ride to be clear and direct. So if you don't indicate precisely where you're going, they're unlikely to go along for the ride. Or, if you say you're going somewhere, but then you veer off course, they will probably want out. If you promise to write about the three major problems facing the New York Giants or about your summer experience working at the county fair, you better fulfill that promise or risk losing your readers.

As a writing instructor who has read thousands of essays over the years, I find nothing is more frustrating than an essay that rambles on and on and says nothing. When I read these essays, I feel like Sandra Bullock and Keanu Reeves on the runaway bus in the movie *Speed*. As the instructor, I have to keep reading, but I feel like the task is going to kill me. Naturally, the grades I assign to these out-of-control essays are much like the maximum posted speeds on our local highways: 55 or 65.

So when you sit down to write your next essay, don't just hit the accelerator and take off. Instead, pull out a map to figure out where you're headed and how you're going to get there. Then, post your destination in a strong thesis sentence at the end of your first paragraph.

What's Your Point of View?

(See Commandment Three in Chapter One: This essay is purposely repeated here since your point of view is an essential part of any essay.)

If you really want to learn how to write, a good writer should practice like I do.

Did you find that introductory sentence confusing? You probably did because the sentence includes three different points of view rather than one consistent point of view. Under those circumstances, confusion is inevitable. As a writer, therefore, you want to make sure that you don't confuse your readers. Before you begin any writing task, you should decide upon your point of view, and you should stick to it.

Point of view is generally defined as the way in which you tell a story. The three general options are referred to as first person, second person, and third person. Here's an overview of each.

First Person. The first-person point of view is the one you use most often in normal conversation or in most autobiographical essays. When you get home at the end of the day, for instance, and you begin to tell others about your experiences, or you begin to write in your journal, you're using the first-person point of view. When you write in the first person, you will use the following pronouns: I and we, me and us, my and our, and mine and ours. Here's an example: "I got pulled over for speeding on my way to school. We all failed our quiz in math class. Then, my friends and I shared a pizza for lunch."

This point of view is appropriate whenever you are speaking or writing about your life. If an instructor asks you to introduce yourself in writing, or if you must describe an emotional moment that you will never forget, the first-person point of view is perfect.

Pulitzer Prize-winning author Russell Baker uses the first person in his essay called "Learning to Write." In this essay, Baker describes a turning point in his life when a high-school English teacher read Baker's essay aloud to the class: "I did my best to avoid showing pleasure, but what I was feeling was pure ecstasy at this startling demonstration that my words had the power to make people laugh. In the eleventh grade, at the eleventh hour, as it were, I had discovered a calling. It was the happiest moment of my entire school career" (188-89).

Second Person. Of the three points of view, the second person is used least often. However, that doesn't mean it's any less important. The second-person point of view is generally used when you want to teach someone how to do something (this essay is written in second person) or when you want to give directions to a specific location. With the second-person point of view, you will use the pronouns "you, your, and yours."

If you're having a party at your house, for instance, and you want to tell your friends how to get there, you might say or write the following: "You should drive north on 87, and get off at Exit 8. Then, you should turn left onto Crescent Road, and look for Lapp Road on your right. Turn right on Lapp, and go to the third house on the right."

With this point of view, you can sometimes leave out the pronoun "you" and go straight to the verbs because the word "you" is understood. You can see this in the last sentence in the example above: "Turn right on Lapp, and go to the third house on the right."

Author Garrison Keillor uses the second person in his teaching essay entitled "How to Write a Personal Letter": "Sit for a few minutes with the blank sheet of paper in front of you, and meditate on the person you will write to; let your friend come to mind until you can almost see her or him in the room with you. Remember the last time you saw each other and how your friend looked and what you said and what perhaps was unsaid between you, and when your friend becomes real to you, start to write" (226).

Third Person. You typically use the third-person point of view when you speak or write about others. When you write in the third person, you will use some of the following pronouns: he, she, it, they, him, her, them, his, her, its, and their. You might describe your instructor, for instance, in this way: "He's pretty tall, he wears glasses, his hair is gray, and his jokes are bad."

Generally speaking, you will use the third person in formal writing – such as term papers – or whenever you want to focus more on the subject of the essay and less on your own thoughts or opinions concerning the subject.

In his essay entitled "Grant and Lee: A Study in Contrasts," Civil War historian Bruce Catton uses the third person to describe generals Ulysses S. Grant and Robert E. Lee: "They were two strong men, these oddly different generals, and they represented the strengths of two conflicting currents that, through them, had come into final collision" (535).

Is it possible to state your personal opinion while writing in the third person? Yes. Just don't make the mistake of changing your point of view. After writing an entire essay in third person, for example, you might be tempted to switch to the first person in your conclusion and write, "I definitely think we should dredge the Hudson River." However, you should really stick with the third-person point of view by writing "The Hudson River should be dredged" or "The government should dredge the Hudson River."

Do the three points of view ever overlap? Yes, they do, especially when you're writing about yourself (first) and about others (third) or when you're trying to teach someone (second), but you're also drawing on your own experience (first) in the teaching process. When those overlaps occur, just make sure they do so because you want them to occur and not because you weren't paying attention to your point of view.

Paragraph Patterns

My youth was a difficult one. I am the only boy in our family, and I have five sisters: one older and four younger. I can vividly recall waking up on a summer day and coming downstairs to find practically all of them – and my mother – on the floor of the living room with large swatches of material and scissors. They were cutting the material and pinning it to white, odd-shaped sheets of lightweight paper. "Can I play too?" I asked, assuming that this activity had to be some kind of game or puzzle.

Every one of those females gave me an odd look, and once they explained what they were doing, I didn't want to participate. Apparently, the odd shapes were designs for summer dresses that they were about to sew, and they were using these patterns to fit all the pieces together. Fortunately, even though I never did learn to sew, I acquired a valuable lesson from this experience: just as a seamstress can use a standard pattern to create an article of clothing, a writer can use a standard paragraph pattern to express his or her ideas.

According to the authors of *The New McGraw-Hill Handbook*, most paragraphs fall into one of four basic patterns: chronological, spatial, general to specific, and specific to general (Maimon, et al., 69-71). Here's an overview of each.

The **chronological** paragraph simply moves through a series of items in the order in which they occurred. For example, if you were describing a particular event, such as a lecture at school, you would begin with the official welcome and the introduction of the speaker, move to the main presentation, and conclude with the question-and-answer session that followed. If you were teaching someone to bake a particular dish, you would start with a list of ingredients, then explain how those ingredients are mixed together, and finish with the specific baking instructions. Finally, even if you are merely explaining your thoughts on a particular issue, you would probably walk your reader through the natural progression of those thoughts.

The **spatial** paragraph is somewhat similar, but instead of providing a time sequence, the writer presents key details as a viewer might observe them. For instance, if you were describing the furniture in your living room, you might move from left to right or from right to left. If you were explaining the history of the faces on a totem pole, you would move from top to bottom or bottom to top. And if you were offering a tour of a circular building, you might move in a clockwise or counterclockwise direction. Whatever approach you choose, just make sure that it follows a logical pattern rather than jumping randomly from one point to another.

The **general-to-specific** pattern is probably the most commonly used pattern because it offers a strong topic sentence up front and follows with the particular details that support that main idea. For instance, if you feel your favorite football team is good enough to go to the Super Bowl, you would probably begin with a basic statement to that effect. Then, you would most likely back up that statement with sentences that include the names and accomplishments of the key players or with statistics that show the team's overall superiority.

Finally, the **specific-to-general** approach would pretty much reverse that process. Fans of the New York Yankees, for instance, might begin by announcing that their first baseman and second baseman recently won Gold Gloves for their defensive superiority. Next, they might announce that the Yankees plan to re-sign all of their key veterans and also offer a free-agent contract to a front-line pitcher. Then, at the end of the paragraph, they might offer their main point that the Bronx Bombers are the early favorite to win the next World Series.

Are any other paragraph patterns possible? Of course. Creative writers are always experimenting with new ways of expressing ideas or combining patterns for a special effect. But these four basic patterns will help you through most of your basic collegiate assignments until you feel confident enough to create a new pattern or special effect of your own.

Begin Your Paragraph with a Topic Sentence

A long time ago, when I was in the midst of working as a high-school English teacher and also working on my master's degree, I was feeling overwhelmed by the amount of reading I was required to do. Thus, I took a speed-reading course to help alleviate the problem. I recall learning a few tricks to save time without decreasing my comprehension, but one suggestion really stood out, and this particular suggestion actually helped me more with my writing than it did with my reading.

Basically, the instructor said, "If you ever find that you have too much material to read and not enough time to read it all, just read the first sentence of each paragraph because most of the key ideas are located there." Obviously, this instructor was referring to the topic sentence of the paragraph and to the tendency of most writers to begin their paragraphs with the topic sentence.

What is a topic sentence? While many students confuse the topic sentence with the thesis sentence, the two are not the same. The thesis sentence usually contains the main idea for the entire essay (and is usually located at the end of the first paragraph), but the topic sentence contains the main idea for a paragraph. Thus, a typical 500-word essay will have only one thesis sentence but may have as many as five to ten topic sentences.

According to Diana Hacker and Nancy Sommers, the authors of *The Bedford Handbook*, a topic sentence "acts as a signpost pointing in two directions: backward toward the thesis of the essay and forward toward the body of the paragraph" (62). For example, in his essay entitled "Camping Out," Ernest Hemingway begins with his thesis that a person "ought to be able to sleep comfortably every night, to eat well every day, and to return to the city rested and in good condition" (196). Then, in the body of his essay, he explains how to avoid insects and how to sleep comfortably before he uses the following topic sentence to introduce his third key subject: "Outside of insects and bum sleeping, the rock that wrecks most camping trips is cooking" (197). That particular sentence points back toward the main idea of sleeping comfortably and points toward the main idea of eating well. In the paragraph that follows that topic sentence, he goes on to list the cooking utensils that are needed in the woods, and in subsequent paragraphs, he explains how to cook fish, how to boil the water for coffee, and how to bake an apple pie.

Hacker and Sommers go on to explain that some writers begin a paragraph with a transitional sentence, and, then, they use the second sentence as the topic sentence (63). For instance, in his essay "Prison Studies," Malcolm X explains how he educated himself by copying the entire dictionary and by reading voraciously while he was incarcerated. Then, near the end of that essay, he uses this transitional sentence to begin a paragraph: "I have often reflected upon the new vistas that reading opened to me" (77). At that particular point in the essay, he has stopped describing his reading habits, and he is ready to describe the effect that all his reading had on him. Thus, his second sentence is his topic sentence, and he writes the following: "I knew right there in prison that reading had changed forever the course of my life" (77). Naturally, he follows up with additional details about how reading allowed him to improve his life and the lives of others.

So can a topic sentence ever appear at the end of a paragraph? Yes, but you probably won't see it there often. Even Hacker and Sommers admit that the placement is unusual and needs to be handled carefully: "Occasionally the topic sentence may be withheld until the end of the paragraph – but only if the earlier sentences hang together so well that readers perceive their direction, if not their exact point" (63). Since the topic sentence at the end of the paragraph is so unusual

and since few students will ever attempt it, I will often force my students to write one by asking them to write a paragraph that concludes with this line: "And that's why I will never . . . ." Naturally, they will have to fill in the end of that line, and, to do so, they have to think of an experience when they did something foolish and learned a valuable lesson. My personal example follows:

"On an early December afternoon many years ago, I was all set to watch the Miami Dolphins play my New York Jets when my wife asked me to do her a favor. 'Jim, would you go up in the attic and get the Advent wreath for me?' Not wanting to miss the kickoff, I rushed upstairs, climbed the ladder into the attic, and located the Christmas decorations. However, rather than move the boxes that were in my way, I decided to reach around them and stretch my foot to the edge of the plywood that covered only a portion of the attic floor. In my haste, unfortunately, I stretched a bit too far, and my foot slipped off the plywood and fell through the insulation and sheetrock into the bathroom ceiling on the second floor. And that's why I will never rush around in the attic again."

So did I ever use those speed-reading tips that I learned so many years ago? Yes, I have become a faster reader, but since I hate to miss any details when I read, I will never read just the first sentences of paragraphs. Instead, I have tried to use that particular piece of advice to remember the importance of having a topic sentence when I write and, most often, to place that topic sentence at the beginning of each paragraph.

Make the Transition to Transitions

Have you ever traveled on a major highway late at night with few other cars to light the way? If so, you know how lost and isolated you can feel at times as you cruise through vast stretches of darkness at 65 miles per hour. Fortunately, most major highways provide you with numerous signs to let you know where you're headed and how soon you might get there. As a writer, you, too, need to provide your readers with proper signage in the form of transitions.

Transitions are the words and phrases that help move readers through your essay. Yes, you could rely exclusively on paragraph breaks to let your readers know you're moving from one idea to the next, but appropriate transitions make the trip more pleasant and less stressful. Naturally, the selection of those transitions will depend on the type of essay you're writing.

Transitions of Time. For example, if you're telling a story in chronological order, or if you want to teach someone to perform a multi-step process, you may want to use words like "first, second, third," or words such as "initially, next,

later, and subsequently." These time transitions are like mile markers on the highway that let readers know a small portion of the journey is complete, but the remainder is still to come.

Transitions of Place. Similarly, if you're giving driving directions or describing a particular place, you'll want your transitions to be as precise as possible to give the reader a vivid picture of what's ahead and what's important. These place transitions are like the service signs on the highway for restaurants, gas stations, and hotels. These transitions include the following: "to the left (or right), above or below, alongside, nearby, and in the distance" among others.

Transitions of Similarity, Example, and Addition. Another situation that calls for transitions occurs when you're pointing out a similarity or providing an example. For a similarity, you may want to use a transition such as "also, likewise, moreover, furthermore, and in the same way." For an example, you may want to use transitions such as (obviously) "for example, for instance, and as an illustration." At times, too, you may want to provide more than one similarity or example to strengthen your point or to make it more persuasive. These additional similarities or examples are like the numerous exit signs that occur near major cities where one exit is not sufficient, and the transitions that introduce these added similarities or examples are as follow: "again, another, besides, in addition, and equally important."

Transitions of Contrast. While a comparison points out similarities, a contrast points out the differences in people, places, products, or ideas. The transitions of contrast are especially important because they change the direction of your essay, much like a U-turn on the highway. Thus, you should use transitions such as "however, conversely, otherwise, by contrast, and on the other hand."

Transitions of Cause and Effect. Equally important are the words and phrases that demonstrate the causes and effects of life's activities. These transitions include words and phrases such as "therefore, thus, hence, consequently, and as a result." Like highway detours, these transitions show connections, and the words

must be chosen carefully. For instance, a word like "subsequently" means one event merely followed another, but a word like "consequently" implies a much stronger connection and may mean that the first event actually caused the second event to occur.

Transitions of Conclusion. Finally, when you get close to the end of your essay, you'll want transitions that let your reader know the trip is just about over. Thus, the most common transitions in this category include words or phrases such as "therefore, in conclusion, to summarize, to finalize, all in all, or as has been said." Simply writing "the end" or "that's all, folks" is much too blunt; a final transition is a kinder and gentler way of showing the highway exit sign and saying good-bye to your readers.

Therefore, before you turn in your next essay, review it carefully, especially in regard to your transitions. After all, if you don't provide transitional words, your readers may be like those highway drivers who feel lost and in the dark. The right transitions in the right places, however, can help your readers see your ideas clearly and make your destination obvious.

A Final Word on Conclusions

In the introduction to her essay on "Friends," Judith Viorst begins with her own personal definition of the word "friend." Then, in the body of that essay, Viorst divides her friends into eight categories, what she calls "varieties of friendship." She has "special-interest friends, historical friends, and cross-generation friends," among others. Once Viorst has divided her various friendships in this way, she concludes her essay by returning to her original definition of a friend, and she alters that definition somewhat by expanding upon it. This return to the introduction allows Viorst's essay to come full circle, to give the reader an echo of what she had said earlier (143-47). As a writer, if you connect your introductions and conclusions in a similar way, your essays will be more powerful and more memorable.

Regarding conclusions, too many students rely exclusively on the traditional ending phrases that these students learned in grade school, phrases like "in conclusion" and "to summarize." While those endings are adequate, they're too much like a referee's decision in boxing. They provide a final word, but they fail to provide the "knockout" blow that creates a long-lasting impression.

When you write an essay, you may want to actually visualize a large wheel, much like Vanna White's *Wheel of Fortune.* Instead of giving that wheel numerous turns, however, you want to provide one complete rotation only. So, if you start with a rhetorical question in your introduction, make sure you answer that question in the body of your essay, and refer to the question again in your conclusion. Or, if you begin with a startling statement, you may want to refer back to that statement in your conclusion. Note, too, that your conclusion doesn't always have to allude solely to your introduction. You can also remind the reader of other significant words, phrases, or ideas from the body of your essay. The key is to make a connection to a point you made earlier. Here are some examples.

In the early part of his essay "Learning to Write," Russell Baker describes his elderly, 11th-grade teacher, Mr. Fleagle, as "stuffy, dull, and hopelessly out of date" (186). Yet, after one particular assignment, Mr. Fleagle was so impressed with Baker's writing that this teacher read the essay aloud to the class and praised the writer exuberantly. Looking back on that experience, Baker viewed it as a turning point in his life, and he concluded with a statement that showed a sharp contrast to his earlier description: "After that, I ranked Mr. Fleagle among the finest teachers in the school" (189).

In an essay entitled "Foul Shots," Rogelio R. Gomez, a Mexican-American author, recalls a basketball game he and his Hispanic teammates played against an all-white team in the suburbs of San Antonio, Texas. Though his team was victorious, what Gomez remembers from that day is the insult the team received when one of the opponents sarcastically threw a bag of Fritos at them. At the time, Gomez and his teammates were so stunned that they failed to say or do anything. Subsequently, the experience haunted Gomez for over 20 years, and in his conclusion, he writes, "For, invariably, whenever I feel insulted, I'm reminded of that day at Churchill High. And whenever the past encroaches upon the present, I see myself rising boldly, stepping proudly across the years, and crushing, underfoot, a silly bag of Fritos" (369).

In a final example, Roxanne Roberts writes about her father's suicide in an essay entitled "The Grieving Never Ends." Early in the essay, Roberts compares life to a can of white paint.

She explains that each event in a person's life adds a tiny drop of color; light colors, like pink and yellow, are for positive events, and dark colors, like brown and gray, are for negative events. A suicide, however, is different: "When a suicide happens, someone hurls in a huge glob of red. You can't get it out. You can't start over. The red will always be there, no matter how many drops of yellow you add" (152). In the remainder of her essay, Roberts discusses suicide in general, her father's suicide in particular, and the negative effects his suicide has had on her life and on the lives of her family members. Fortunately for Roberts, she has also experienced many positive events during the 20 years since her father's death, and she reflects upon them in her conclusion, a conclusion that returns to her earlier comparison: "A lot of wonderful things have happened in those years, hundreds of shimmering droplets added to the mix. When I stir the paint now, it is a soft, dusky rose. A grownup's color, with a touch of sweetness and a touch of melancholy" (157).

When you conclude a speech, your audience members usually have time to ask you questions about your major point. When you write an essay, unfortunately, your readers rarely have that opportunity to ask you questions to clarify or illustrate your point. Thus, your essay's conclusion should be memorable, one that will reverberate in your reader's mind long after your wheel of fortune has stopped spinning.

Chapter 6

Ten Steps to Writing a Research Paper

1. Choosing a Topic for Your Term Paper

On your first day of class, you probably received a syllabus which outlined the major components of the course: required textbooks, supplemental materials, test dates, due dates for major assignments, and other information with specific details about how the final grade is determined. If one of the major assignments for the course is a term paper due near the end of the semester, you may be tempted to push the assignment aside with the thought, "I'll worry about that later." However, the sooner you begin work on your term paper, the more likely it is that you will receive a good grade, so you should start thinking about your topic as soon as possible.

A "term" paper, after all, is so named because, ideally, you should be working on the paper throughout the entire term. If that were not the case, your professor might refer to the assignment as "half-of-a-term paper" or "a-week-near-the-end-of-the-term paper" or, for the real procrastinators, "a-night-before-the-due-date-for-the-term paper." Yes, the first week or two of classes are hectic, especially for new students, but at least thinking about a topic for

the term paper is a great way to begin. Here are three questions to consider.

Did your professor assign a topic? Some professors, for example, assign general topics such as a "living author" or "a subject related to The Revolutionary War" or "a subject covered in the textbook." If you have an assigned topic, you should begin by looking at the possibilities within that topic, so you can get a basic idea of what's available. If you've read every work written by Stephen King, for instance, you might want to write a paper about him. Or, if you live in Saratoga County, you might want to explore the significance of The Battle of Saratoga during the Revolution. Finally, if someone in your family suffers from depression, you might want to write about that subject for your social science course. Note, too, that most teachers are open to other ideas you might have, even if that idea doesn't appear at first glance to fit the assignment.

Did your professor give you the freedom to choose a topic? If you have complete freedom to choose, you have three basic options: (1) you can write about something you already know well, such as a hobby, a passion, or a lifelong interest; (2) you can write about something new which interests you and about which you want to know more; or (3) you can write about a subject that doesn't interest you at all, but you think that subject will interest your professor.

Generally, the third choice is not a good one, but many students make the mistake of trying to impress the professor. That doesn't work well because if you're not interested in the subject, you will probably get bogged down in your research, and your final product will reflect your lack of enthusiasm. Thus, a subject that bores you will probably bore your professor, even if it's in his or her area of expertise. Most instructors who give you the freedom to choose would rather see you write about your area of expertise or see you educate yourself about a new technology, advancement, or trend. If you're really interested in the subject, your excitement will show through in your work, and your instructors may be enlightened, as well. Note, too, that if you choose a new topic, you really need to start early and stay disciplined, so you can learn enough to present a good paper.

Does your professor want an informative paper or a persuasive paper? An informative paper simply provides the basic information about the subject. For instance, if you were to write an informative paper about an upcoming election, you might provide details about the candidates such as their political parties, biographical and educational background, work experiences, and positions on various issues. Once you've presented that information, you would leave it up to the reader to decide which candidate is superior.

By contrast, a persuasive paper might include all of the information listed above, but the paper would also recommend a particular candidate. Obviously, the persuasive paper is more difficult to write because once you recommend one candidate, you have to back up your choice with facts, reasons, statistics, and any other information you feel is convincing. Obviously, you won't do well if your teacher is expecting a persuasive paper and you provide only the informative paper or if the reverse is true.

So, as you consider a topic for your term-paper assignment, you can approach the task as a dreaded chore, put it off until the last possible moment, and, then, plow through it just before final exams. Or, you can view the task as a challenge and an adventure, one that will be interesting and engaging for both you and your professor. Why not start thinking about your topic today!

2. Finding a Focus for Your Term Paper

If you've ever used a manual camera with a zoom lens, you know that the first image you see will probably be vague or fuzzy because your subject is too close or too far away. Thus, you have to adjust the lens until your subject becomes clear. A similar adjustment may be necessary as you prepare to write your term paper. If the topic is too narrow or too broad for the expected length of the assignment, you may have to expand the scope of your paper or zoom in a little tighter, so the subject will be clear to your readers.

At the college level, most instructors assign a term paper that is between five and ten pages. If you've never written a term paper before, that length may sound intimidating or overwhelming. However, once you begin gathering information on a broad, general topic, you'll be surprised at how quickly those pages fill up.

For instance, if you decide to write about author Stephen King, you could easily write five to ten pages about his life, his many novels, and his awards. Unfortunately, that wouldn't

be an interesting paper because it would read too much like a shopping list of his accomplishments. Instead, you may want to narrow your focus and write on only one or two of his novels and compare and contrast them in some way or connect them to another aspect of life or society.

By contrast, if you want to write about a new female novelist who has only written one book, you may have to take the opposite approach because you can't find five to ten pages of information about her. When that occurs, you can still write about that author, but you may have to include her with other authors in a broader category such as "new female voices" or "the next generation of American novelists." Narrowing or broadening a topic requires some work, of course, so here are five pre-writing activities that you may find helpful.

Freewriting or Brainstorming.
When you free write, you force yourself to write for a certain amount of time, and you let your ideas go straight from your brain to the page, or the computer

screen, without allowing the "editor" in you to interrupt the flow of the ideas. "Focused freewriting" is similar to brainstorming because you start with a certain subject – such as the tentative topic for your term paper – and you write down anything that comes to mind on that topic. Yes, you may find that most of what you write with these activities may be useless, but if you discover one idea that is really useful, you may have refined your topic.

Journaling. Journaling is similar to freewriting or brainstorming, but instead of writing for only a short period of time, you write regularly over an extended period. This method works well for a term paper because you have so much more time with which to work. Journaling allows you to dig much deeper, and you'll probably find that your ideas will pervade your thoughts as you perform other activities. Within a week or two, the perfect idea may just pop into your head while you're washing the dishes or vacuuming the rugs. Yet, that "pop" may not have occurred if you hadn't laid the groundwork for it with your journaling.

Asking and Answering the Reporter's Questions. Typically, newspaper reporters use six key questions when they write their stories: "Who? What? Where? When? Why? and How?" As you attempt to answer these questions on your subject, you may discover one aspect of your topic that you didn't consider previously. For example, you might begin writing about "why" people suffer from depression, but, then, as you explore the other five questions, you may find that "when" they suffer or "how" they suffer is a much more interesting and manageable topic for your term paper.

Browsing. Most people associate browsing with a department store or a shopping mall, but have you ever considered browsing in a library or on the Internet? If you want to write about the Revolutionary War, for instance, you might go to the library shelf where all the books about that war are located. Then, instead, of starting to read one book cover to cover, you can simply glance at the table of contents and the chapter headings to find one particular aspect of that war that intrigues you: a specific battle, an individual participant, or an unusual cause or consequence. Naturally, you can do the same thing electronically by using a computer search engine or by taking advantage of one of the many databases that your college library provides for you.

Diagramming, Mapping, or Clustering. If words begin to overwhelm you in your research, you may want to add drawings to your words. Diagramming, mapping, and clustering are visual ways to help you see connections and relationships among your ideas and your details. You might, for instance, surround certain words with rectangles, circles, or triangles to show similarities, or you might use lines and arrows to show connections. This visual technique is especially effective if you want to focus on causes and/or effects, or if you want to see an actual timeline of when certain events occurred.

Typically, when photographers shoot a subject, they don't just take one shot and walk away. Rather, they may take numerous shots with various settings, exposures, and angles in order to find the one perfect combination that leads to the desired photograph. When you write a term paper, your pre-writing activities will also allow you to find a focus for your term paper and allow you to communicate that idea to your readers.

3. Starting Your Research

Writing a research paper is a bit like preparing a meal or a special dessert, especially during the gathering stage of the process. Just as a chef has to gather all of the ingredients and all of the cooking utensils beforehand, you, too, must gather certain information. Here's a four-step overview of what you need to gather to write a strong research paper.

1. First, gather as many materials on your topic as possible: books, magazines, newspapers, pamphlets, database information, and website information from reputable sources. Generally, website information from education sites (.edu) and government sites (.gov) is more objective and reliable than information from organizational sites (.org) and commercial sites (.com) because the latter sites are trying to get you to support their cause or to purchase their products or services.

2. Then, preview the materials, and read selectively. Once you've gathered as much information as you can find, you should, obviously, begin reading it, but don't overwhelm yourself by immediately trying to read every word of every document. For example, if you're writing about the Battle of Saratoga and one of your books on the Revolutionary War contains only one chapter on that particular battle, read only that chapter. If you have time later to read the entire book, you may do so but only after devouring everything that pertains specifically to your topic.

3. Next, keep thorough records of your sources. In fact, you may want to start putting together your works cited page or your reference page as you write your paper. Most students save that step until the entire paper is written, but if you can add each source as you refer to it, the final documentation process will be easier and much less stressful.

Generally, for your works cited page, you should collect three kinds of information. First, make sure you record the full name of the author or authors. Next, record the full title of the work. Then, record the work's publication information which is different for each type of source:

• Book – the publisher and the year.

• Magazine or newspaper – the name of the publication, the date, and the page number.

• Document retrieved from a database – the name of the database and the web address.

• Information from an Internet website – the name of the school, government agency, organization, or company that set up the website, and the web address (without http://), which is sometimes referred to as the URL or Uniform Resource Locator.

4. Finally, look beyond the normal sources for information or consider non-print sources. This is especially true if your topic lends itself to non-traditional sources. For instance, if you're writing about depression, try to interview a person who has suffered from depression or someone who works with people who are depressed. Or, if your topic doesn't lend itself to an interview, consider attending a public meeting or an event that might be related to your topic. Or, visit a museum or a historical site that is connected in some way. Typically, teachers really appreciate students who think in new ways about their subjects and explore out-of-the-ordinary sources. Again, you have to keep thorough records about these sources, so you can properly document that information.

When chefs finish preparing a meal or a special dessert, they not only get to taste that work of art, but they also get to watch others enjoy that particular specialty. Similarly, when you write a strong term paper, you'll not only enjoy the satisfaction of a task done well, but you'll also experience the joy of your teacher's positive reaction to the paper and the A or the A+ that goes along with it.

4. Developing a Thesis

Have you ever been the victim of a broken promise? Perhaps a friend failed to follow through on an agreement. Or, maybe a business person neglected to perform as expected. Sometimes, too, unfortunately, loved ones will break your heart. In each of those cases, the disappointment can range from mere frustration to outright anger. While a college term paper doesn't usually generate such intense emotion, the thesis of your paper is the promise you make to your readers, a promise that you don't want to break.

Some students confuse the subject of a paper with the thesis, yet a strong distinction exists. The subject is generally the starting point: a living author such as Stephen King, a Revolutionary War event such as the Battle of Saratoga, or a psychological disorder such as depression. The thesis, by contrast, is not only much more specific, but a strong thesis also provides precise directions for the paper. For instance, you might contrast two of King's prison stories and make the argument that *The Green Mile* is actually an extension of *The*

Shawshank Redemption. Or, you might explain that America's most notorious traitor, Benedict Arnold, was one of the heroes in the Battle of Saratoga. You might even explain the three major effects of depression on teenagers.

Once you decide upon your thesis, you should make sure to place it in the appropriate spot – the last sentence of the first paragraph. That placement is essential for you as a writer and for your readers.

For you as the writer, the thesis serves as your compass to keep you moving in the right direction. Without a clear destination in mind, you may get distracted and drift off course. To prevent this drifting, some students actually write their thesis on an index card, and they attach the card to their research notebook or their computer screen to keep them focused on the main idea of the paper.

The thesis also helps your reader to follow the flow of your paper. For instance, if a paper doesn't have a strong thesis with clear directions, the readers may hesitate or pause and wonder where you're headed. Some readers may, in fact, not finish reading because they can't tell where you're going, and they don't want to be surprised or disappointed by your eventual destination. The strong thesis with clear directions, however, is like a leisurely guided tour through an old castle with lots of interesting exhibits and stories throughout.

One final thought to consider regarding your thesis is that you should not feel locked in to that particular itinerary; as you conduct your research and write, you should always consider your thesis "tentative." After all, even though you begin with what you think is a great thesis, storms may occur. In fact, three situations may occur which could prevent you from completing the paper with that original thesis.

First, you may discover that you can't find any information to support your original thesis. Next, you may come up with an even better idea for a thesis. Finally, you may even discover that your original thoughts on a subject were totally incorrect, and you may change your mind completely. If one of these situations does occur, you have to be flexible enough as a writer to realize it and be willing to edit your thesis or revise it accordingly. Some students are so stubborn that they persist with a poor thesis only because they already submitted the thesis and the outline to their instructors, and these students don't want the hassle of trying to explain the change to their instructors. Yet, most instructors want you to remain objective throughout the research process because they want the process to be a time of discovery for you rather than simply an attempt on your part to prove what you already believe.

Thus, your thesis is really a statement that goes through three stages. First, it's a compass to guide you as you research and write your paper; then, it's a storm that might throw you off course or force you to change directions; and, finally, when you put it in the final draft of your paper, it's a promise to your readers, one that you don't want to break.

5. *Organizing Your Ideas for Your Term Paper*

When most people think of writing tools, they usually think of pen or pencil and paper, a typewriter, or a computer. And, yes, these are the practical tools to record your thoughts, so others can read them. However, the even more useful tools of writing are the various techniques you can use to express yourself, and you have a menu of nine basic choices.

1. Narration is nothing more than telling a story, and you use this most basic technique every single day. During the school day, you tell your friends and classmates what you did the night before, and when you get home, you tell your family what you did that day at school. Each story, though, must have a point. A story without a point – a main idea or a thesis – is like an endless carnival ride, one that readers will want to abandon. If you're writing about Benedict Arnold and the Battle of Saratoga, for example, you may want to narrate all the key events in chronological order, the order in which they occurred.

2. Description is simply showing your readers how a person, place, object, or idea looks, sounds, smells, feels, and, if appropriate, tastes. Normally, description is used along with narration to add color and excitement to your stories. When describing, you don't necessarily have to include details about all five senses, but you should at least go beyond the visual since that is what most writers focus on first. For instance, if you are writing about depression, your major emphasis might be the utter emptiness and loneliness that some depressed people feel.

3. Comparison and Contrast are used to point out the similarities and differences between two or more options. This is another technique you use often, especially when you spend your money. When buying a new winter coat, for example, you may visit various stores or look at numerous catalogs or online websites to find the coat that fits your preferences and your budget. Similarly, if you're writing about some of Stephen King's novels, you may have to compare and contrast them to make your point.

4. Exemplification simply means using examples to back up a statement or an argument. When you suggest an idea in class or at work, for instance, someone might ask, "What makes you think this will work?" A typical response might be two or three examples of situations where you know your idea has succeeded. So, if you're arguing in your paper that Benedict

Arnold was a great American hero at the Battle of Saratoga, you'll have to back up your argument with examples of his actions or exploits in that particular battle.

5. Causation is the technique that allows you to explain the causes that precede and the effects that follow a certain event. This technique is used often in history classes when teachers ask you to write about the causes and/or effects of major wars. Generally, in a short paper, you have to choose between causes or effects, but in a longer paper, you may have room to discuss both. In fact, you might actually use a timeline to demonstrate a whole chain of events leading up to and, then, following the event that is the cornerstone of your paper. If you're writing about depression and teenagers, for example, you could explain the social, emotional, and physical causes and also explain the social, emotional, and physical symptoms if the problem goes undiagnosed and untreated.

6. Classification and Division serve to bring organization and simplicity to a complex subject. You actually use these techniques at home when you divide your eating utensils in the silverware drawer in your kitchen or when you classify your clothing items by inserting them in certain drawers in your bedroom dresser. To visualize this technique, you might imagine your subject as a pizza pie that needs to be sliced into a certain amount of pieces to match each of your categories. If you are writing about Stephen King, for example, you might explain that all of his novels fall into four distinct types.

7. Process Analysis is usually referred to as "How To" writing because the writer is attempting to teach the reader how to perform a certain task. However, process analysis also includes "How" writing which explains how something happens; with "How" writing, though, the writer doesn't expect the reader to imitate the process. Again, if you were writing about Stephen King, you might use King's non-fiction book entitled *On Writing – A Memoir on the Craft* to show how King

became one of the best-selling authors of all time, but you wouldn't expect the reader to have that same extraordinary success.

8. Definition is an unusual technique because it cannot stand alone. You may start with a basic explanation of your subject, but, then, you would have to work with one or more of the other writing techniques to make your points about that subject. Thus if you were writing about depression, you would have to define it first before you could explain the causes or effects. Another option might be to contrast depression with other ailments such as schizophrenia or bi-polar disorders. You could even show how teenage depression is different from post-partum depression.

9. Persuasion is another technique that cannot stand alone. When you write a persuasive paper, you're trying to convince your reader to believe as you do or to take a certain action. In fact, all advertising is a form of persuasion as advertisers are urging you to buy their product or service. Thus, you can use narration to persuade – as Jesus did in His parables – or you can use causation to explain how implementing a certain idea or plan will lead to a beneficial effect. Also, the Benedict Arnold examples mentioned earlier demonstrate how persuasion can be used with narration and exemplification to argue the thesis that Benedict Arnold was an American hero in the Battle of Saratoga.

Will you write an entire term paper using only one of the first seven techniques? Probably not. Just as you need to combine definition and persuasion with other writing techniques, you will, most likely, write your paper with a combination platter. Thus, as you outline your paper, you might want to brainstorm ideas for all nine techniques. Then, you can choose one as your primary technique and one or two others as your supplementary techniques. Brainstorming in this way will help you choose the proper tools for the job of explaining your topic, and you should be able to write an excellent term paper.

6. *Documenting Your Sources*

Have you ever received a compliment you didn't deserve? Maybe you purchased cookies to bring to a party, and your friends admired your baking ability. Or perhaps you hired a contractor to install a hardwood floor, and your guests praised your handiwork. When these situations occur, you can do one of two things: you can pretend you baked the cookies or installed the floor and deceive those close to you; or you can give credit to the baker and installer and also let your friends and guests know how they, too, can acquire that same product or service. Similarly, when you write a term paper, documenting your sources allows you to give credit to those who provided the information and to help your readers find those same sources.

Giving Credit. When you take information from various sources for your paper, you have to acknowledge and give credit to the writers who provided you with that information. If you fail to do so, you are essentially stealing that information and implying that you are the original source. In other words, you are accepting a compliment that you don't really deserve. In academic circles, that's called plagiarism, and it's a serious offense that could, depending on the level of the offense, lead to a failing grade on an assignment, a failing grade in the course, and a suspension from school ("Plagiarism," *The Newbury House Dictionary* 654). Thus, you're much better off if you simply give credit to your source.

Helping Readers. In addition to giving credit to your sources, you also want to let your readers know how to find those sources, so your readers, if necessary, can also go to those sources. If, for instance, you find a new book about depression and teenagers, and if you use some information from that book in your paper, your professor may also want to read that same book. By providing the reader with the author, title, and publication information, you make it easy for the reader to find the book in a library or a bookstore or online.

The next question you may be asking yourself is, "Do I have to document everything in my paper?" Fortunately, the answer is "no." You do not have to document two types of information: personal opinion and common knowledge.

Personal Opinion. If you are writing an informative paper, your instructor may not want your personal opinion in the paper. However, if you are writing a persuasive paper, you will need to express your opinion, but you don't need to cite yourself as the source. If, for instance, you feel that Benedict Arnold is the most underappreciated American soldier in history, you could write, "Most Americans remember Benedict Arnold only because of his traitorous actions after the Revolutionary War, but his exploits during that war are remarkable and should be appreciated by historians." (In your research paper, you should avoid the first-person point-of-view pronouns, such as "I" and "we" and use the third-person point of view exclusively.) Naturally, once you state your opinion, you need to support that opinion with information from your sources.

Common Knowledge. Common knowledge is generally referred to as information that everybody knows or information that can be found easily in a variety of sources. For instance, most people know that Stephen King has written some best-selling novels such as *Carrie*, *The Shining*, *Pet Sematary*, and *The Green Mile*. Thus, you wouldn't have to document that information when you refer to his works in general.

How about Stephen King's birth date? Do you know what year he was born? Most likely, you don't. However, you could probably find that date easily by looking at one of his books, by checking an encyclopedia, or by finding a website about him. So, even though that information may not have been "common knowledge" for you when you began your research, you wouldn't have to document it because that type of biographical information is readily available. As a general rule, if you see certain information in at least three different sources, that information is considered common knowledge and does not have to be cited. If you have any doubts whatsoever, though, about whether to cite certain information, you should cite your source because, as mentioned earlier, if you fail to document your sources properly, you will be guilty of plagiarism.

So where did you buy those cookies, and who installed that hardwood floor in your dining room? Once your friends and guests realize that you didn't bake the cookies or install the floor, they'll probably move on to the next question: If you didn't do the work, who did? The same is true for your readers. They're not surprised or offended when you're not the original source of information. Instead, readers are generally pleased by your effort to find the information and by your willingness to share your sources with them.

7. *Avoiding Plagiarism*

Certain football coaches are reluctant to have their teams throw the ball because, according to the cliché, "When you throw a forward pass, three things can happen – and two of them are bad." Yes, these coaches fear that their quarterbacks will throw an incompletion or, worse yet, an interception. Still, however, their quarterbacks do throw the ball once in a while because the coaches also recognize the positive possibility of a completed pass. Plagiarism, on the other hand, offers no positive possibilities whatsoever. As a student, if you are caught plagiarizing, three things can happen, and all three of them are bad.

Plagiarism is, essentially, a theft of intellectual property. When you take another person's ideas without giving that person credit, that act is the same as if you broke into that person's house and stole the television ("Plagiarism," *The Newbury House Dictionary* 654). Some students plagiarize because they don't know any better. Others are simply not as careful as they should be with their documentation. Still others are unwilling to do the work, and they hope they won't get caught.

You should know, however, that the faculty and the administration at most colleges will not tolerate plagiarism. According to the *Plagiarism Policy* pamphlet at Hudson Valley Community College, the College "has a strong policy against plagiarism because when students plagiarize, they threaten the integrity of the entire institution, and they devalue the legitimate intellectual accomplishments of all students." So what can you do to avoid plagiarism? You can learn to use all of the following correctly: quotations, paraphrases, and summaries along with in-text citations and a list of sources.

Quotations. When you copy directly from a source, you have to put the copied material in quotation marks to indicate that the material was originally composed by someone else. Generally, you should include quotations "when a source's exact words are important to your point and make your writing more memorable, fair, or authoritative," say Elaine P. Maimon, Janice H. Peritz, and Kathleen Blake Yancey, authors of the 2007 edition of *The New McGraw-Hill Handbook* (358). Does that mean you should fill your entire paper with quotations? No. Anyone can simply copy quotes; your teachers would much rather see you paraphrase or summarize what you read and use quotations only for special effect.

Paraphrases. When you paraphrase, you take your source's information, and you put that information into your own words, usually in a way that is much more concise with fewer specific details. Unfortunately, some students view a paraphrase as if it were a translation into a new language, and they simply substitute synonyms for the key words or phrases. To paraphrase correctly, however, you should change both the sentence structure and the overall vocabulary, so that your paraphrase has your own unique style rather than the style of the original author (Maimon, et al., 2009, 353).

Summaries. When you summarize, you're also putting the source's information into your own words, but you're doing so in a much shorter format. According to Lynn Troyka and Douglas Hesse, authors of the *Simon & Schuster Handbook for Writers,* the summary is the technique you'll use most often in your research, and you'll use it primarily to focus on main ideas. Thus, you may have to break down the original source into smaller segments and, then, extract the main idea from each segment. At that point, you may have to accentuate certain ideas, eliminate others, and organize your selected ideas to fit the overall pattern of your paper (557-60).

Once you've chosen the appropriate quotations and once you've finished writing your paraphrases and your summaries, you need to cite all those sources in two places: (1) immediately after the quotation, paraphrase, or summary in an in-text citation and (2) at the end of your paper in a complete list of sources.

In-text Citations. Generally, an in-text citation will give your reader a general reference to the source of your information. For example, you might include the author's name in the paragraph itself, as this essay does in the paragraph on "Summaries." Or you might include the author's name within a set of parentheses (a parenthetical reference) at the end of the quotation. Finally, you might use a parenthetical reference at the end of the paragraph that includes either a paraphrase or a summary, as this essay does in the

paragraph on "Paraphrases." You might even use a footnote or an endnote to indicate that general information about the source is located at the foot of the page or at the end of the paper. The information included in these citations and the placement of the citations will depend on the documentation style you are using.

List of Sources. At the end of your paper, you must also provide a list (alphabetized by author) of either the works mentioned in your paper or the works consulted during the research process. (Again, the exact format will depend on the documentation style you are using.) Generally, you have to provide the author's name, the title of the work, and enough of the publication information, so that your reader can also find that same source.

Is it acceptable to provide only the in-text citations or only the list of sources at the end? No. You need to provide both, and if you fail to do so, you are guilty of plagiarism. And the punishments for plagiarism are severe based on the level of the offense. According to the *Plagiarism Policy* pamphlet at Hudson Valley Community College, for a minor offense or a Level One violation, you "may receive a failing grade for the assignment." For a "significant" offense or a Level Two violation, you "may receive a failing grade for the course." Finally, for a repeated offense or a Level Three violation, you "may receive a failing grade for the course" and "may be suspended or expelled from the College." Note, that if you commit any of the three levels of violations, your name will be forwarded to various authorities on campus. Note, too, that if you feel you have been unjustly accused of plagiarism, you do have the right to appeal.

Thus, as mentioned earlier, "if you are caught plagiarizing, three things can happen, and all three of them are bad." Obviously, then, you will want to avoid plagiarism by keeping thorough records of all your sources and by properly documenting those sources according to the style that is required by your instructor or appropriate to your subject matter.

8. *Citing Sources – MLA or APA Style?*

When you are invited to a party, how do you determine what to wear? Do you base your clothing decision on the location of the party, on those who will be in attendance, or even on the theme or the occasion for the party? Most likely, you decide based on one or more of the factors mentioned, and you choose a style and an outfit that are appropriate. When you write a term paper, you also have to consider style, and the documentation style you choose will be based primarily on the subject of your paper and on your teacher's expectations.

Believe it or not, when you write a term paper, you have numerous documentation styles available. The two most common, however, are the MLA style and the APA style.

MLA Style. According to *The Purdue Online Writing Lab*, the style of the Modern Language Association "is most commonly used to write papers and cite sources within the liberal arts and humanities" ("MLA Formatting and Style Guide"). Thus, if you are taking a writing course, a literature course,

a language course, or an art course, your instructor may ask you to use the MLA style. Note, however, that if you're taking a writing course, but the subject of your paper is not in the arts or humanities, your instructor may ask you to use a different style. Note, too, that some instructors who teach outside the realm of the arts and humanities may also ask you to use the MLA style.

The MLA style has two required components and one optional component. First, you must include parenthetical references for your sources. Basically, that means any time you take information from a source and use it as part of a quotation, a paraphrase, or a summary, you must include the author or authors' last name(s) and the page number for the source in a set of parentheses after that information is mentioned (Maimon, et al., 2009, 381). Since the essay you are reading is about writing, this essay is written in MLA style, and the source for the information in the previous sentence is included at the end of that sentence in a parenthetical reference. (Exceptions to the general rule about author and page do exist, so be sure to consult the MLA guidelines for sources that do not fit the normal pattern.)

Next, you must also include a list of "works cited" at the end of your paper. So, if you mention any source in your paper (either in the text itself or in a parenthetical reference), you must include additional information about that source on your works-cited page. Generally, these sources will be listed in alphabetical order by the author's last name, and each citation will include the author's name, the full title of the source, and publication information about the source. This information will make it possible for your readers to find your sources if your readers wish to consult those same sources. (Again, exceptions to the general rule about author, title, and publication information do exist, so be sure to consult the MLA guidelines for sources that do not fit the normal pattern.) You should know, too, that some instructors will ask you for a "works consulted" list in place of, or in addition to, a works cited list. Obviously, those instructors want to see a complete list of all your sources – sometimes referred to as a bibliography – even if you didn't refer to all of them in your paper.

Finally, though you are not required to do so, you may also include explanatory notes and acknowledgements at the end of your paper. These notes can be helpful when you want to "offer the reader comment, explanation, or information that the text can't accommodate" or when you want to make "evaluative comments on your sources" ("Are Notes Compatible with MLA Style?").

APA Style. The style of the American Psychological Association is typically used in "many of the social and behavioral sciences"

("About APA Style"). That means if you are taking a course in sociology, psychology, business, or medical subjects, you may be required to use the APA style. The APA style is similar to the MLA style because the APA style also requires parenthetical citations within the text and a complete list of sources – referred to as "references" – at the end of the paper.

The major difference between the two styles concerns the placement of dates within the parenthetical references and on the list of sources at the end of the paper. The APA style requires the author's name and the year of publication in all in-text citations. In addition, the APA style requires that the date immediately follow the author's name on the list of sources (instead of placing the date at the end of the publication information as is done in the MLA style). The APA style places a greater emphasis on the date of publication because readers in the behavioral and social sciences want the most current information available. In fact, some instructors in those fields will tell you that they don't want you to use any sources that are more than three years old. Finally, you should know that the APA style "discourages the use of explanatory content notes to supplement the ideas in your paper, but they are an option" (Maimon, et al., 2009, 452).

When you first start using either the MLA or APA documentation style, you may feel overwhelmed by the complexity of the style and by the numerous rules that pertain only to specific sources. However, like any other activity, you will soon become accustomed to the patterns, and you'll probably find yourself helping your friends and classmates learn to use the style as well. Now, if you could only figure out what to wear to that party.

9. *Revising Your Paper*

When I was a boy, I always helped my dad with home-improvement projects. Since he was a plumber by trade and a carpenter and an electrician through experience, he performed all of the difficult tasks while I handed him tools and brought him sodas. Then, when he finished, he allowed me to complete one of the most important tasks of all: "Jim, clean up this mess."

As a boy, of course, I thought cleaning up was simply a menial task that anyone could perform. Now that I'm a grown man, however, I realize that the cleanup is an important part of the process, and not everyone can perform the task thoroughly and well. In fact, cleaning up the three major parts of an essay or a term paper may be the most difficult task of all.

First, you should make sure that your introduction is interesting and strong. Too many students settle for a bland opening statement such as "This paper will be about . . ." or "The subject of this paper is . . ." Some students have a weak introduction because they aren't willing to dig up anything interesting, but others simply don't know how to begin or what they're trying to accomplish.

Basically, a strong introduction should accomplish four objectives: grab the readers' attention, present the general plan of development for the paper, provide some basic background information, and make the thesis – or main idea – clear. An effective introduction may use one or more of the following techniques: a question, a joke or a story, a quotation or a bit of dialogue, a detailed description, a comparison, a vivid example, a definition, an allusion, or a startling statement, statistic, or fact.

If you're writing about Stephen King, for example, you might take a quotation from one of his works. If you're writing about the Battle of Saratoga, you might include an interesting statistic. Or, if you're writing about depression, you might start with a definition. The introductory device that is appropriate for you and your paper will depend in large part on the topic of your paper.

Next, you have to look at the body paragraphs of your text which support the main idea of your paper. As you evaluate each paragraph, you should ask yourself these questions:

- Does the paragraph have a transitional word or phrase?

- Does the paragraph have a strong topic sentence?

- Does the paragraph support the thesis?

- Does the paragraph reinforce a previous point or make a new one?

- Does the paragraph give specific evidence to develop its point?

- Does the paragraph use outside sources to support its point?

- Does the paragraph indicate the credibility or expertise of the outside source?

- Does the paragraph cite the source properly?

- Do the paragraphs fit together seamlessly with all the other paragraphs?

Lastly, you need to look at your conclusion. Again, many students are content to simply write "In conclusion" or "To summarize" and, then, restate the thesis. While you should definitely restate your main idea, your overall conclusion should be more powerful. After all, the conclusion is the last thought your reader will grasp, and you want that final thought to be memorable. Thus, you may want to use one of the techniques mentioned earlier (a question, a story, a quotation, etc.), or you may want to use a call to action.

For instance, you may want to use a final story about Stephen King to reiterate your thesis. You may want to ask a thought provoking question about the Battle of Saratoga to intrigue your reader long after the paper has been read. Or you may want to recommend that major health plans cover the cost for the treatment of depression. Again, the concluding device you use will depend on your topic and your thesis.

Overall, you want your introduction, your main text, and your conclusion to work neatly together. What often happens, unfortunately, is that many students are finishing the main text as the deadline approaches, and they have little time to write a strong introduction and conclusion. Ideally, you want to leave yourself plenty of time before the deadline, so you can write a few introductions and conclusions before choosing the most effective. After all, if you don't leave yourself enough time to clean up and polish all those messy paragraphs, you'll probably feel more like the helping child and less like the master craftsman.

10. Proofreading Your Paper

When I was in college almost 50 years ago, I was using a typewriter rather than a computer, and I didn't have a spell checker or a grammar checker on my machine. Fortunately, today, I have access to these modern devices, and I usually find and correct most of my mistakes rather quickly. Fortunately, too, most of my students are smart enough to use the spell checkers and grammar checkers on their computers. Unfortunately, too many students rely on them exclusively. Since these modern tools are not perfect, however, here are five old-fashioned proofreading techniques for you to consider.

Let your paper sit overnight. The mistake that some students make is they proofread their papers right after they finish writing. This is a problem because you can't see your own errors at that point; you're still too close to the actual writing of the paper. Ideally, you should finish the paper well in advance, so you can let it sit overnight before you proofread it. A full night's rest will give you the separation you need to look at the paper with fresh eyes in the morning.

Believe it or not, some of your errors will jump out at you at that point, and you can make the appropriate changes.

Let someone else read the paper. You can also benefit by having a second set of fresh eyes, someone who has not seen the paper before. This person may be a classmate, a friend, a relative – anyone who is serious and objective. After all, if you were a professional writer, you would probably have a professional editor or a professional proofreader looking over your work. Thus, until you reach that level as a writer, you should find someone who is willing to help you, and you can return the favor by offering to read for that person, as well.

Read your paper aloud – slowly. If you don't have anyone who is willing or capable of reading for you, you can help yourself by reading the paper aloud and by reading slowly. When you read your own work without speaking, you tend to see words that aren't even on the page because you thought of writing those words, and you meant to write them, but you didn't. When you read aloud, though, you notice that words are missing, and you might also notice that certain word combinations don't work well together. Note, too, that you should read aloud even your punctuation marks: comma, hyphen, apostrophe, colon, semicolon, dash, and period. Otherwise, you may skip over these marks too quickly and defeat the overall purpose of the slow, methodical reading.

Read your paper syllable by syllable. Yes, this method is time consuming and requires you to be meticulous, but you will catch most of your spelling errors this way. For example, if you see the words "con-sum-ing" and "me-tic-u-lous" broken down by syllable, you're much more likely to see a missing letter, a repeated letter, or an incorrect letter.

Read your paper backwards. This method sounds really crazy, but, again, it's especially effective for catching spelling errors. When you read from left to right and top to bottom, you usually find yourself reading not only for spelling errors but also for content. Thus, thinking about content may prevent you from seeing your spelling mistakes. Reading from right to left and bottom to top should prevent you from focusing on the content and allow you to focus exclusively on the spelling of each word. Thus, you should read this sentence in this way: "way this in sentence this read should you Thus."

Is proofreading really that important? Yes, it is. After all, you could have the best paper in the world, but if your instructor is constantly distracted by spelling, grammatical, and punctuation errors, you're probably not going to receive the grade you desire. So rather than view proofreading as a minor task at the end of the research process, try to finish your writing well in advance of your deadline, so you can take your time and proofread carefully and thoroughly.

New MLA Guidelines for 2016 (8th edition)

Our kitchen stove at home has a drawer at the bottom where we keep some of our pots and pans. One particular set includes three pots that sit inside one another: a large pot that we use for frying meatballs, a medium pot that we use for cooking omelets, and a small pot that we use for boiling water for tea. Naturally, for storage purposes, the small pot sits inside the medium pot which sits inside the large pot, and this idea of one small container sitting inside a larger container sitting inside a third container is one of the major visual images to keep in mind regarding the new MLA Guidelines (*MLA Handbook,* 2016, 8th ed.).

In the previous editions of the *MLA Handbook*, the editors tried to provide explanations and sample citations for each type of source such as a book, a magazine or newspaper article, a journal article, a film, a sound recording, etc. As the years passed, however, modern technology made more and more types of sources available: online books, databases, websites, blogs, podcasts, and e-mail messages among others. Rather than create even more explanations and examples, the 2016 edition of the *MLA Handbook* tries to simplify the process by focusing on the basic elements of any

source. As the introduction to the book explains, "now more than ever we need a system for documenting sources that begins with a few principles rather than a long list of rules (3). The text goes on to call these principles "commonsense guidelines," and adds that "A work in a new medium thus can be documented without new instructions" (3).

For instance, an example of a small pot is any work that stands on its own such as a book by one author. So a researcher who wants to cite a book now only needs to provide four basic elements: author, title, publisher, and year. Under the new guidelines, the place of publication is no longer necessary, nor is the medium (print or web). Below is an example of a recent novel under the old format and the new format, and the underlined elements from the old format are no longer needed.

Old Format

Quindlen, Anna. *Miller's Valley*. <u>New York:</u> Random House, 2016. <u>Print.</u>

New Format

Quindlen, Anna. *Miller's Valley*. Random House, 2016.

An example of a medium pot would be a larger work such as an anthology that includes a number of shorter works such as short stories, poems, or articles. The short work itself and the author make up the small pot inside the bigger container, the anthology. For example, former tennis player Arthur Ashe once wrote an article (small pot) entitled "Send Your Children to the Libraries" which is included in an anthology (medium pot) entitled *The Simon & Schuster Short Prose Reader*. For this source, the researcher would have to include the same four elements mentioned above – author, title, publisher, and year – but also add three additional elements: title of the anthology, editor(s), and page numbers. Again, the place of publication and the medium are no longer necessary, but the new format requires the abbreviation "p." or "pp." for page numbers. Below are examples of citations for the Ashe article from the book under the old format and the new format; again, the underlined elements from the old format are no longer needed.

Old Format

Ashe, Arthur. "Send Your Children to the Libraries." *The Simon & Schuster Short Prose Reader*. Ed. Robert Funk, Susan X Day, and Elizabeth McMahan. Upper Saddle River, NJ: Prentice Hall, 1997. 286-89. Print.

New Format

Ashe, Arthur. "Send Your Children to the Libraries." *The Simon & Schuster Short Prose Reader*, edited by Robert Funk, Susan X Day, and Elizabeth McMahan, Prentice Hall, 1997, pp. 286-89.

Finally, an example of a large pot would be a library database which includes a number of publications (medium pots) which include a number of articles (small pots). Using the same Ashe article mentioned above, a researcher who didn't have access to the *The Simon & Schuster Short Prose Reader* could still find the article in a database which includes *The New York Times*. Ashe initially published his article in *The Times* in 1977, and that article is still available today in the *ProQuest* database. To summarize, the article is the small pot inside the newspaper – the medium pot – and the database is the large pot which holds both the newspaper and the article. To document the article from the database instead of the textbook, the researcher would still need the author and title of the article and also require the name of the newspaper, the date of publication, the page number(s), and the name of the database. The medium and the date of access are no longer required, but the new guidelines do require the web address (without http://). Below are examples of citations for the Ashe article from the database under the old format and the new format; the underlined elements from the old format are no longer needed.

Old Format

Ashe, Arthur. "Send Your Children to the Libraries." *New York Times* 6 Feb. 1977: S2. *ProQuest*. Web. 8 June 2016.

New Format

Ashe, Arthur. "Send Your Children to the Libraries." *New York Times*, 6 Feb 1977, p. S2. *ProQuest*. proxy.hvcc.edu:2048/ login?url=http://search.proquest.com/ docview/1231 19290?accountid=6155

To summarize, then, the new guidelines suggest that researchers always provide the basics of author, title, and publication information for stand-alone sources, the small pots. When those sources are included in a larger pot or pots, however, the editors recommend that researchers look for (and provide when possible) seven types of information: title of container, other contributors, version, number, publisher, publication date, and location. Naturally, many sources will not have all seven. Thus, when citing sources, researchers should remember that the primary purpose is to give readers enough information to find the sources wherever they may be located.

Research – Then and Now

I'll never forget my first research assignment. My teacher asked me to put together a short history of the community in which I lived. So I walked to the center of our small village, I found the oldest man in our town, and I asked him to tell me everything he remembered.

Okay, so maybe I'm not really that old, but I think I have officially crossed over from the cool, young teacher to the old curmudgeon. I've become one of those guys who says, "I remember when I was in school . . . ," or "Students today don't know how good they have it."

Obviously, the research process has changed dramatically during the past 50 years. I wrote my first research paper when I was a senior in high school during the spring of 1969. I chose to write about the *USS Pueblo*, an American ship that was captured by North Korea in January 1968, because the ship was supposedly spying in Korean waters. The captain, Lloyd M. Bucher, and his 82 crew members were held hostage and tortured for 11 months before they

were finally released. Naturally, this story was big news at that time, and I wanted to know more about it.

So, first, I googled the words "Pueblo" and "Bucher," and I found 10 million articles on the subject. Then, I printed the first five articles on the list, I read them, I highlighted them, and I wrote the paper. The whole process took maybe an hour. No, that was not the case. The research process was a bit more complicated back then.

First, I went to our school's library, and I began to look through *The Readers' Guide to Periodical Literature*. This was a small, green, weekly periodical that catalogued all the magazine articles written during the previous week. Eventually, these weekly editions were combined to form bigger volumes that covered a month or two or even an entire year. The hardbound version of the annual edition weighed about 40 pounds, and each library had two professional weightlifters on the staff to help researchers go through these volumes. Today, in fact, since those old volumes are no longer needed, the government uses them to reinforce bridge supports along the Hudson and Mohawk Rivers.

As I looked through *The Readers' Guide*, I also had to consult the list of magazines that our library carried to see if the articles I sought would be available. Since I attended a small, Catholic school, our periodical collection was somewhat limited. (I think we had *Time*, *Newsweek*, and *Sports Illustrated*.) Then, once I found a few articles that I thought were appropriate and were available, I had to go to the stacks of magazines that were shelved in a special section. At that point, too, I usually said a short, two-part prayer: I prayed that, first, the magazine itself would be in the right spot, and, second, that the article would still be in the magazine. Believe it or not, some Catholic-school-boy classmates were known to steal a magazine or to rip an article out of a magazine if they needed it for their own research papers.

Why would anyone steal or rip an article out of a magazine if he could just as easily make a copy? Because he couldn't just as easily make a copy. Our school library didn't get its first copier until later that year (a big deal, believe me). So if my prayers were answered

and I actually found the article I needed, then I had to do something almost unimaginable to today's students: I had to read the article and actually take notes on it. While that particular step involved a lot more work than printing and highlighting the key information, I have a feeling I had a better understanding of my material as a result.

Finally, once I had all my ideas and sources organized, I had to sit down at an old manual typewriter, with erasable bond paper, and pound the keys until I got blisters on my fingertips. If I made a mistake, I had to actually erase the error and type it again. If I decided to move a paragraph, I had to retype the whole page. And if I wanted to check the spelling and the grammar when I was finished, I had to do it myself. Sometimes I wonder how I ever survived the twentieth century.

So am I really an old curmudgeon? No, not really. I love the students at Hudson Valley Community College, and I love helping them with their research papers. But when one of them starts to complain about how hard the whole process is, I get a faraway look in my eyes, and I say, "Son, let me tell you about the research process when I was a boy."

Scrapbooking Your Way to a Term Paper

After my daughter Maria graduated from college, she came home and took over her sister's bedroom. Yes, Maria had a bedroom of her own, but while Katrina was away at school, Maria spread her "Spain stuff" all over the floor of Katrina's room because Maria needed some space to put together a scrapbook of her senior trip. As I looked at Maria's mess, I realized that what she was doing is very similar to what all students should be doing as they prepare their term papers. If you're in the midst of writing your own term paper, here are three simple steps to keep in mind.

Gather as much information as you can. As part of her final college course, Maria had the opportunity to spend three weeks in Spain. (Yes, I was extremely jealous, but don't tell Maria.) She spent the first two weeks living with a family in Sevilla and attending daily classes where she learned about various aspects of the Spanish culture. On the weekends, she visited nearby tourist attractions and swam in the Mediterranean Sea. Then, she spent her final week in and around Madrid where she had

the opportunity to tour museums and cathedrals and see a bullfight. During those three weeks, she took numerous pictures and collected and purchased various souvenirs. (Yes, I got a tee-shirt.) By the time she got home, obviously, she had enough photos, pamphlets, brochures, postcards, menus, maps, coins, and ticket stubs to easily fill her scrapbook.

As a writer, you should already be in the midst of a similar gathering process. Once you decide upon a general topic for your paper, you should locate as much information as you can find on that topic. Use the library to find books, use the library's databases to find articles, use the Internet to find statistics, charts, and pictures, and use the people around you – students, teachers, librarians – to help you find other sources that you may not have discovered on your own. For example, you might be able to attend a public meeting on your topic, you might interview an expert on your subject, or you might visit a particular site that has a significant connection to your topic. Ideally, you want to have more information than you need to complete the assignment, so you can pick and choose the information that is most useful and relevant.

Choose a main idea and an overall organizational plan. As I glanced at Maria's materials, I got the impression that she was focusing primarily on the art and architecture of Spain. She had postcards of numerous famous paintings – such as *Guernica* by Pablo Picasso – and she had her own photographs of homes, schools, churches, restaurants, and businesses. Naturally, those photographs also include the faces of the students and teachers who accompanied her. Regarding the organizational plan, the layout appears to be in chronological order. The photos on one side of the room show her departure from New York City, then the souvenirs along one wall chronicle her time in Sevilla, and, finally, the other side of the room includes a bit of everything from her time in Madrid. What's in the middle? All of her scrapbook supplies: the scrapbook itself, scissors, tape, stickers, markers, highlighters, stamps, ribbons, etc.

Once you've gathered all of your information, you, too, have to decide upon a main idea, and you have to make sure that it's appropriate for the length of your paper. After all, if your topic is too broad, you won't be able to cover it thoroughly, but if your topic is too narrow, you'll probably come up short. Your main idea will also help you determine your organizational plan. Like Maria, you may want to use the chronological approach if you're telling the story of a person's life, an event, or a movement. If, however,

you're analyzing two subjects or exploring the connections among a string of incidents, the compare-and-contrast technique or the cause-and-effect approach might be more appropriate. Finally, if you are writing a persuasive paper, you may need to use examples, definitions, or process analysis to make your point.

Put everything together, and show your work to someone. Personally, I didn't think Maria would ever finish her scrapbook. She took her time and enjoyed the process thoroughly. Fortunately for her, she could take her time because she had no real deadline. Yes, Katrina complained when her room was still cluttered at Thanksgiving, and my wife and I were anxious to see the finished scrapbook, but we weren't going to critique Maria's work in a serious academic way.

Obviously, your situation is different. Your teacher has a set deadline, and your term paper might count for a quarter or more of your final grade. Thus, you should try to work on the paper regularly, and you should try to finish your first draft well in advance of the final deadline. By finishing early, you can show your draft to someone who can offer constructive feedback. Then, you can make your final draft even stronger by incorporating the suggestions you feel are appropriate.

Naturally, those of us who work in The Writing and Research Center are here to answer all of your writing questions and to read your work and offer our feedback. And since I probably won't be going abroad anytime soon, I would also love to see the scrapbooks from your overseas adventures.

Roll Up Your Sleeves, Spit On Your Hands, and Finish That Term Paper

A while back, my dad was helping me install a 12-by-20-foot carpet in our living room. We had already installed the padding underneath the carpet, and we had the new rug pretty close to where we wanted it, but we were struggling to move it just a few more inches, so it would lie perfectly up against the walls. That's when my dad – a retired, 82-year-old plumber-steamfitter – got serious.

He rolled up his sleeves, spit on his hands, rubbed them together to get a good grip on the carpet, and said, "Let's move this thing." Sure enough, within seconds, we had the carpet exactly where it belonged, and we were ready to trim it and secure it by installing the baseboards. Fortunately, that blue-collar, get-serious-about-your-work mentality can also help you with your term paper.

Writing a term paper can be a long, arduous process, but some parts of the process are so much easier than others. Choosing a topic, for example, and researching that topic can be fun and exciting. You're reading, you're learning, you're asking questions, and you're answering them. Usually, too, you're doing these things early in the semester, so you're not worried or nervous yet about due dates or deadlines. Then, at some point, you're ready to write your first draft.

The first draft is also exciting because so much is possible. You can play with words, with ideas, with organizational patterns; essentially, you can write anything you want because you know you're going to go back and revise everything later. This is usually the surprise stage of the process because as you write, new thoughts and phrases might come tumbling out, thoughts and phrases that you weren't even aware of earlier. Then, once that first draft is completed, you can share it with someone: a friend, a family member, a significant other. You can be like a little kid again, saying "Mommy! Daddy! Look what I made." Then, you and your reader can discuss your paper's strengths and weaknesses, and you can move on to your final draft.

Unfortunately, the final draft is the heavy lifting of the writing process. That's when you have to go in and make all your final decisions about your introduction and your thesis, your organizational pattern, your transitions, and your conclusion. You have to make sure that your point of view is consistent throughout and that you don't go off on tangents. You also have to make sure that your sources are documented properly within the paper itself (usually in parenthetical references) and at the end of the paper (on your works-cited or reference page). The entire task can feel overwhelming because the final deadline is approaching, and you may be in the midst of a similar task for another course or two. At this point, you have to roll up your sleeves, spit on your hands, and get to work.

Roll up your sleeves. Basically, you have to remove all distractions, anything that will get in your way as you attempt to complete your term paper. Tell your friends you can't go out. Tell your family members they're on their own. Or hire a babysitter if you have to. Basically, you need to gather all your resources, and you have to sit down at your keyboard for a good chunk of time, enough time to allow you to finish.

Spit on your hands. This part sounds unsanitary, and it may well be, but metaphorically, you have to get a better grip on yourself and on the task at hand. You can't procrastinate any longer. You can't daydream. And you can't give less than your full attention and effort. If you really want to lift that final draft from the level of a C or a D grade up to the level of an A or a B, you have to be ready to work.

Get to work. If you've ever lifted and carried anything that's really heavy, you know that you should make sure you're evenly balanced. You should lift properly with your legs rather than your back. You should breathe deeply. And you should exert yourself to the fullest. The same basic principles apply to writing. You have to maintain perspective. You have to concentrate only on what you're doing. And you have to persevere until the task is completed. Yes, you will still have to complete some other chores – such as proofreading and editing – after that final draft is completed, but the heavy lifting will be done.

Though writing a term paper can be a long and arduous process, the completion of that process should give you a strong sense of achievement and satisfaction. Having read thousands of term papers over the years, I know that the difference between a C and a B or a B and an A can be determined by the final push and the final effort on the final draft. As you approach your final deadline, make sure your final effort on your term paper is a strong one.

Chapter 7

Six Essays on Proofreading

These essays were first published in *The Editorial Eye*.

The Proofreader's Lament

I can now empathize with retired cops. They used to be in the spotlight. They once stood in the center of the action, stopping cars with one hand, waving pedestrians across the street with the other, and blowing their whistles at anyone who thought of challenging their authority. But that was before expressways and traffic lights. Now, there is little human work to do.

As a proofreader, I'm going through the same process. I used to stop the writers and point out misspelled words. I used to wave a manuscript through if it contained no errors. If anyone tried to slide anything by me, I blew the whistle. I had authority. But that was before floppy disks and spell checkers.

When I began proofreading, all our writers wrote either in longhand or on typewriters. Naturally, they made some mistakes. After they wrote the draft, it went to typesetting, and the operators there made additional mistakes. By the time the text came to the proofreading department, I was ready. I went through red pens regularly. Not anymore.

First came the computers with floppy disks. Each writer had a terminal where he or she composed, copied to a floppy disk, and set the work to typesetting. The information on the disk was entered directly into typesetting equipment, and the typesetting operators didn't have a chance to make errors. Although the writers still made mistakes, the use of floppy disks cut my work in half.

Then, spell checkers were installed at each terminal. If a writer misspelled a word while composing, the spell checker whistled. To correct the error, the writer could change the spelling manually or let the spell checker do it. The writer could even use the spell checker to scan the document when it was completed to double check the overall spelling. And when the writer finished, he or she copied the text to a floppy disk and sent it to typesetting. Between the floppy disk and the spell checker, my work was practically eliminated.

Sure, everything still goes through proofreading, but we rarely find anything. Have you ever tried to proofread something knowing that there are no errors in it? It's like directing traffic in the old neighborhood, which now has a traffic light and lies below the overpass to the expressway. There's nothing to do.

So what's next for me? I'm thinking about becoming a writer. How hard can it be when my machine checks my spelling for me? To prove how easy it is, I'm going to activate my spell checker for the last paragraph of this article. I won't even bother to proofread it when I'm done. As

long as the spell checker remains silent, I'll be okay. Here goes . . . .

I've always wanted to be a winter. When I was in grade school, I won all the selling bees. When all the other kids were getting nervous, I remained clam. One item, I spelling a word backwards just to I could sit down and take a rust. By downfall was my typing. I wasn't coordinated enough, and my taping errors looked like spelling errors. I new better. Now with these new spell checkers, I won't have any difficult. I'll be a grate writer for cretin.

The Proofreader's Curse

The curse may start at any time. A friend may ask you to check his or her résumé for typographical errors. Or you may work as a teacher and get paid for finding mistakes. Or, worse yet, you may actually work as a professional proofreader. In any case, once you start, you're hooked. Your life will never be the same again.

Proofreading – the art of finding and correcting errors in written communication – is a curse, an addiction. You can't simply punch in and out like most workers; you're on call 24 hours a day.

Other professions don't have this problem. My father, for example, worked as a plumber. Yes, he installed or fixed water pipes all week long in his regular job and, sometimes, at home, and, yes, he often got calls from relatives and neighbors asking him to fix their plumbing as well. But he could also avoid his work by hopping in the car to go for a ride or by playing golf.

My mother was a telephone operator. All day long at work, she answered the phone. When she got home, however, she often took the phone off the hook or simply refused to answer. Even though she's now retired, some days, she still won't answer. If I absolutely need to get through to her, I have to use our signal: call, let it ring once, hang up, and call again. Otherwise, she'll let it ring.

Proofreading is another story. Even after proofreading all day at work, I can't simply go home and read the paper. I'm addicted after all. Misspelled words jump out at me. Misplaced commas try to dance by. Dangling modifiers dangle. Who else do you know who reads the paper with a red pen nearby?

If I go out to eat, it's worse. I notice spacing problems in the menu. I find type styles that are inconsistent or inappropriate. And when I look at the prices, I assume that they must be incorrect. Unfortunately, my red pen does me no good in a restaurant.

Reading the mail should be an escape, but it isn't. Many of my friends use contractions incorrectly. My sister has a problem with subject-verb agreement. And my bank statements and insurance policies need to be completely overhauled.

Even moving away from written communication doesn't help. I watch television and wonder why everyone feels "badly" about the problems of the world. I call a friend, and he suggests that "you and me" go bowling. Even when I go shopping alone, I ask myself, "Shouldn't it be 'Toys 'R We'?"

What can a proofreader do about this curse? Nothing, except learn to live with it. As long as people make mistakes – and I make as many as the next person – proofreaders will be needed. We may not be loved, but we'll be needed.

The Proofreader's Dilemma

"Can you do a quick proof on this, Jim? I need it in ten minutes."

Anybody who has ever done any proofreading has probably heard a similar request. I don't know about you, but my immediate response is negative. Oh, I won't say "No" to the request. I'll say "Sure," and I'll put aside whatever I'm working on to do the "quick proof." After all, it's usually a superior or a friend who needs help. But I don't like it."

After the petitioner has left my office, I start growling. Then, I start talking to myself. Pretty soon, I'm steaming. "A quick proof'?" What do I usually do? Slow proofs? And why the rush? If he were more organized, he wouldn't need to rush around at the last minute looking for "a quick proof."

By the time I finish my tirade, three minutes have passed. And since I know he will be back in eight minutes instead of the requested ten, I have about five minutes left to work. Do I jump right in at that point? Not yet. I like to examine the project slowly, to see if I can reasonably be expected to complete

the assignment. This is the dilemma; I can handle it in one of two ways.

I can decide that the job can't be done that quickly. What are you, crazy? Or I can view the job as a challenge, shift my proofreading skills into high gear, and attempt to break the all-time, land-speed record for meeting unreasonable requests.

If I fail, no one will mind because, like Don Quixote, I have attempted to reach the unreachable star. If I succeed, I can begin preparing my induction speech as the first member of The Proofreaders' Hall of Fame.

But wait. There's one more thing. What does the original request for a "quick proof" really imply? My co-worker doesn't want me to find any errors in his document. He just wants me to sign off on it. Then, if any errors exist, I'll have to take the blame. I'll bear the sin. I'll be the scapegoat.

What if I do find an error? There's no way the document can go back to typesetting, be corrected, and be proofread again in ten minutes. So I

140 Writing Is Hard by Jim LaBate

may as well take my time and do a thorough job rather than one that's either quick or not quick enough. If I find a mistake, my co-worker will be relieved that the copy was checked one more time before publishing an error. And if I don't find a mistake, but it takes me more than ten minutes, maybe he'll go somewhere else next time for his "quick proof." Or, better

yet, maybe he will get things done on schedule and not require special favors.

But what if no mistakes exist, and I can get the job done in ten minutes?

"Ladies and Gentlemen, I'd like to thank you for coming here today. I am, indeed, honored to be selected as the first proofreader . . . ."

The Proofreader's Fear

"Falling asleep on the job."

Generally, this phrase suggests that someone simply isn't paying attention: a clerk gives incorrect change to a customer; a truck driver makes a wrong turn; an accountant copies an incorrect figure on a tax return. However, falling asleep on the job is not just a figure of speech for a proofreader; it's a hazard of the profession.

If I fail to catch a misspelled word or a grammatical error, I won't be fired immediately. No one will condemn me for imperfection. But when my eyes close, my head drops, and I snooze, I take with me my pride, my reputation, and my honor.

To remind us of the stigma of falling asleep on the job, we have a sleeper beeper in our proofreading department. These gadgets were sold on late-night television many years ago as an aid to cross-country truck drivers. The sleeper beeper attaches to your ear, and nothing happens as long as your head is upright. As soon as your head

drops, though, the liquid in the beeper activates a small alarm that wakes you up – ideally before you crash your rig.

The sleeper beeper in our department is a painful reminder of a proofreader who literally fell asleep on the job. Later, after being razzed unmercifully by his co-workers, he left to seek a new profession. He probably moved, changed his name, and grew a beard as well. The only thing he left behind was the sleeper beeper he had received as a gag gift. Even though he's no longer here, his disgrace lives on as a company legend.

Many instances might cause me to fall asleep on the job. Some of the things I proofread are monotonous and dry. Sometimes, I stay up too late watching a ball game. And once in a while, I'm distracted because I'm worrying about paying the rent on my proofreader's salary. Nonetheless, excuses will not bail me out.

What can a proofreader do to avoid falling asleep on the job? I try to proofread as much as possible early in the morning when I'm alert. I avoid mid-afternoon proofreading whenever I can. If I must proofread when I'm sleepy, I exercise a bit or get something to drink first. And if those tricks don't work, I conjure up the frightening image of myself in another part of the country, with a beard, a new name, and a copy of the want ads.

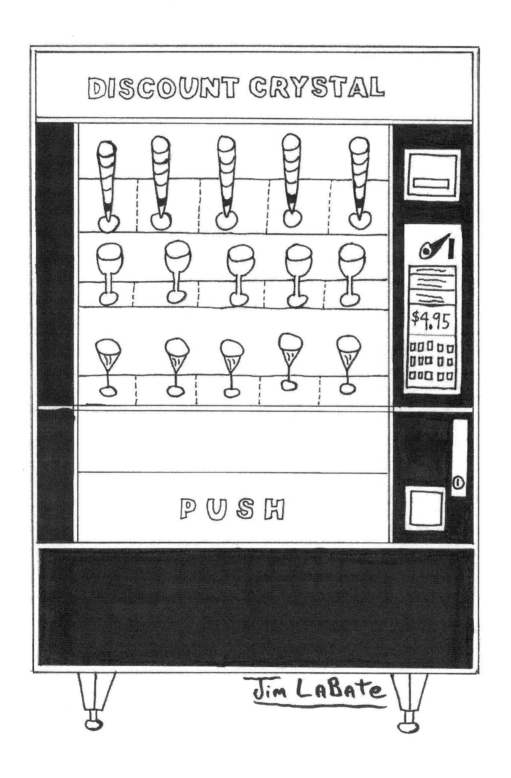

The Proofreader's Wall

When protesters began to destroy the Berlin Wall in 1989, I watched the television reports with interest. However, unlike most observers, I did not identify with the people who wielded picks and sledgehammers or with those who were drinking champagne, or even with those who danced in the streets. Instead, I identified with the guards.

Why? Because as a proofreader, I'm a guard myself. I take orders from those above me, and part of my job is to make sure that the colloquial words and phrases accepted in everyday speech do not cross the border into print. Yes, a day may come when my superiors will accept such words and phrases in formal writing, but until that day comes, I'll guard the wall.

The job is not easy. Lately, for example, many writers are trying to smuggle the word "importantly" across the line. "No way," I explain to my petitioners. "Not without the proper paperwork."

Technically, the word "importantly" is an adverb. If someone talks or acts as if he's special, we might say, He talked importantly," or "He acted importantly." But I've rarely seen the word used that way. As a matter of fact, the only place I've ever seen it used correctly is in a dictionary that explains its proper usage.

No, the people who are trying to slip this word into formal writing have been watching too much television and listening to too many public speakers. You've probably heard it yourself. A speaker lists persuasive arguments and concludes with the strongest point: "Most importantly, I believe . . . ." What the speaker is really saying is, "Here's my most important point," or "What is most important is . . . ."

When I first heard the phrase used in this way, I passed it off as simply another common mistake – like "ain't" – that knowledgeable writers would avoid. But that's not the case. As more people hear and say the phrase, more writers are trying to use it as well. Somebody has to stand up and say "No."

Why? Because the incorrect use of "importantly" is important. It's not a misspelled word. It's not a mistake in punctuation. It's not even a regional expression. It's simply an incorrect usage of a legitimate word, a word easily understood – and easily misused.

If I let this one slip by, the rest will definitely follow: "hopefully" ("Hopefully, we'll win the game") and "badly" ("I feel badly that your cat died").

See what I mean? One small crack in the wall will lead to a crevice. A crevice will become an opening.

And an opening will lead to picks, sledgehammers, champagne, dancing in the streets, and frivolous language.

Although such actions are to be commended in a political situation where people are stifled and freedom of expression is restrained, that's not the case here. If our standards are not upheld, our language will deteriorate. If our language is not protected, our civilization will falter. And, most important of all, if our civilization falters, I'll be unemployed.

The Proofreader's Pain

In 1969, Elisabeth Kübler-Ross wrote a book called *On Death and Dying.* In the book, she defines the five stages people go through once they realize they have a terminal illness. Although I'm not foolish enough to equate discovering a proofreading error with death, I did find myself going through similar reactions recently when I let a mistake slip through.

"You spelled Irondequoit (a suburb of Rochester, New York) incorrectly in the last issue of your newsletter, Jim."

Denial.

"No way," I replied. "That's part of the masthead, and it never changes." I was partially correct. The name wasn't misspelled in the masthead but in the statement of ownership. If only I had been careless enough to misspell the name in the masthead also, no one would have noticed.

Anger

When I finally acknowledged my error, I wasn't yet ready to accept full blame. Not only was I angry with myself, but I was also angry with the other proofreaders who had missed it. I was also angry with the customer who always reviews the newsletter before it's printed. Why hadn't any of them caught the error?

Bargaining

Maybe no one will notice, I reasoned. How many people actually know the correct spelling of Irondequoit anyway? And who bothers to read the statement of ownership, which appears only once a year? If anybody calls or writes to complain. I'll say we did it on purpose to see if anyone were paying attention. Then, I'll congratulate the person for paying such attention to detail, and we'll both feel great.

Depression

Nobody with any intelligence will accept such a ridiculous explanation. I'll have to admit the truth. I'm totally to blame. I'm a failure. I'm paid to find and correct errors, and

I let one slip through. How will I face my boss, my co-workers, my wife, my children, or my friends?

Acceptance

After a while, I snap out of my funk. "It's not your first mistake, and it won't be your last," I tell myself. "Just don't make that particular mistake again."

When I'm finished with the last stage, I can go on to the next job. The whole process takes 10 to 15 minutes. Unlike death, which offers no second chances, proofreading offers another chance with every manuscript. And if I am as conscientious as I should be, I can use the next opportunity to redeem myself.

Chapter 8
Eight Articles on Plagiarism

The History of Plagiarism

(See Commandment Ten in Chapter One: This essay is purposely repeated here as background information for the following essays on plagiarism.)

I can remember vividly the first time I became aware of the word "plagiarism." I was in junior high at the time, and I was reading an article in the sports' pages about a local athlete who had earned a scholarship to play basketball at a major university. Unfortunately for this particular athlete, the article stated that he would be unable to play during the upcoming semester not because he was injured physically but because he had injured his academic reputation and had been found guilty of plagiarism. I was stunned, and I knew at that precise moment that plagiarism must be a serious offense.

"So what is plagiarism?" I said to my English instructor when I went to school the next day.

"Plagiarism is a lot like stealing," she said, "but instead of stealing something solid like a wallet or a purse, you are stealing someone's ideas. You

are pretending that those ideas are your own, and you are trying to get credit for them." Then, like any good teacher, she took that opportunity to explain plagiarism in more detail to the entire class later that afternoon ("Plagiarism," *The Newbury House Dictionary* 654). Over 50 years later, obviously, that lesson still stays with me.

So does Hudson Valley Community College have a policy on plagiarism? Yes. According to the HVCC *Plagiraism Policy*, "A student is guilty of plagiarism any time s/he attempts to obtain academic credit by presenting someone else's ideas as her/his own without appropriately documenting the original source."

Most colleges today have a similar policy regarding plagiarism, but, interestingly enough, plagiarism hasn't always been considered such a serious offense. In the long ago past, for example, students and writers were actually encouraged to take the wisdom of their elders and predecessors, and no one was expected to cite their sources. According to

Brian Hansen, author of "Combatting Plagiarism," the ancient Greeks called this "mimesis," or imitation, and the absence of citations "was grounded in the belief that knowledge of the human condition should be shared by everyone, not owned or hoarded. The notion of individual ownership was much less important than it is today" (782).

So when did ownership of ideas become so much more important? Hansen goes on to say that two factors contributed to the change in thinking; the invention of the printing press and the introduction of copyright laws "advanced the notion that individual authorship was good and that mimesis was bad" (784). Thomas Mallon agrees with this view. In his book entitled *Stolen Words: Forays into the Origins and Ravages of Plagiarism*, Mallon writes, "plagiarism didn't become a truly sore point with writers until they thought of writing as their trade" (3-4). Thus, as a student, you should be aware that plagiarism is not only a college issue that professors worry about but also a real world issue that involves professional writers and concerns everyone.

Unfortunately, since the invention of the printing press in 1440 spurred the ownership of creativity, another recent invention has threatened to undermine the corresponding individual ownership of ideas. Hansen writes

that "The advent of the Internet makes committing plagiarism easier than ever" (783). This is especially true for a generation of students who grew up with computers and for a while became accustomed to the free file sharing of music. In other words, some students assume that if it's on the Internet, it's free for the taking, and these students may simply "copy" text from the Internet and "paste" it into their term papers. That could be a problem.

The problem isn't necessarily the using of the information. After all, the Internet always has the most current information, and teachers definitely want you to have up-to-date information in your research. The problem occurs when you fail to cite the source of your information. Just as composers and musicians demanded to be compensated when their music was shared on the Internet, writers and researchers demand to be acknowledged and recognized for their work, and teachers expect their students to cite their sources.

So as you begin working on your term papers for this semester, make sure you take meticulous notes and document your sources properly. Then, you will, most likely, avoid the consequence of damaging your own academic reputation by being accused of plagiarism.

Pressure, Procrastination, and Lack of Practice Can Lead to Plagiarism

The Oxford English Dictionary defines plagiarism as "the wrongful appropriation or purloining, and publication as one's own, of the ideas, or the expression of the ideas (literary, artistic, musical, mechanical, etc.) of another" (947). In that definition, the word "purloining" is a rather unusual word, one that means theft. Yet, the word brings to mind Edgar Allan Poe's short story "The Purloined Letter," and that story's theme is closely related to the practice of plagiarism.

In Poe's story, the narrator describes a detective who cannot find the stolen letter because the thief has hidden it in plain sight. In some ways, students who plagiarize are doing the same thing. They have purloined the words or ideas of another and hidden them in the open text of their research papers by failing to cite their sources. Why do students steal and hide their theft in this way? According to various authors and educators, three of the main reasons why students resort to plagiarism are pressure, procrastination, and lack of practice.

Pressure actually comes in many forms. Many parents and teachers have extremely high expectations for their children and students. Thus, some students may do whatever is necessary to meet those expectations. In addition, some students put high expectations on themselves because they want to be accepted into the best graduate schools or be hired by the most prestigious professional firms. Finally, some students face academic pressures that are related to finances or extracurricular activities. For example, some students have to maintain a certain grade point average in order to retain their financial aid or scholarships, and other students must maintain a certain grade point average in order to participate in sports or other college activities (McCabe and Drinan, qtd. in Lathrop and Foss 93).

But is taking a chance on plagiarism worth the risk? Probably not. After all, if a student is found guilty of plagiarism, he or she may face certain punishments such as failing the assignment, failing the course, being suspended from school, and having a certain "Scarlet Letter" attached to one's permanent transcript. Surely, those punishments are much more serious and have more long-term consequences than a legitimate grade that fails to meet expectations.

Procrastination is another reason why some students plagiarize, especially first-year students who haven't yet mastered time-management skills. In their book entitled *Student Cheating and Plagiarism in the Internet Era,* authors Ann Lathrop and Kathleen Foss say that most students don't start the semester thinking about plagiarism. During those first few weeks of classes, almost everyone is still optimistic and has good intentions of properly completing their assignments. Due to poor planning, however, and, sometimes, due to unforeseen circumstances, certain students find themselves at the end of the semester with too much work and too little time. As a result, these students may panic – and plagiarize (27).

Fortunately, plagiarism isn't the only solution to this problem. Believe it or not, some teachers actually do have hearts. In addition, these teachers probably faced a similar dilemma at some point during their own college experience, and they may be willing to empathize and accept a late paper or offer an extended deadline. Yes, students may lose a few points as a consequence, but, again, a lower grade is still better than the scar of plagiarism. So before students seriously consider plagiarism, they should think, instead, about talking to their instructors and trying to find a workable solution. After all, communication is always better than fear and isolation.

Finally, some students plagiarize because they lack confidence in their own writing abilities due to a lack of practice (Harris). Sure, most students have written personal essays before, but when it comes to conducting research and explaining their findings, some inexperienced students freeze. Thus, they simply copy what they've read without citing their sources, or they simply change a few words and assume that it's okay. Yet, copying without citing or making only minor changes usually result in plagiarism.

A better solution in this case is a visit to The Writing and Research Center. There, professional instructors and peer tutors can demonstrate how to use quotations, paraphrases, and summaries to express ideas discovered through research. In addition, those who work in The Writing and Research Center can offer instruction on how to properly cite sources or evaluate what the student has already written. Naturally, students will still have to do their own work, but the advice and experience of seasoned writers can help immeasurably.

At the end of Poe's story, the purloined letter is finally discovered but not by the detective who was searching for it. Instead, the narrator's friend, C. Auguste Dupin, found the letter because he knew the man who had hidden the letter, and he used that knowledge to discover the letter's whereabouts. So is it possible to get away with plagiarizing a term paper? Yes. However, since most teachers know their students and their writing ability, the chances are good that the teacher will not be fooled, and the student will pay a heavy price for an academic offense that can be avoided.

Unintentional Plagiarism – Is It Possible?

Have you ever been pulled over for speeding on the highway? If so, you know that you can handle that situation in one of two ways: first, you can bow your head humbly, admit your mistake, and accept your ticket from the officer; or, second, you can try to talk your way out of it. If you choose the second option, however, you should also know that one particular excuse will not work. You cannot claim that you "didn't know the speed limit." If you try that particular line, you are definitely going to receive a ticket.

If you're caught speeding, you can claim that you're on the way to the hospital. You can claim that your accelerator got stuck. You can even claim that you're trying to make it to class on time to take a critical exam. But you cannot claim ignorance of the speed limit. After all, claiming that you didn't know you were speeding is a lot like claiming that you didn't know you were plagiarizing. As a licensed driver and as a college-level writer, you are expected to know both the speed limit and the rules of documenting sources.

So why, then, do you sometimes hear students and teachers talk about "unintended plagiarism?" Is it possible to steal another's words or ideas without intending to do so? Probably. Does it happen at Hudson Valley Community College? Most likely. But should the excuse, "I didn't know I was doing anything wrong," be an acceptable explanation for an academic offense? Before answering that question, here are a few examples to consider.

In 1970, former Beatle George Harrison wrote and recorded a song entitled "My Sweet Lord," a song that produced earnings of over two million dollars. Unfortunately for Harrison, a songwriter named Ronald Mack claimed that Harrison had essentially recorded Mack's 1963 hit "He's So Fine" – recorded by the Chiffons – with different words. When the claim went to court, Harrison himself admitted that the songs were "strikingly similar," and he admitted that he had heard the Chiffons sing the song "at least a few times" (*ABKCO Music v. Harrisongs Music,* 24 Nov. 1982). Thus, while Harrison did not consciously steal Mack's song, the court ruled that Harrison had "subconsciously plagiarized" (*ABKCO Music v. Harrisongs Music,* 19 Feb. 1981).

As another example, in an article entitled "Dear Teacher, Johnny Copied," teachers and authors Louise Jackson, Eileen Tway, and Alan Frager wrote that young students often plagiarize unintentionally for three main reasons. First, a student "might internalize a piece of writing so thoroughly as to be sincerely unaware some months later that it is not his or her own" (qtd. In Lathrop and Foss 170). Second, some students lack confidence in their own work, so they innocently copy the words of another. Finally, some students simply do not realize that they need to let others know the source of their information (Lathrop and Foss 170-171).

So do Harrison's case and the circumstances of the young children parallel the situations that may occur on a college campus? Yes. Definitely. In fact, in all of the situations mentioned, those in authority agree that unintentional plagiarism does occur. However, plagiarism, even when it is unintended, does have consequences.

In Harrison's case, he had to surrender a substantial portion of his earnings from the song (*ABKCO Music v. Harrisongs Music,* 19 Feb. 1981). In the children's cases, the children have to be informed that their copying is inappropriate, and they need to be educated about proper documentation. And in the case of college students who plagiarize, they will, most likely, face an academic sanction. These sanctions generally depend on the extent of the plagiarism and range from failing the assignment to failing the course to being suspended from school.

The punishment occurs because most colleges expect their students to know about plagiarism and to document sources properly. In fact, the HVCC pamphlet on plagiarism specifically states "when it comes to plagiarism, ignorance is not an excuse" (*Plagiarism Policy*). So, as a college student, if you're cruising toward the end of the semester and you're tempted to speed up the completion of your work by plagiarizing, just remember that if you get pulled over, the excuse about not knowing won't work. You will be ticketed, and you will face consequences.

Plagiarism Isn't Confined to College Campuses

Whenever I talk to college students about plagiarism, I always see a few who are not at all interested in the subject. These bored students begin staring out the window or doodling in their notebooks or drifting off into dreamland. Finally, one of them will become so bored that he or she will try to stir up some controversy by asking what many of them are already thinking. The question usually sounds something like this: "Besides teachers, does anybody else really care about plagiarism?"

"Yes," I say emphatically, and, then, I go on to explain that plagiarism – taking the words or ideas of another and using them as one's own ("Plagiarism," *The Newbury House Dictionary* 654*)* – negatively affects not only students but also teachers, preachers, historians, politicians, journalists, and novelists.

For example, a while back, Louis Roberts, a classics professor at the State University of New York at Albany was accused of plagiarism. While writing a book on the history of Cyprus, Roberts failed to use quotation marks and failed to cite some of his sources. When the University became aware of his plagiarism, an investigation ensued, and, eventually, Roberts was removed from his position as chairman of the department and

director of the doctoral program. After 40 years in education, Roberts retired in disgrace and moved away (Wechsler).

Similarly, a preacher who was accused of plagiarism was the Reverend Martin Luther King Jr. He may be one of the most esteemed civil rights leaders in American history, and he even won the Nobel Peace Prize in 1964. Unfortunately, approximately 20 years after King's death, researchers discovered evidence that King plagiarized his 1955 doctoral dissertation from Boston University. Since that initial discovery, additional researchers have found other examples of plagiarism in King's writings. Though the charge of plagiarism will never erase what King accomplished during his lifetime, one of his biographers, David Garrow, admits "it will diminish his reputation" (Turque and Joseph).

In 2002, two of this nation's most famous historians – Doris Kearns Goodwin and Stephen Ambrose – were both accused of plagiarism, and their professional reputations suffered as well. Though the accusations against Kearns Goodwin were not as numerous as those against Ambrose, she arranged for a "substantial" settlement to be paid to the original author of the material (Wiener 183). Ambrose, meanwhile, tried to defend himself in numerous ways before finally admitting, "I don't know that I'm all that good at academics" (Stack, qtd. in Wiener 191).

In 2006, the mayor of Amsterdam, New York, Joseph Emanuele III, found himself in political trouble when he plagiarized a speech delivered by President George W. Bush five years earlier. Emanuele had been asked to speak at a ceremony commemorating Pearl Harbor Day, and he failed to mention that Bush delivered the same speech for the same occasion in 2001 ("When the Words Aren't Yours, Say So"). This incident recalled another politician, Joseph Biden, who made a similar mistake when he first ran for president in 1988. At the time, Biden plagiarized the speech of a British politician, and when the plagiarism was discovered, Biden withdrew from the presidential race. Naturally, after serving as vice-president, Biden has a much stronger reputation than he did previously, but the journalists who cover his actions will probably never let him forget his earlier error (Woodlief).

Journalists, too, however, are guilty of plagiarism. In the recent past, two of this country's biggest newspapers had to discipline writers when these newspapers fell victim to plagiarism. First, in 2003, Jayson Blair, a relatively young journalist, was discovered to have stolen parts of over 30 articles he had written for *The New York Times*. Then, a year later, *USA Today* discovered that Jack Kelley, who had written for the paper for over 20 years and had been a Pulitzer-Prize nominee five times, had also plagiarized parts of at least 20 stories. In both cases, the offenses were so bad that not only were the writers themselves out of work, but their supervising editors were also either fired or forced to resign (McCormick).

Finally, novelists sometimes find themselves taking the words of other writers. In one case, the novelist also happened to be a college student. Kaavya Viswanathan was a freshman at Harvard when her agent notified her that a publisher wanted to publish a coming-of-age novel she had begun to write. When the book was finally written and published, however, readers noticed similarities between Viswanathan's book and two books written by another author. When confronted with the evidence, Viswanathan apologized to the original author and explained that she had unconsciously absorbed the first author's material because she read the original books numerous times while she was in high school (Smith).

So, besides teachers, does anybody else really care about plagiarism? Obviously, the answer is yes. Plagiarism is not merely an academic issue that exists solely on college campuses. Plagiarism is a serious matter that affects numerous professions, and this theft of intellectual material can have costly and long-lasting consequences.

Giving Credit to Avoid Plagiarism

A while back, I wrote a short novel that took place in 1964. Naturally, I wanted to capture the feel and the details of that time period, so I drew upon my own memories, but I also conducted research. I looked at old newspapers and magazines, I viewed old movies, and I read books that chronicled that era. As I read, I found the name of a book entitled *Living Legacy: How 1964 Changed America.* "Now there's a book I need to read," I thought. "I wonder who wrote it." Fortunately, my initial source not only provided me with the title but also the author, the publisher, and the year of publication. That thorough documentation made it easy for me to continue with my research.

When most college students think about documentation of sources, they consider only the negative side. These students know that if they don't document properly, they will be accused of plagiarism – taking the words or ideas of another and using them as one's own ("Plagiarism," *The Newbury House Dictionary*

654*)*. Fortunately, documentation also has a positive side. When you document your sources properly, you serve two distinct purposes.

First, you acknowledge and give credit to the authors who provided the original information, and, second, you help your readers who may also want to read that same information in its entirety. In my case, my first source was a book called *October 1964* by David Halberstam. Basically, Halberstam wrote a baseball book about how the St. Louis Cardinals defeated the New York Yankees in the World Series and ended their 15-year dynasty. Since Halberstam is a Pulitzer Prize-winning author himself, he knew enough to credit his sources – including Joseph J. Mangano, whose book I sought – and to give me, the reader, all the information I needed to find any of those sources. Thus, when you write your research papers, you should also credit your sources and help your readers in this way.

"But," you may be asking," do I have to document every little thing?" No, you do not. You do not have to document your personal opinion, and you do not have to document common knowledge.

You do not have to document your personal opinion because your name is already on the first page of your paper, and readers will naturally assume that the opinions expressed within the paper are yours unless you say otherwise (with proper documentation, of course). Before you insert your personal opinion, however, make sure that your instructor is looking for your opinion. Some instructors assign purely informative papers and are not looking for your opinion. If, on the other hand, your instructor assigns a persuasive paper, you can feel free to express your opinions.

Common knowledge does not have to be documented either because most people will be aware of the information if it falls into that general category of "something everybody knows." For instance, if you were writing about George W. Bush, you wouldn't have to document the fact that he was the president of the United States because your readers know that. In addition, you wouldn't have to document other information about Bush such as the year he was born (1946), his college alma maters (Yale and Harvard), or his years as governor of Texas (1995-2000). While these three pieces of information aren't quite as well known as the fact that Bush was the president, they, too, qualify as common knowledge because they can be found easily in a variety of sources. Thus, even if you didn't know a particular fact when you started your research, if you see that fact in three different sources, you can probably assume that it is common knowledge and does not have to be documented. Should you feel uncertain about whether certain information is common knowledge or not, you should just go ahead and cite the source to be safe.

Writing a college research paper is a great way to educate yourself about both your chosen topic and about the research and writing process in general. In addition to the benefit you receive as a writer, your readers will also benefit from the information you discover, but only if you care enough about your readers to give them the information they need.

Three Ways to Wreck Your Research Paper

Over the years, I've assigned and read numerous research papers. Some are excellent and are a pleasure to read. Others are mildly interesting and show flashes of insight. Still others are a chore because the students who wrote them didn't care enough to write them properly. These students had a vague idea of what they were supposed to do, but they didn't take the time or invest the effort to explain their ideas thoroughly. Generally, these weaker students – let's call them Quentin, Peter, and Sammy – quote quickly, paraphrase poorly, and summarize sloppily.

Quentin is the quick quoter. When he puts together his research paper, he doesn't actually write the paper. Instead, he gathers quotations. Like a coin collector, he simply finds quotes on his subject and copies them. He doesn't think about the quotes. He doesn't evaluate the quotes. He doesn't even connect the quotes in a relevant way. He just strings them together like a child's colorful necklace. Then, he adds an introduction and a conclusion and calls it a research paper. Typically, 80% of Quentin's paper is direct quotes.

Obviously, Quentin receives low grades on his papers because his teachers expect more from him. They want Quentin to be a bit more selective and discerning with his quotes. According to the authors of *The New McGraw-Hill Handbook*, you should "use quotations when a source's exact words are important to your point and make your writing more memorable, fair, or authoritative" (Maimon, et al., 2009, 358). In other words, you should use quotes to support the points you make in your writing, not to substitute for your writing. I tell my students that if more than 20% of their paper is made up of quotations, that's too much. I would much rather see my students put their source information in their own words in paraphrases and summaries.

The only difference between a paraphrase and a summary is the length. A paraphrase is usually the same length as the original while a summary is much shorter. Generally, teachers want their students to paraphrase or summarize because the teachers want to see that their students understand the original work well enough to express it in a way that is clear, correct, connected to the thesis of the paper, and documented appropriately. Unfortunately, some students fail in this regard.

Peter is the poor paraphraser. He knows that he should put his information in his own words, but he doesn't do it well. The following examples show a hypothetical quote and how Peter might paraphrase that quote. Here's the quote: "In Vietnam, the United States was engaged in a costly and lengthy war that divided Americans and led to a change in presidential leadership." Here's Peter's paraphrase. "In Vietnam, the United States was involved in an expensive and long war that separated Americans and resulted in a new chief executive."

As you can see, Peter merely changed four key words ("engaged, costly, lengthy, and led") and the ending phrase ("presidential leadership"). Thus, the amount of change is substantial, but the effect of the change is insignificant. Peter's mistake is that he looks directly at his original source as he makes his changes, and he retains the exact sentence structure of the original writer. What he should do, instead, is look away from the source as he paraphrases and use his own writing style to communicate the idea. For example, he might write the following: "The Vietnam War was such a long and expensive ordeal that Americans cried out for change." Naturally, once Peter writes his paraphrase, he should check it against the source to make sure that the main idea is accurate and undistorted,

and he should cite his source. Failing to cite is Sammy's mistake.

Sammy is the sloppy summarizer. Sammy knows that summaries usually provide general background information and are much shorter than the original source (usually about 20 to 25% of the original). In addition, Sammy typically does a good job of condensing the information and presenting it with his own style and flair. In fact, he does such a good job of summarizing that he doesn't feel he has to credit his source in the text itself. "I changed that a lot," he might say in his defense, "and I listed the source at the end of the paper."

Unfortunately, if Sammy, or any student for that matter, fails to acknowledge his source in both the body of the paper *and* on his list of sources at the end, he is guilty of plagiarism – taking the words or ideas of another and using them as one's own ("Plagiarism," *The Newbury House Dictionary* 654). Essentially, Sammy is being a bit careless with his documentation and implying that he is the original source of the information. That's a major mistake that could lead to serious academic consequences.

Quentin, Peter, and Sammy are obviously fictional characters. Their tendencies, however – to quote quickly, to paraphrase poorly, and to summarize sloppily – are common among college students. If you want to avoid a wreck of a research paper, you should avoid those tendencies; then, you can drive off with an excellent research paper that is a pleasure to read.

Classroom Strategies to Prevent Plagiarism

Do you ever sit in class and wonder why your teachers do certain things? Why, for example, do teachers make such a big deal about plagiarism – taking the words or ideas of another and using them as one's own ("Plagiarism," *The Newbury House Dictionary* 654)? Or, why do teachers ask you for handwritten writing samples in class or make you speak in front of the entire class? Believe it or not, your teachers do such things because they care about academic integrity. They want to make sure that you and your classmates are all treated fairly and all have the opportunity to succeed on your own merits. Here are seven basic strategies that many teachers use to allow you to succeed.

1. Background Information. Some teachers may assign you a term paper at the beginning of the semester and never mention the assignment again until the paper is due. This particular approach can be troublesome for students who have never written a research paper before, for those who struggle with proper documentation, and for those who procrastinate. Without the proper guidance, these students may complete the assignment incorrectly and fail,

may document sources incorrectly and plagiarize, or may wait too long to get started and be tempted to cheat. Thus, most teachers will take the time to explain the assignment thoroughly, to suggest topics and sources of information, and to show students how to document their sources and how to avoid plagiarism. As the HVCC pamphlet on plagiarism states, "when students plagiarize, they threaten the integrity of the entire institution, and they devalue the legitimate intellectual accomplishments of all students" (*Plagiarism Policy*).

2. Practice, Practice, Practice. If you've ever played a sport or a musical instrument, you know how important it is to practice. Yes, performing a drill over and over or playing the scales regularly can seem monotonous at times, but the constant repetition will eventually turn you into a relaxed and natural performer. The same is true in the classroom. Despite student complaints, teachers may assign similar tasks on numerous occasions because your teachers want you to be able to perform certain basic tasks without referring to your textbook for assistance. Then, once you've achieved success on the basics, you can, most likely, move forward and tackle more difficult tasks on your own.

3. Specific Assignment. You've probably noticed that some teachers will allow you to write about any topic whatsoever while others will assign particular subjects, will force you to narrow a general topic into a more specific topic, or will require that you secure approval of a topic before you begin. The teachers in the latter category are probably better for you because they're challenging you to do better work. Anybody, after all, can write a five-page paper on the basic theories of capital punishment versus life imprisonment. The more difficult task is to find recent studies and statistics for particular states or countries to determine which option is more effective at reducing murder rates. Like an archaeologist, the deeper you dig into a particular subject, the more likely you are to discover something of value.

4. Multi-step Process. You've probably noticed, too, that some teachers only want to see your final paper while others want to see various components along the way: topic, tentative thesis, outline, and a preliminary list of sources. Some teachers may even require you to keep a term-paper log and ask you to record your progress on a weekly basis. This multi-step process serves two major purposes: first, it keeps you on course and prevents you from going off on tangents, and, second, it keeps you on schedule and prevents you from trying to do all the work at the last minute. While these preliminary steps may seem annoying at the beginning, they usually make the larger, more difficult tasks easier to complete at the end.

5. Handwritten Writing Samples. British author E. M. Forester once said, "How can I know what I mean until I've seen what I've said" (qtd. in Troyka 2)? For most of us, our thoughts are a jumbled mass in our brains with no order or coherence. When we write, however, we begin to sort those thoughts in a way that makes sense and allows us to express ideas that we hadn't quite formulated previously. Teachers know this, and they want you to write with pen and paper periodically

because writing at the computer isn't quite the same. Some students rely too much on the spell checker and the grammar checker while others are too quick to edit and delete ideas that may, upon reflection, be worth saving.

6. Highlighted Copies of Sources. Have you ever heard of active reading? No, it's not reading a book while you're walking on a treadmill or riding an exercise bike. Instead, active reading requires you to highlight key ideas in a text or to write your own comments or questions in the margins. Again, this may seem like more work initially, but when you go back to your sources to begin writing, you'll find it so much easier to find the main ideas and to remember why you felt certain thoughts were more important than others. Your teachers can also use your highlighted sources to help you find information that you may have missed or to make connections that you didn't see.

7. Oral Presentation. The best way to truly learn a subject is to try to teach that subject to others. When you write a research paper, you are, essentially, preparing a lesson plan for your readers to learn what you learned during the research process. When you take the next step and present that information orally, you have to absorb it even further. After all, you don't want to simply read that paper to your audience. Rather, you'll want to present your findings in a way that is both interesting and powerful. You will want your listeners to be fully engaged in what you have to say. Your teachers, obviously, do this all the time, and they want you to have the benefit of this experience, as well.

Do all of these seven strategies also deter you from plagiarizing your term paper? Of course, they do. When your teachers see different portions of your work or see the paper at various stages, they know you are less likely to copy, steal, or buy a paper from someone else. But preventing plagiarism is not the primary motive behind why teachers assign these tasks. All seven strategies are time-tested and proven ways to help you become a better researcher, a better writer, and a better communicator.

A Most Uncomfortable Conversation

Generally speaking, I am a pretty curious and conversational guy. Thus, if I find myself on the elevator with someone or waiting in line at the grocery store, I will ask a question or make a comment just to see if the person next to me wants to talk. However, near the end of each semester, I find myself dreading a certain conversation that I have to initiate with a student. That conversation concerns plagiarism, and the dialogue is usually uncomfortable.

Plagiarism, as you probably know, is taking another person's ideas and passing them off as your own ("Plagiarism," *The Newbury House Dictionary* 654). Students who plagiarize are committing a serious academic offense, and if found guilty, they may face serious consequences such as failing the assignment, failing the course, and in the case of a repeat offender, being suspended from school.

"But what's the big deal if I plagiarize?" some students may ask; "Nobody gets hurt." Physically, that's true. Academically, however,

plagiarizing is just not fair. For example, let's compare two students.

Serious Sally begins her research as soon as she receives the assignment from her teacher. Sally works diligently throughout the semester and even finishes her paper early, so she can get feedback from a specialist in The Writing Center and from her instructor. Finally, on the due date, she hands in her best work and receives an A on her paper.

Procrastinating Patty, meanwhile, has more important tasks to tackle. She works part-time at the mall, she travels to Buffalo to see her boyfriend every other weekend, and she likes to watch reality shows and spend time on Facebook. Thus, as the due date for the term paper approaches, Patty is desperate. In her desperation, she buys a paper from an online source, submits it as her own, and also earns an A.

Is that scenario fair to Sally? Of course not. Patty cheated, and she should be punished. That's why teachers are especially diligent in their desire to detect plagiarism, and, fortunately, the detection is not that difficult in many cases. Here are three ways that teachers can discover if a student has plagiarized.

First, most teachers are familiar with the writing styles of their students. Thus, if a student turns in a paper that is drastically different from what he or she has submitted all semester, the teacher will likely become suspicious and initiate the dreaded conversation.

Next, if a teacher is suspicious about the legitimacy of a paper, the teacher can use Google to see if a portion of the paper appears anywhere on the Internet. For example, I had a student once who was not a very good writer, who rarely came to class, and who did not communicate well when called upon. Still, at the end of the semester, this student turned in an unbelievable paper, one of the best I'd ever seen. Consequently, I found one unique sentence in the paper, I typed the entire sentence within quotation marks (so Google would look for those words in that exact order), and I submitted it to a Google search. Within seconds, Google found the entire paper on the home page of a student from another state. Apparently, the original writer was so proud of his paper that he put it on the Web for everyone to see. Again, I faced a difficult conversation.

Finally, many teachers have access to a computer program called "Turnitin," and these teachers may require their students to submit research papers to the program for review. Like Google, Turnitin will compare the papers to what is available on the Internet, but it will also compare the papers to what is available in various databases which are updated regularly and which may contain material that is not available on the Internet. So while modern technology allows devious students to "copy" information from a source and "paste" it into a paper without citing the source, similar technology also allows instructors to catch students who are committing academic fraud. Naturally, a conversation with the student will follow.

Personally, I hate these conversations because they're awkward and embarrassing for both parties. As the teacher, I have to ask the student if he or she really wrote the paper in question. Typically, I already know the answer, but the student has to make a decision. Some students will admit the truth immediately and apologize, but others will attempt to continue the fraud by lying or pleading ignorance. Only when confronted with the actual evidence will these students confess, and some of those students will become defensive, angry, or hostile.

Obviously, no students want to find themselves in this predicament. Believe me, teachers don't want to be there either. So if you find yourself stressed out at the end of the semester and facing a term-paper deadline, don't fall into the trap of plagiarism. After all, the chances are good that you will be caught, you will have to endure a most uncomfortable conversation, and you will be punished.

Chapter 9
Literary Techniques

Similes Are Like Smiles; Metaphors Are Laughter

My favorite lines in all of English literature are not from a Shakespearean play, not from a romantic love sonnet, and not from a modern short story. Instead, my favorite lines are from an old poem written by Solomon, a former king of Israel. The poem appears in The Bible in the book of *Proverbs*, and the writer uses four similes to describe four human experiences:

Like apples of gold in settings of silver is a ruling rightly given.

Like an earring of gold or an ornament of fine gold is the rebuke of a wise judge to a listening ear.

Like a snow-cooled drink at harvest time is a trustworthy messenger to the one who sends him; he refreshes the spirit of his master.

Like clouds and wind without rain is one who boasts of gifts never given. (*NIV Study Bible*: Proverbs 25:11-14)

As a writer, you, too, can create vivid descriptions with similes – and metaphors.

Basically, a simile is a comparison using the words "like" or "as." (The words "seem" or "appear" are sometimes used for similes, as well.) If you think writing is difficult, for example, you could simply write, "Writing is difficult." However, if you want to be more imaginative, you could use a simile to describe different degrees of difficulty. "Writing is like driving a taxi in New York City," or "Writing is as difficult as threading a needle in a tornado." Similes make your writing more colorful and more interesting for your readers.

When using similes, however, you should compare things that are essentially different. For instance, "Writing is like printing," or "Writing is as difficult as typing" do not qualify as similes because you're comparing two pretty similar activities. Similes should give readers a unique way of looking at a particular subject.

Professional writers use similes often. In his essay entitled "A Nonsmoker with a Smoker," Phillip

Lopate describes his girlfriend's craving for a cigarette in this way: "It's almost as though there were another lover in the room – a lover who was around long before I entered the picture, and who pleases her in mysterious ways I cannot" (70). Later, in that same essay, Lopate writes that his girlfriend's cigarette is "like a weapon in her hand, awakening in me a primitive fear of being burnt" (74). Lopate's use of similes gives more feeling and more life to his essay.

Similes are also closely related to metaphors because they both use comparison, but a fine distinction exists between the two. In fact, a metaphor is actually stronger than a simile because a metaphor is a direct comparison without using the words "like" or "as." So when Leola Evans describes the destruction of a tornado in the essay "Wind" by William Least Heat-Moon, she could have used a simile and said, "The car was like an accordion." Apparently, however, she wanted a more forceful image, so she used a metaphor instead:

"The car was an accordion" (35). The absence of the words "like" or "as" shows that the car wasn't just scratched or dented; it was crushed completely.

Here are a few more examples of metaphors. In the essay, "More Room," Judith Ortiz Cofer describes her grandmother's Bible in this way: "God's word was her security system" (55). In "The Jacket," Gary Soto writes that his old, ugly jacket "had become the ugly brother who tagged along wherever I went" (257). And in his famous "I Have a Dream" speech, Martin Luther King Jr., uses two metaphors when he says, "Now is the time to lift our nation from the quicksands of racial injustice to the solid rock of brotherhood" (506).

When I talk about writing, I often tell jokes or funny stories to connect with my students. If they smile, I know that the joke was okay, but if they laugh, I know that the joke was really funny. When you write, keep that distinction in mind; similes are like smiles, but metaphors are much stronger. Metaphors are laughter.

Personification Can Make Your Writing Come Alive

When my two daughters were younger, one of our favorite books for nighttime reading was *The Giving Tree* by Shel Silverstein. This book chronicled the lifelong relationship between a boy and the tree that loved him. At each stage of the boy's journey into manhood and, eventually, old age, the tree gives him whatever he needs. This timeless story of love and companionship will endure not only because of the story's theme and Silverstein's drawings but also because of the author's strong use of personification. As a student writer, you can also use personification to make your writing come alive.

Basically, personification is giving human characteristics to anything that is not human. In other words, when you personify something, you're making it like a person. In *The Giving Tree*, for example, the tree talks to the boy, shows him affection, plays hide-and-seek with him, and experiences both happiness and sadness.

The personification of nature is also evident in familiar, everyday phrases such as "the weeping willow,

the whispering wind, and the nagging cold." Personification is even more evident in fables where animals are portrayed as if they were people. From your own childhood, you probably remember the story of "The Three Little Pigs and the Big Bad Wolf" or "Goldilocks and the Three Bears." In addition, most modern cartoon characters – such as Mickey Mouse, Donald Duck, Winnie the Pooh, and Nemo – also rely on personification.

Poets, too, make extensive use of this technique. In his poem entitled "Stopping by Woods on a Snowy Evening," Robert Frost personifies the narrator's horse: "My little horse must think it queer / to stop without a farmhouse near" (224). When Carl Sandberg describes the city of "Chicago," he writes, "Come and show me another city with lifted head singing so proud to be alive and coarse and strong and cunning" (17). And no one who has read Emily Dickinson can forget her personification of death: "Because I could not stop for death – He kindly stopped for me" (350). As a student writer, however, you should realize that personification is not limited to fiction, fables, cartoons, or poetry. You can use personification to enliven your personal stories and your essays.

For instance, if you're writing about a subject that seems dry, you may want to bring it to life by comparing it to a person. Let's say, for instance, that you're struggling with a calculus course. The simple word "struggling" doesn't quite portray what the course is doing to you on a daily basis, so you might go further and compare the course to a boxer: "That calculus course is beating me up every single day and leaving me bloody and swollen."

You can also use personification when you're writing about abstract ideas that are somewhat hard to grasp. If, for example, your instructor asks you to write about wisdom, you could use a metaphor and write that "wisdom is a dear friend who comes with a gift." Or, you could use personification and write that "wisdom is the janitor who arrives only after I have made a big mess." As a final example, the Bible describes wisdom in numerous ways, but one particular description portrays wisdom as a woman crying out to those who need her: "Come, eat of my bread and drink of the wine I have mixed. Lay aside immaturity, and live, and walk in the way of insight" (*NIV Study Bible*: Proverbs 9:5-6).

When most students consider personification, they think of it primarily as a technique for professionals: poets, novelists, and essayists. However, if you begin to use personification in your own writing, it may undergo a transformation. Instead of coming across like a dry telegram, your writing may begin to sing and dance and laugh – just like a real person.

These Allusions Are Real

How would you feel if someone referred to you as "Scrooge"? Or, how would you react if you were speaking and a listener said, "Your nose is getting longer"? Finally, what would you say if someone called you "The Scarecrow"?

In each case, you would probably be offended – and rightfully so. After all, the first person is comparing you to the miserly employer in the Charles Dickens' novel entitled *The Christmas Carol*. The second person is calling you a liar by referring to the classic children's story "Pinocchio" by Carlo Lorenzini. And the third person is saying you need a brain, like Dorothy's friend in *The Wizard of Oz* by Frank Baum. No, the purpose of this essay is not to teach you how to trade literary insults, but to emphasize the use of allusions.

An allusion is an indirect reference to a well-known person, place, or event from history, from mythology, from literature, or from other works of art. Allusions are often used for three reasons: to catch the reader's attention, to provide a short but vivid description, and to make a strong connection.

To Catch the Reader's Attention. People who write newspaper and magazine headlines use allusions frequently to catch the reader's attention. For instance, articles about Daylight Savings Time might allude to the Biblical verse "Let there be light" (NIV Study Bible: Genesis 1:3). Stories of betrayal might refer to William Shakespeare's line in Julius Caesar: "Et Tu, Brutus," and situations that defy logic might be described as a "*Catch 22*," after the 1961 novel by Joseph Heller. One more obvious example is the title of this essay which alludes to the homonym "illusion," which, like a mirage, is not real.

To Provide a Short but Vivid Description. Speakers and authors often use allusions as a shortcut. Instead of having to describe how cheap someone is, the speaker or author can just say the person is a "Scrooge." Then, the listener or reader who is familiar with *The Christmas Carol* will immediately understand the comparison.

One example of an allusion that appears every spring involves the National Collegiate Athletic Association's basketball tournament. Certain schools – like Duke, Cincinnati, and Kansas – are traditional powerhouses, and they usually qualify for the tournament each year. Other schools, however, seldom make it to the tournament. As a result, when these schools unexpectedly qualify, sportswriters across the country refer to them as "Cinderella" teams. "Cinderella," of course, is the fairy tale about the young housemaid who wasn't even expected at the ball. Yet, when she arrived in a beautiful dress and glass slippers, she attracted the attention of the handsome prince. When these Cinderella teams eventually lose, the allusion is extended. The sportswriters will write that the clock has struck midnight, and these teams have to return to reality.

To Make a Strong Connection.
As a writer, you, too, may want to use an allusion occasionally to make a strong connection with your reader. If you want to emphasize an extremely important day in your life, for instance, you might refer to it as "D-day." This allusion applies to the World War II Allied invasion that liberated France from German occupation and served as a major turning point in the War (June 6, 1944). Or, if you want to describe a particular failure in your life, you may call it your "Waterloo," a reference to Napoleon Bonaparte's final defeat in Belgium on June 18, 1815.

An allusion is similar to an inside joke between the writer and the reader. Thus, before you use an allusion, you should be reasonably sure that your intended reader will understand it. If, for instance, your reader is young and not interested in history, references to D-day and Waterloo will not be understood or appreciated. But, if your reader is young and familiar with popular music, you could introduce a story about failure by alluding to the Britney Spears' song "Oops, I Did It Again."

If you use an allusion, do you have to document the source? No. If you're simply referring to a person, place, event, or work of art, no documentation is necessary. Thus, allusions can add life to your writing without making you feel as if you're writing a research paper.

As a baseball fan, I am tempted to conclude this essay by saying this is the "bottom of the ninth," an allusion to the last inning of a typical game. Since this may be the first time some of you have ever thought about using allusions in your writing, I'd rather refer to the beginning of the game. Thus, as the umpire says right after the playing of the national anthem, "Play Ball!"

Parallel Structure Is Poetic, Persuasive, and Powerful

Two of the more famous speeches of the previous century were delivered in the same city – Washington, D.C. – within three years of each other: President John F. Kennedy's Inaugural Address on January 20, 1961, and Martin Luther King Jr.'s "I Have a Dream" speech delivered on August 28, 1963. Obviously, these two speeches received a lot of notoriety because of the power and positions of the speakers. However, both speeches are still remembered today in part because both Kennedy and King used parallel structure in their presentations.

Parallel structure, or parallelism, is the repetition of certain words and/ or phrases and/or patterns to make the message – either spoken or written – more powerful and more memorable. One of the simplest examples, and yet one of the most memorable, is the phrase Julius Caesar uttered when he referred to his conquest of Zela (part of modern Turkey) in 47 B.C.: "I came. I saw. I conquered." Caesar used the pronoun "I" three times for emphasis. Yes, he could have said, "I came, saw, and conquered," but that

one sentence doesn't have the same dramatic effect as the three shorter, parallel sentences. Kennedy and King also used repetition in their speeches.

When Kennedy spoke as President for the first time, he wanted to stress both the potential and the danger that were present in the nuclear age. Thus, he repeated the phrase "all forms" and followed it with contrasting prepositional phrases: "For man holds in his mortal hands the power to abolish all forms of human poverty and all forms of human life." At the same time, Kennedy also wanted to contrast the presence of a higher power with the power of men: "the rights of man come not from the generosity of the state, but from the hand of God."

As you can see from these examples, Kennedy repeated certain phrases to draw attention to them, yet his contrast also highlighted the extremes. This use of parallel structure with contrast is evident later when he said, "United, there is little we cannot do . . . Divided, there is little we can do." Finally, Kennedy concluded with, perhaps, his most famous line: "Ask not what your country can do for you – Ask what you can do for your country."

Similarly, when Martin Luther King Jr., delivered his "I Have a Dream" speech almost three years later, he repeated the words "shall" and "will" to highlight his hope for the unity of mankind and for the elimination of differences: "I have a dream that one day every valley shall be exalted, every hill and mountain shall be made low, the rough places will be made plain, and the crooked places will be made straight, and the glory of the Lord shall be revealed, and all flesh will see it together" (508).

Later, King emphasized that unity again when he repeated the word "together" after the infinitive form (to) of various verbs: "With this faith we will be able to work together, to pray together, to struggle together, to go to jail together, to stand up for freedom together, knowing that we will be free one day" (508).

Finally, as King approached his conclusion, he wanted to stress the need for freedom for all people, from all sections of the United States, so he used the phrase "Let freedom ring" eight times, and he followed each one with prepositional phrases that designated different sections of the country: "So let

freedom ring from the prodigious hilltops of New Hampshire. Let freedom ring from the mighty mountains of New York. Let freedom ring from the heightening Alleghenies of Pennsylvania! Let freedom ring from the snowcapped Rockies of Colorado! Let freedom ring from the curvaceous peaks of California! But not only that; let freedom ring from Stone Mountain of Georgia! Let freedom ring from Lookout Mountain of Tennessee! Let freedom ring from every hill and molehill of Mississippi. From every mountainside, let freedom ring" (509).

As an orator speaking at a dramatic moment in American history, King's exaggerated repetition was unusual yet effective. As a college writer, however, you won't need to repeat any phrase eight times; two or three examples are generally sufficient to make your point. Still, if you do have the opportunity to use parallel structure, you should consider doing so. For instance, instead of writing two thoughts that are not parallel such as, "My head ached, and I was hungry," you could make those thoughts parallel by writing either, "My head ached, and my stomach growled," or, "I had an aching head, and I had an empty stomach."

Likewise, instead of writing, "Parallel structure is poetic and persuasive, and it has a lot of power," you could write, "Parallel structure is poetic, persuasive, and powerful."

Chapter 10
Specific Writing Tasks

Make a Strong First Impression on Paper

When you think of first impressions, you probably think of your physical appearance, your clothing, your speech, and your manners. While all these things are important in a general sense, they probably won't influence your teachers or affect your grades as much as the first written assignment you hand in for a particular course. So to make a strong first impression on paper, consider the following six tidbits of advice.

First, make sure your assignment is typed and handed in on time. You're in college now. That means handwritten papers are no longer acceptable. Even if you don't have a computer or a word processor at home, as a college student, you probably have a computer account on campus and numerous computer labs available to you. Take advantage of them, and give yourself plenty of time to complete the assignment on schedule. A first assignment that is typed and on time may lead your professors to think that you are organized and prepared.

Next, write to the correct length. If your professor asks you to write two full pages, don't write one or three. Believe it or not, teachers have a specific purpose in mind when they assign the length of an assignment. They may want you to be precise and direct in a short assignment, or they may want you to provide examples and background information in a longer paper. Writing to the requested length may lead your instructors to conclude that you can follow directions and are willing to do so.

Third, use a strong thesis early in your paper. Your thesis is your main idea, and your thesis belongs, generally, at the end of your first paragraph. Your thesis also lets your reader know where the essay is headed and how it's going to get there. Here's an example of a strong thesis: "The Hudson River should be dredged for four main reasons." A strong thesis in the proper location will let your instructors know you are serious about what you have to say.

Also, use transitions to move your readers from one idea to the next. If you're writing about the four reasons for dredging the Hudson, you should use words like "first, second, third, and fourth" to separate your reasons. Yes, a new paragraph will indicate that you're moving on to a new idea, but without a transition, the reader might not know if the new idea is still part of the previous reason or a new reason altogether. Transitions make your writing more clear and make you appear ordered and logical.

Fifth, have a strong conclusion. Just as your thesis introduces your main idea, your conclusion reminds the readers of that idea and allows them to remember your idea and think about it. You may want to conclude with a summary, a challenge, or a call to action. A strong summary shows that you are secure and confident.

Finally, use the spell checker and the grammar checker on your computer and proofread carefully. In the days before computers, teachers may have been a bit more lenient. They might have forgiven a spelling error, for example, if it looked more like a typing error. Today, however, you can't let anything slide by. Your professors expect you to use the tools available to you. Your professors also expect you to catch the errors that the computers miss. A paper that is free of spelling errors and typos will show you to be a competent and careful writer.

First impressions – either positive or negative – are hard to overcome. This semester, take your time with that first writing assignment and make a great first impression on your instructors.

Writing the College Application Essay

As a student, you may soon have to write one of the most important essays of your life. No, this essay won't be part of a final exam, and this essay won't even be written for a particular course. Instead, this essay will be part of your college application.

If you decide to continue your education, your college application essay may well determine whether or not you are accepted at the college of your choice. Obviously, then, you want to do a good job. Here are some guidelines to keep in mind.

Start Early. Good writing takes time. The last thing you want to do is write your essay the day before your application has to be postmarked or received electronically. Ideally, you should begin the writing process at least a month ahead of your deadline. This will give you plenty of time to brainstorm ideas, gather thoughts, write a first draft, get feedback from others, revise your essay, and proofread the final version. If you're really struggling to get started, you may

want to look at sample application essays you can find on the Internet.

Write About Something You Love. Obviously, each college has its own essay guidelines, but most are general enough to give you some choice and some freedom to express yourself. So instead of pretending to be interested in a particular topic that you think will impress the admissions officer, choose a topic that you really understand and love. This will allow you to write a much stronger essay. Typically, the essay question or writing prompt will ask you to write about some aspect of your past, your present, or your future.

Essays that focus on the past will usually ask you to write about a person, an event, or an experience that influenced you in some way. If you write this type of narrative, make sure you use plenty of transitional words or phrases (such as first, later, eventually, etc.) to move your reader smoothly through the story. Also, try to avoid clichés or colloquial expressions such as the following:

"She will be a forever friend"; "The event just blew me away"; or "The experience was totally awesome."

Essays that focus on the present may ask you to describe yourself, your family, your favorite activity, your heroes, your philosophy of life, or your opinion on a current controversial issue. When you write description, you may be tempted to pull out a thesaurus to impress the college admissions officer with your vocabulary. If you use a thesaurus, make sure you also use a dictionary to determine the precise meaning of the word you're considering. Using a word incorrectly or using a word that doesn't fit with the rest of your essay may be even worse than using a cliché or a colloquial expression.

Finally, essays that focus on the future may ask you to explain what you hope to accomplish at the school you've chosen or what you hope to achieve with the education you obtain there. Obviously, you should be as specific as possible and be aware of the school's strengths. Thus, you should be familiar with the school's catalog or web page, and you should have a clear idea of both your short- and long-term goals. Try to present yourself as a serious student with a definite plan rather than as another average student who is simply climbing the next rung on the educational ladder.

Explain What Makes You Unique. Your application and the transcript that accompanies it will tell the school about your grades, your accomplishments, and your activities. Your essay, however, is the only chance you have to set yourself apart from all the other applicants. So, if you volunteered at a local day-care center, try to explain your motivation for doing so. Or if you played football, let the admissions officer know why the game is important to you.

Edit Thoroughly. Once you finish your essay, make sure you get some constructive criticism from a parent, a teacher, or a trusted friend, and make all the appropriate changes. Then, run your essay through the spell checker and the grammar checker on your computer, and proofread your essay meticulously. After all, your essay should demonstrate not only your thoughts but also your ability to express those thoughts logically and correctly.

How to Write a Résumé

About 50 years ago, when I applied for my first job after college, writing my résumé was a major project. First, I had to type the résumé on my manual typewriter using erasable paper, so I could later correct any errors. Then, I had to bring my original to a printer or copy center and purchase 50 copies on a better quality of paper. Finally, I had to distribute those copies to potential employers at job fairs or through the mail. In other words, every potential employer saw the same copy of my résumé, and no customization was possible. Obviously, modern technology has drastically improved the process, but writing a résumé still requires a basic format and good deal of work.

Essentially, a résumé includes four key components: your contact information, your education, your work experience, and anything else that might help you get a job. Let's look at each component.

Contact Information. Most people place their information in the center of the page on the top portion of their résumé, but others like to put it in one corner or the other. Whatever location you choose, be sure to include the following: name, street address, city, state, zip code, phone number, and e-mail address. Some people put their name in bold type and also use a larger font while others put everything in bold with a larger font. Your font size and type may depend on the job you're seeking. A conservative law firm, for example, might appreciate a standard font and size, but a creative talent agency might want to see something with a little flair.

Education/Work. Many students or recent graduates will place their educational details next, before their work details, because their educational accomplishments might be more impressive than their work experience. However, if your work experience is more remarkable than your level of education, you may want to reverse the two. Again, the decision may depend on the job you're seeking. A big company with a manager-trainee program might want a recent college graduate, but a small, family-run business might prefer a job candidate who has experience in that particular field.

Education. With both education details and work details, you should list your most recent activity first. For instance, if you have both a four-year diploma and a community-college diploma, you should list the four-year school above the two-year school. Also, if you are still in school – studying for a master's degree, perhaps – you should list that first, and be sure to include an expected graduation date. In addition, if you have any special academic accomplishments or honors, you may want to include them in this section. For instance, if you made the Dean's List, earned a high grade point average, or won a departmental award, you should let your reader know that.

Work Experience. As mentioned earlier, always start with either your current job or, if you're currently unemployed, your most recent position. For each position, try to include the start date and the end date (unless, of course, you're still employed there, which you should indicate). Also, try to mention the employer's name, address, and contact information along with a bulleted list of your job responsibilities.

For that list, try to start each description with a strong verb such as "*managed* a team of cashiers, *filmed* trainee videos, or *balanced* the books monthly." Naturally, you'll want to highlight any specific experience that will connect easily to the job you're seeking.

Anything Else. For the final section of your résumé, you should include volunteer activities, special hobbies or interests, or other unique skills or experiences that might make you more attractive to potential employers. For instance, if you teach adult Sunday school classes at your church and you're seeking a job that includes dealing with the public, that personal-interaction experience may demonstrate that you'd be a good fit for the position. Or if you have a degree in financial management, but you also have a computer-repair business on the side, that computer knowledge may give you an edge over other candidates with similar academic credentials. Finally, if you're bilingual or have experience living overseas, that background may also give you an edge for certain job opportunities.

The final important detail regarding your résumé is proofreading. When you send it off to a potential employer, that one sheet of paper or electronic file may be all that employer knows about you. Thus, you want to make sure that you don't have any errors in spelling, grammar, or punctuation. You should also make sure that you don't have any glaring spacing issues or font inconsistencies. Your résumé should demonstrate that you are professional and precise rather than careless and capricious.

By the time you finish, you should have one basic résumé that you can use for any position, but you should also be flexible enough to adapt that basic résumé to fit a particular job. For one job, for instance, you might want to highlight your education, but for a different job, you may want to highlight your experience. Modern word-processing programs make such adaptations easy, so you may as well use the technology to your advantage. Otherwise, you'll feel like you're an old man, composing on an old typewriter, and later rushing off to the copy center and the post office.

Hello and Good-bye: How to Write a Cover Letter

"Hello" and "Good-bye" are two of the most common greetings in our daily lives. We typically salute one another with "Hello" when we meet at school, at work, or in the neighborhood, and we usually say farewell with "Good-bye" as we exit those same locations to return to our homes. Interestingly, those same two words provide the basic framework for a standard cover letter.

What is a cover letter? Essentially, a cover letter accompanies your résumé when you send it to an employer to apply for a job. In theory, you could just send your résumé to the employer to express your interest in working there because your résumé should include all of the following: your educational qualifications, your work experiences, your special abilities or talents, information about your references, and your contact information. Thus, if the employer only had one job available and if you were a good fit for that position, that employer could look at your résumé and contact you to set up an interview. In reality, however, the job-application process is a bit more complicated.

Oftentimes, employers are looking for numerous employees in a variety of jobs. Thus, when you apply, you need a cover letter to identify which job piques your interest. Fortunately, the cover letter itself is not complicated and, in fact, may be one of the easiest writing tasks ever. Basically, the cover letter involves three short paragraphs, and all you have to do is say "Hello" and "Good-bye" and add an extra tidbit or two in the middle.

Hello. In your first paragraph, you simply have to mention the job you're applying for and how you found out about the position. One simple and straightforward sentence is usually sufficient. For example, you might write, "I am applying for the editorial assistant position (ED2) in your Cleveland office, a position that is advertised on your company website." By mentioning the job title with its company designation (ED2) and the position's location in Cleveland, you differentiate your letter and résumé from the others that might pertain to other positions. In addition, mentioning the company website helps the employer figure out the best place to advertise job opportunities.

Tidbits. The second paragraph will be the longest of your three paragraphs, and you may want to add something here that is not included on your résumé. For instance, if you know someone who also works in that Cleveland editorial office, you may want to mention that person's name and describe your connection. Or if you are familiar with the employer's publications because you are a long-time subscriber, you may mention that too. And what if you don't have any extra tidbits to offer? Under those circumstances, you might simply highlight one or two major points from your résumé and introduce them with the phrase, "As the enclosed résumé indicates, ..." Essentially, in this paragraph, you want to show a strong connection between you and the position, but you want to do so in a concise manner.

Good-bye. Finally, your last paragraph should be, like the first paragraph, brief and to the point. You want to thank the reader for his or her time and also mention the best way to contact you, most likely with a phone number or an e-mail address. Some people who are a bit more assertive may add, "I will call you next week to make sure you received my information." That approach may be okay in certain situations – such as if you know the reader well – but most employers do not want to be bombarded with phone calls.

Once you've written the body of your letter, make sure you also precede the body with the date and your home address plus the name,

title, and address of your recipient. If the job notice doesn't provide a specific name and title, try to dig up that information and include it. Doing so will show initiative on your part. If you can't find the information, try to address the letter with one of the following: "Dear Sir or Madam" or with a job description such as "To the Personnel Manager" or "To the Director of Human Resources." Note, too, that you should always follow your salutation with a colon (Dear Mr. Keefe:).

Finally, before you send out your cover letter, let someone else read it. Ask a friend, a classmate, a co-worker, or a significant other, someone who knows you well and also wants to see you succeed. This person doesn't necessarily have to be an English major or a grammar expert, though that expertise is helpful. He or she simply needs to see that the letter reads smoothly and makes sense. You, on the other hand, must double check everything else such as the spelling of the recipient's name and address and all of your contact information. Making certain that everything is just right demonstrates your attention to detail, a characteristic that most employers seek and appreciate.

When you apply for a job, you are essentially saying "Hello" to an employer, but you don't want that employer to say "Good-bye" in return. Instead, you want to receive a job offer, so you can say "Hello" to that employer each day when you arrive at the workplace. So as you prepare to apply, try to write the best cover letter you can, and perhaps you will secure that coveted position.

Write a Movie Review To Practice Your Critical-Writing Skills

The month between the end of the fall semester and the beginning of the spring semester is usually a time of rest, relaxation, and recovery for most students. However, some ambitious students do take a course during the intersession, and others work on their academic skills in an unusual, non-credit-bearing way.

I have had students come to me and ask me to give them a writing assignment. These students are looking for a writing challenge, and they want some feedback on their writing before the new semester begins. Thus, since I want to provide a reasonable task that will not overwhelm the student with research, I will typically ask the student to write a review of the last movie he or she has seen. Writing a movie review is an excellent way to practice the critical-writing skills that most instructors are looking to evaluate. Here are four simple steps to get started.

First, write a short summary of the movie and identify all the key elements: the time and place of the story, the main characters and the actors and actresses who portray those characters, and some of the details concerning the conflict without revealing the resolution of that conflict. After all, you don't want to reveal the ending to someone who hasn't yet viewed the movie. For example, I saw the movie *Bella* (2006) a while back, and my short summary of the movie follows.

"Jose (played by Eduardo Verastegui) is a former soccer star turned chef who works in his brother's restaurant in modern-day New York City. Jose's soccer career ended prematurely, however, because of a tragic accident that continues to haunt him. Nina (Tammy Blanchard) works as a waitress in that same restaurant and she faces a difficult situation of her own. In an effort to ease his own suffering, Jose offers to help Nina, and they both begin the process of recovery."

Second, once you've introduced the key elements, you should begin to point out the movie's strengths, the features that captured your

attention or amazed you in some way. These features may include the visual images, the soundtrack, the dialogue, the acting, the costumes, or the special effects, among others. As you write, try to be as specific as possible, and try to avoid the standard movie clichés such as "the actors were totally believable in their roles," or "the action kept me on the edge of my seat."

For instance, in the case of *Bella*, one of the most interesting features was the unusual flow of the story. Rather than use a straight chronological order, director Alejandro Gomez Monteverde uses numerous flashbacks to reveal the cause of Jose's sufferings, and Monteverde also allows the characters to gradually reveal key details that come into play later. This non-linear approach to the story keeps the viewers engaged throughout the movie and leads to interesting conversations afterwards.

Third, you should also provide your readers with the movie's weaknesses, again being as specific as possible. Some weaknesses may be obvious such as an actor who appears to be playing himself rather than the character (Hugh Grant comes to mind) or a distracting inconsistency like an elevated train in midtown Manhattan (as occurred in the movie *Spider-Man 2*). Other weaknesses may not come to mind until much later when you realize something is missing, or something didn't quite make sense.

In *Bella*, for instance, I assumed one ending and was surprised to see a different outcome altogether. When I thought about it afterwards, I don't think the director gave viewers enough hints that the movie would turn out the way it did. In addition, I felt like the ending came too quickly and left too many unanswered questions, almost as if the director were setting the movie up for a sequel.

Finally, you should weigh the strengths and the weaknesses to determine your overall judgment of the movie. Using my example, for instance, I would definitely recommend *Bella* because the strengths easily outweigh the weaknesses. In other cases, however, the final decision is not as obvious, and you might want to qualify your decision by indicating that the movie is worth seeing but not at full price in the theater. By contrast, some movies are terrible in every respect but still worth seeing on the big screen because of the special effects (such as the 2005 version of *King Kong*).

Obviously, this short essay is not going to turn you into the next Roger Ebert, a now deceased reviewer for *The Chicago Sun-Times* and the former co-host of the television show *Ebert and Roper at the Movies*. However, actually composing a movie review should make you a better writer because the process forces you to summarize briefly and to evaluate seriously a work's strengths and weaknesses. If you can master those skills, you will likely succeed in any college course that requires extensive writing.

Write a Love Letter This Christmas

The Christmas season is approaching, but you're feeling like Ebenezer Scrooge because you're broke. You can't afford to buy that new toy for your little brother. Your boyfriend or girlfriend will have to do without that special piece of jewelry. And Mom and Dad won't be getting that gift certificate for a weekend getaway. What can you do? You can still give one of the most memorable gifts of all by writing a love letter this Christmas season.

A Christmas love letter is basically a thank-you note. The note gives you the opportunity to express in letter form why someone is special to you. For example, you might thank your mom or dad for encouraging you to go to college when everyone else said you couldn't succeed. Or you might thank a longtime friend for always being willing to listen when you suffered through difficult relationships. You might even thank your boyfriend or girlfriend – or spouse – for simply sharing the day-to-day pleasures of life with you.

If you think this sounds hokey and if you think the recipient of the letter will not really appreciate it, think again. Here are three examples.

In an essay called "Thank You," author Alex Haley describes thank-you letters he wrote on Thanksgiving to three influential people in his life: his father, his grandmother, and his grammar school principal.

Though Haley felt the letters were long overdue and though he felt guilty for always taking these people for granted, each of the recipients was extremely grateful for the affection and appreciation. In fact, all three wrote back to Haley expressing their gratitude for his thoughtfulness (352-56).

Another similar example occurs in an essay entitled "How to Write a Personal Letter" by Garrison Keillor. In this essay, Keillor states authoritatively that "Letters are a gift" (225).

He says letters are especially useful for shy people who "don't shine at conversation" (225) or for people who have difficulty expressing their true emotions verbally. And in his conclusion, Keillor states that letters are gifts that won't be discarded: "Probably your friend will put your letter away, it'll be read again – a few years from now – and it will improve with age" (227). From personal experience, I can tell you that what Keillor says is true.

Over 40 years ago, I wrote a love letter to my family as a Christmas gift. In the letter, I included a separate paragraph for each family member. In these paragraphs, I thanked my mom and dad and each of my five sisters for special moments I had shared with them.

I recalled Dad's farewell advice when he put me on an airplane for my two-year Peace Corps assignment in Costa Rica: "Do a good job, Son." I described my sister Kathy's wedding day and how her evening departure with her husband made me acutely aware of how our family was changing. And I closed with a paragraph to my deceased sister, Peggy, who died when she was four. In that particular paragraph, I remembered how her short life was so full of energy and how her death simultaneously devastated our family and strengthened it. All the family members received a copy of this letter, and I'm pretty sure they all still have their copies almost half a century later.

Whenever I teach Composition II, I usually assign the thank-you letter as an early-semester writing assignment. The students' letters are typically sincere, touching, and heartfelt, and I always encourage the students to pass them on to their loved ones. Typically, too, the students who follow my advice return with sweet stories about how the letters were enjoyed and treasured. I think if you write a love letter this Christmas, both you and your loved ones will be glad you did.

Don't Summarize When You Should Analyze

When you return from the movies and when your friends or family members ask you about the film you just viewed, how do you answer? Do you start at the beginning and give a long, detailed summary of every incident all the way through to the climax and the conclusion? Or do you give a quick analysis ("Fantastic!" or "What a waste!") and then gradually explain the reasons why anyone should, or should not, pay full price to see this particular movie?

You probably take the second approach. After all, most people want to know your general reaction first and the reasons later. Plus, they probably don't want all the specific details, either because they've already seen the movie or because they're thinking about seeing it in the near future. Yet, when college instructors ask a similar question in the form of a writing assignment, many students make the mistake of writing a summary when they should be writing an analysis. Let's look at the differences between the two.

A summary – sometimes referred to as an abstract – is essentially an essay that explains the key idea of an article, a book, or a creative work of art. The summary should be much shorter than the original work and purely objective. In other words, you shouldn't include your personal opinion in a summary. Thus, if I were to summarize the folk tale of "The Three Little Pigs," I might write something like this:

"Three pigs each had to build a home. The first didn't want to work too hard, so he built his house of straw and went off to play. The second was pretty busy, so he built his house of sticks and went off to the fair. But the third was a bit more ambitious. He wanted a strong, sturdy house, so he took his time and carefully built a house of bricks.

"All three houses appeared to be sufficient and safe until the big, bad wolf came along. He blew down the first and second houses and forced those two pigs to run to the third pig's house for safety. Since the wolf could not blow down the brick house, he climbed to the roof and went down the chimney. But the pigs had a hot fire and a boiling pot of water waiting for him, and they boiled him, ate him for supper, and lived happily ever after."

The summary, then, simply gives the basic details of the story without any comments or interpretation. Jack Webb used to offer the same advice on the old television show *Dragnet*: "Just the facts, ma'am." An analysis, though, is quite different.

When you write an analysis – sometimes referred to as a critique or a review – your readers expect personal comments and interpretation. In some cases, you may have to include a summary before your interpretation, but in most cases, your professors have already read the work in question, and they don't want the summary; all they want is your analysis.

When you write an analysis, you need to come up with a main idea, generally referred to as your thesis. Then, you need to support your thesis with other information that may involve classification, comparison and contrast, personal experience, or other details that help to persuade the reader to believe as you do. Your analysis, then, is more like a newspaper editorial than a straight news story. Thus, if I were to analyze the same folk tale, I might write something like this:

"The tale of 'The Three Little Pigs' is a wonderful, classic fable that teaches a vital lesson: If people don't take the time to do a task correctly, they will eventually face sad consequences. This children's story is closely related to the adult version which appears in The Bible as the parable of the house built on the rock (*NIV Study Bible*: Matthew

7:24-27). When Jesus, a carpenter, told this parable, he was probably thinking of his own construction experience. He knew that a strong foundation was essential and that a house built on sand could not survive the symbolic heavy rains that are bound to occur. Personally, I heard the story of 'The Three Little Pigs' many times as a boy, but I had to experience the lesson first-hand to fully comprehend.

"During my undergraduate days at Siena College, I built an academic house of straw and sticks because I didn't think I'd ever go on to graduate school. Eight years after graduating from Siena, though, I changed my mind. As a result, when I applied to a certain graduate school, the big, bad wolf in the admission's office blew right through my application, and said, 'No way.' Since then, I've tried to become more and more like that industrious third pig. I'm trying to learn more from the lessons of others and less from personal failure."

As you read this critique, you probably noticed two major differences from the earlier summary: the length and the point of view. Generally, an analysis is longer and more developed than a summary. Also, an analysis generally uses the first-person point of view (I) rather than the third-person point of view (he, she, it, and they), though a more formal analysis may require the third-person point of view.

Obviously, this one short essay can't tell you everything you need to know about writing summaries and critiques. If, however, you understand the differences between the two and know your instructor's expectations beforehand, you may receive a positive review for your work.

Use Writing to Express the Silence

How many times have you heard someone say the following phrase about an unusual or exhilarating experience: "I can't put it into words"? Poet Edgar Lee Masters said basically the same thing in his poem entitled "Silence." His main idea is that some experiences or situations can't be expressed verbally in words, yet he uses written words in his poem to express that thought. And therein lies the beauty of writing. Writing is a way to express the silent moments of our lives.

Some of the examples that Masters mentions in his poem are the "silence of the sick, the silence of a great hatred or a great love, a deep peace of mind, an embittered friendship, and a spiritual crisis." He also mentions the "silence of defeat, of those unjustly punished, of the dying, of those who have failed, and the silence of age." Have you experienced any of those silences? I know I have.

I think most of my silent moments have occurred when I've needed to say "good-bye." For example, at age 21,

when I left my family to work in the Peace Corps in Costa Rica, I couldn't speak at the airport's departure gate. I didn't know what to say, and I'm sure I couldn't have said it anyway.

Two years later, I thought it would be easy to hop on another plane to come home. Yet, before I left the small town of Golfito, where I'd taught and coached the village's teenagers, I got choked up again. A busload of those students came to the airport to say good-bye to me, and even though I knew I'd probably never see any of them again, I could only hug each one and try my best not to break into tears.

Fortunately, those speechless moments stay with us for a long while, and to with time and meditation, we can eventually put our experiences into writing. When I witnessed the birth of our first daughter, Maria, for instance, I was overwhelmed by the miracle of her appearance in the delivery room. I tried to absorb it all because I knew I couldn't speak. Later that evening, I described her birth to my parents and to

my extended family members, and later,
I wrote a short poem about her arrival,
a poem called "Maria Christina":

Miraculous baby.

Miraculous birth.

Miraculous mother.

Miraculous mirth.

Miraculous moment.

Miraculous wife.

Miraculous miracle.

Miraculous.

Life.

Naturally, after we brought Maria
home, I experienced so much more
with her, and I recall playing with her,
dressing her, feeding her, burping her,
walking with her, singing to her, and,
finally, setting her in her crib for a nap
or a night's rest. The one experience
I recall most vividly, though, is when
she would fall asleep in my arms.

I experienced such a lightness when
she finally let go of her tears or her
exhaustion, and even though I could
put her down at that point, I didn't
want to let go of that warm sensation.
Thus, whether I was walking with

her or sitting in the rocker with her, I
would often just hold on and experience
that tender silence, what Masters
called the "silence of a deep peace of
mind." Eventually, I put words to my
feeling, and I wrote this short poem
entitled "Sleeping in My Arms":

From the mountains to the valleys,

From the cities to the farms,

Nothing is more soothing

Than you sleeping in my arms.

You can silence all the cannons,

Turn off all alarms.

Nothing is more peaceful

Than you sleeping in my arms.

I'd give up all possessions,

All money, luck, and charms

To experience this moment

With you sleeping in my arms.

So will you experience moments
that you will find difficult to "put into
words"? Of course, you will. Life is
full of moments that we cannot absorb
fully as they occur. Thus, we are left to
simply experience them, to hold on to
them, to reflect upon them, and, when
we are ready, to write them down.
Writing is the only way to express
the silent moments of our lives.

Chapter 11
Authors on Writing

What Stephen King Says About Writing May Frighten You

I have to admit that for a long time, I wouldn't read anything written by Stephen King. I was always afraid that his horror stories would keep me awake at night. After reading numerous term papers about this author, however, I finally asked my class to recommend a King story or two that wouldn't frighten me. Surprisingly, I liked what I read.

I began with a friend's copy of *The Shawshank Redemption*. Then, I went to the library and borrowed King's serial bestseller, *The Green Mile*. Next, I read his electronic novella called "Riding the Bullet" on my computer. In fact, I so enjoyed King's storytelling that I actually purchased his non-fiction book called *On Writing – A Memoir on the Craft*. Now this is a scary piece of work.

This book is scary because King, whose works have always been popular with college students, actually reinforces what college writing instructors have been saying for years. Three key areas that King covers have to do with the three R's: Reading, 'Riting, and Revising.

Reading. If you want to be a writer, according to King, you only have to do

two things: "read a lot and write a lot" (145). King's first exposure to extensive reading occurred when he was about six years old. Since he was sick at home for most of that school year, King claims that he read "approximately six tons of comic books" (27), and, eventually, he began to write his own stories.

Today, many of the people I meet – both students and non-students alike – say they don't have time to read. King has an easy answer for that excuse: Turn off the television. He calls television an "endlessly quacking box" (148) and says that turning it off to make time for reading will improve not only the quality of your writing but also the quality of your life. To drive home his point on the reading-writing connection, King adds, "You cannot hope to sweep someone else away by the force of your writing until it has been done to you" (146).

Writing. Writing instructors are forever telling their students to "write about what you know." King takes that advice and expands upon it: "Write what you like, then imbue it with life and make it unique by blending in your own personal knowledge of life, friendship, relationships, sex, and work" (161).

In his *Memoir*, King mentions that he enjoys writing primarily about situations and "what if" questions. As examples, he cites the following novels and the situations and the questions they are based on: *Salem's Lot* – "What if vampires invaded a small New England village?" *Desperation* – "What if a policeman in a remote Nevada town went berserk and started killing everyone in sight?" *Cujo* – "What if a young mother and her son became trapped in their stalled car by a rabid dog?" (169-70). You may not be able to write a best-selling novel like King, but if you write about what you know and love, your writing will be real and true.

Revising. King uses a door to emphasize the difference between writing and revising. When you write, King suggests you close the door to the outside world to isolate yourself for writing and to remove all distractions that might keep you from writing. Then, when you finish your first draft, King feels you must open the door to begin the process of revising (57, 155, 209, and 271-84).

Once the door is open, you are ready to show your work to one or more readers. For King, his "Ideal Reader" is his wife, Tabitha, and he suggests that all writers have at least one person who can read objectively and point out strengths and weaknesses (215). Some students let their professors perform this task, but if you can show your work to a trusted reader beforehand, you'll probably receive a higher grade for a revised second draft than you would have received for a rough first draft.

King's *Memoir* isn't solely about reading, writing, and revising. He focuses, too, on other aspects of good writing such as vocabulary, grammar, punctuation, narration, description, dialogue, pace, plot, theme, characterization, symbolism, and research. As he discusses each of these subjects, he also writes about the autobiographical details that led him to his current ideas on these matters. He even includes a special section on the accident he endured in 1999 and how it affected his outlook on writing in particular and on life in general (253-70). If you're a Stephen King fan, you'll love this book. But even if you're not, you'll learn an awful lot about the craft of writing from one of today's most popular storytellers.

Writing Is Like Surgery

I've been thinking about writing and surgery quite a bit lately. Usually, I think about writing a lot because I work all day in The Writing and Research Center, and I write fiction in my spare time. I've also been thinking about surgery recently because I've been reading the works of Richard Selzer, the surgeon/author who visited our campus a while back. And the more I read by Selzer about his medical experiences and his writing, I realize that writing is, in fact, a lot like surgery.

Selzer, who is a Troy native and a graduate of Union College in Schenectady and Albany Medical College (all in New York), commented on the similarity between the two professions in a 1992 interview with *Publisher's Weekly*: "A pen is the same size as the scalpel. When you use a scalpel, blood is shed; when you use a pen, ink is spilled on the page" (Steinberg 48).

As I pondered that quote, I recognized both a similarity and a difference between the two activities. Writing is like surgery because both writers and surgeons are going below the surface. Both practitioners are trying to determine if something within the body needs to be inspected, cleaned, or removed. The difference, however, is that surgeons are operating on others while writers are operating on themselves.

Something needs to be inspected. I once worked with an older gentleman who had undergone numerous medical procedures, some of which were quite complicated and invasive. At one point, this man wasn't feeling well at all, and he was convinced that something was wrong inside. He was so convinced, in fact, that he pestered his surgeon to perform exploratory surgery to discover the problem. Only when the surgeon consented and, subsequently, operated and discovered that everything was working smoothly did my co-worker finally convince himself that he was okay.

Writers sometimes experience a similar uneasiness about their lives, and these writers may need to perform exploratory surgery on themselves, often in a journal. One cliché about writing asks the following question: "How can I know what I'm thinking unless I write my thoughts down on paper?" The writing serves as a form of therapy to help the writer clarify his thoughts. Selzer himself experienced such uneasiness in 1986 when he was sued for malpractice by the family of one of his patients. By the time the trial took place, Selzer had retired from surgery and the patient was deceased, so Selzer wrote that the experience "was like two ghosts being brought to the courtroom to do battle" (Steinberg 49). Even though the case was eventually dropped, Selzer found the whole experience disheartening, and he claims that he survived only by writing about it: "My only defense was to take my notebook to court every day. That was all I could do to converse with myself" (Steinberg 49).

Something needs to be cleaned.

Recently, a good friend had to go in for surgery. He was experiencing unusual back pain that wasn't related to physical exercise or strain. His doctor thought the pain might be related to the heart, and, sure enough, when the surgeon operated, he had to clean out my friend's arteries; if they had not been cleaned, my friend may have died.

As human beings, we, too, may have certain experiences from our past that we need not remove necessarily but to clean out. For example, if we've endured an extremely difficult experience that has helped us in some way, we may need to write about that experience in order to reap the true benefit. For example, when I was 12, my four-year-old sister, Peggy, died from various medical complications. This was my first experience with death, and I found myself reflecting often on Peggy's short life, her unexpected death, and the wake and funeral that followed. Consequently, I found myself writing about Peggy for various school essays, and later,

I wrote both a poem and a short novel about what had happened. Though I will never remove Peggy from my memory, cleaning up those memories and making sense of them through writing has helped me to appreciate the delicate and precious thread that is our life here on this earth.

Something needs to be removed.

When I was teaching at the high-school level about 30 years ago, I was also coaching the girls' tennis team. While the girls were running laps one day, one of the girls came up to me and said, "Mr. LaBate, I don't feel well; may I go home?" Part of me, the hard-nosed coach part, wanted to say, "You'll be fine; just keep running." Fortunately, the softer part of me said, "Sure. I hope you feel better tomorrow." When she got home, however, she felt even worse, and her parents brought her to the hospital where the surgeon later removed her appendix.

As individuals, do we have things in our lives that we may need to remove, as well? Of course we do. Isn't that what songwriters do all the time? After all, most love songs deal with either the initial period of a relationship, where the two individuals are totally enamored with one another, or the breakup that often follows. Unfortunately, most of us have been through similar breakups at one time or another, and we may need to express our anger or frustration and remove that hurt from our lives before we can move on to another serious relationship.

So, if writing is, indeed, like surgery, do we have to be medically trained in order to inspect, clean, or remove the experiences of our lives? No. All we really need is a willingness to explore, to go below the surface of our lives. As Red Smith, a sportswriter for *The New York Times* once said: "There's nothing to writing. All you do is sit down at a typewriter and open a vein" (Charlton 39).

"Bird by Bird" with Anne Lamott

In 1994, author Anne Lamott published a book of essays entitled *Bird by Bird*. On the surface, that title sounds like an odd choice from a writer who at that time had written four novels and a memoir about the first year of her son's life (*Operating Instructions: A Journal of My Son's First Year*). The book, however, is not about birds; instead, Lamott was referring to a family story about the writing process, and the essays in the book – subtitled "Some Instructions on Writing and Life" – cover various aspects of writing from "Getting Started" to "Publication."

The "bird-by-bird" story actually referred to Lamott's older brother who was facing a writing task of his own. Like many ten-year-old boys, John had procrastinated for three months and, then, panicked the day before the assignment was due. As Anne tells it, "he was at the kitchen table close to tears, surrounded by binder paper and pencils and unopened books on birds, immobilized by the hugeness of the task ahead" (19). Fortunately for the children, their father, Kenneth, was a writer himself, and he had

published novels and magazine articles. So, based on his own experience, he remained calm and offered his fatherly wisdom: "Bird by bird, buddy. Just take it bird by bird" (19).

This idea of breaking the writing task down into smaller parts is one of the key ideas in the book and one that writers everywhere should absorb. In fact, just a page earlier in the same book, Lamott quotes American novelist E. L. Doctorow who offers similar counsel: "Writing a novel is like driving a car at night. You can only see as far as your headlights, but you can make the whole trip that way" (18). Lamott goes on to say that "This is right up there with the best advice about writing, or life, I have ever heard" (18).

In this book, Lamott has various chapters on different aspects of writing, but three stand out. First, in "Getting Started," she says that when she teaches writing, she often encounters students who don't know what to write about or who feel as if they have nothing to write about. To encourage them, Lamott quotes American short-story writer Flannery O'Connor who once said, "Anyone who survived childhood has enough material to write for the rest of his or her life" (4). Lamott then asks these struggling students to begin by writing about their memories as honestly and as precisely as they can. At first, the writing may seem insignificant and have no purpose, but gradually "the miracle happens" (9). Her writers "begin to string words together like beads to tell a story . . . it is a matter of persistence and faith and hard work" (7). Overall, Lamott is both honest and optimistic about the writing process. She readily acknowledges how difficult writing can be, but she also promises a reward and satisfaction for those who persevere.

Later in the book, Lamott has a chapter on first drafts. What most writing instructors call "rough drafts," Lamott calls "Shitty First Drafts." According to Lamott, "All good writers write them. This is how they end up with good second drafts and terrific third drafts" (21). Basically, Lamott lets her readers know that even professional writers struggle through the early versions of their work. Thus, she encourages writers to "let it all pour out and then let it romp all over the place, knowing that no one is going to see it and that you can shape it later" (22). For this method to work for college writers, of course, they must leave themselves enough time to work on those second and third drafts before the teacher's deadline.

Finally, Lamott also includes an essay on "Someone to Read Your Drafts." Some college writers may assume that getting feedback from a reader is something that only occurs in a classroom; surely, professional writers don't need constructive criticism. Lamott destroys that illusion when she writes that "there may be someone out there – maybe a spouse, maybe a close friend – who will read your finished drafts and give you an honest critique, let you know what does and doesn't work, give you some suggestions on things you might take out or things on which you need to elaborate, ways in which to make your piece stronger" (163). Lamott herself adds that she shows all of her work to one of two readers: one who is a fellow writer and her best friend, and another who is a librarian who reads voraciously but has never written a word. Her message here is that she would rather have these individuals catch her mistakes or inconsistencies rather than an editor or an agent; obviously, students too can benefit in the same way if a reader catches the writer's errors before the teacher grades the work.

In the final chapter, "The Last Class," Lamott admits that most of the aspiring writers in her classes will never be famous or on the bestseller lists; many will never even be published. Still, she encourages all of them to continue writing. She compares writers to musicians and adds that "the literary life is the loveliest one possible, this life of reading and writing and corresponding" (232). Bird by bird, and word by word, Anne Lamott has made a convincing case that writing is a healing and life-changing experience.

What William Kennedy Taught Me About Writing

As one of the organizers for literary events on our campus, I had the opportunity to spend a full day with Pulitzer Prize-winning author William Kennedy. He spoke to two classes; he shared lunch with a small group of students, faculty members, and employees; he lectured to a big crowd; and he attended a dessert reception afterwards. Thus, I was able to listen in as Kennedy shared some interesting thoughts about the writing process in general and about the writing of *Ironweed* in particular.

Research. During a visit to a Macroeconomics class, one of the students asked Kennedy about his research on the Depression and on *Ironweed*'s main character, Francis. In response, Kennedy said that he "didn't have to do too much research" because he had lived through the Depression in Albany and, thus, knew quite a bit about it. He did, however, add that to get a feel for the life of Francis, he spent quite a few, full days with a homeless alcoholic while writing some feature stories on Albany's neighborhoods. Thus, Kennedy was echoing the classic

writers' advice to "write what you know and research what you don't know."

Types of Writing. During that same Macroeconomics class, Kennedy also discussed his work as a newspaper journalist for *The San Juan Star* in Puerto Rico and also for the Albany *Times Union*. Journalism, he acknowledged, is a great training ground because the daily deadlines force writers to write quickly and write often. Those same, never ending deadlines, however, can often stifle or prevent creative writers from fulfilling their desires to write fiction. Kennedy himself readily admits that he "quit journalism numerous times" early in his career as a writer because while journalism paid the bills, he really wanted to write novels.

Subject Matter. Another student asked Kennedy about how he decided upon the subject matter for his novels. Essentially, the student was asking if Kennedy wrote to please his readers or to please himself. Kennedy emphatically emphasized that creative writers should always write to please themselves because "readers don't know what they want until they read it." He added that he himself was not interested in imitating recent bestsellers; instead, he wanted to explore a terrain that had never been chronicled before: the lives and stories of New York's capital city. Even when *Ironweed* was rejected by 13 publishers, Kennedy persisted with his chosen subject matter, and that book eventually was published and earned him the Pulitzer Prize in 1984.

Writer's Block. During a Composition I class, a student asked Kennedy, "How do you overcome writer's block?"

"I don't," Kennedy responded quickly. Rather than try to "overcome" writer's block, Kennedy said that when he finds it difficult to finish a particular project, he simply "puts it on the shelf." Then, he works on other projects until he feels ready again to tackle the troubling task. He explained that writers sometimes can't see the solution to the problem, but if the unconscious mind is allowed to think about the problem while accomplishing other tasks, the writer will eventually figure out a solution and return to implement it. Later, he mentioned, as an example, that he was about to finish a play that he "put on the shelf ten years ago."

Marketing. During the luncheon, one participant asked Kennedy how he came up with the title *Ironweed*. He laughed as he said that the initial title for the book was actually "Lemonweed" because from his youth, he associated the lemon with bitter characteristics like those of some of the novel's characters. As he got older, though, he noticed that the connotation of the word "lemon" changed with the popularity of the song "Lemon Tree" by Peter, Paul, and Mary, and with the advertising for cleaning products such as Lemon Pledge. In addition, some people in the publishing industry warned him that if he used his original title, some book reviewers might compare the novel to a bad, used car. Thus, Kennedy sought a new name for the book and found it in the *Field Guide to North American Wildflowers*. When he came across that name – which refers to the fact that the stem is so sturdy – he knew immediately that it would work well and serve as a great metaphor for the book's protagonist.

Near the end of the day, in my introduction to Kennedy's lecture, I mentioned that Kennedy is not a reclusive author who gives the world only his books. Rather, he is a writer and an educator, a neighbor and a friend, who is more than willing to share both his writings and his thoughts on writing with those around him. Hudson Valley Community College was privileged to have William Kennedy on campus, and I am grateful I had the opportunity to share the day with him.

Do You Have What It Takes to Become an Outlier?

According to *The American Heritage College Dictionary,* an "outlier" is "one whose domicile is distant from one's place of business" (970). Since the earliest recorded use of this word dates back to the 17th century, one can assume that an outlier lived in the country, far away from the central activities of his work in a town or a village. In 2008, however, author Malcolm Gladwell broadened the definition of the word in his best-selling book called *Outliers: The Story of Success.* And it's Gladwell's definition that may well determine whether you have what it takes to be a successful writer.

According to Gladwell, outliers are "men and women who do things that are out of the ordinary" (17). His definition focuses not on the person's physical separation from the town but on the activities that go well beyond the normal or the average. This is especially true in regard to a person's effort and devotion to a particular skill. Gladwell states that one of the main ingredients to "success" is a commitment to work, and he claims

that in order to achieve success, one has to commit 10,000 hours to the task.

Ten-thousand hours is essentially five years of full-time work (40 hours per week times 50 weeks times five years = 10,000) or ten years of half-time work. How did Gladwell come up with this particular number? He based it in part on a 1993 study of musicians. In the study, researchers analyzed the practice time of violinists at the Academy of Music in Berlin, Germany. The musicians were separated into three groups: at one extreme were those who would likely become world-class experts; at the other extreme were those who would most likely never play professionally but would probably become music teachers; and the third group was made up of those between the two extremes (Ericsson, et al.)

And while many people might assume that the musicians' natural ability separated the best from the worst, the true indicator of success was the amount of practice time. Based on the research, all the musicians began playing around the age of five and practiced two to three hours per week. This continued for roughly three years. At the age of eight, however, some students began practicing up to six hours a week, and that number increased as they aged: "eight hours a week by age twelve, sixteen hours a week by age fourteen, and up and up, until by the age of twenty . . . well over thirty hours a week" (Gladwell 38). By then, the best performers had accumulated 10,000 hours of practice while the middle and bottom groups had only totaled 8,000 and 4,000 hours respectively (Gladwell 38).

The same researchers later studied professional pianists and reached the same conclusion. In fact, they never found a so-called "natural," a gifted musician who could rise to the top on talent alone without putting in the required 10,000 hours of practice time.

Does this same rule apply to all professions? Yes. According to neurologist Daniel Levitin: "In study after study of composers, basketball players, fiction writers, ice skaters, concert pianists, chess players, master criminals, and what have you, this number comes up again and again . . . But no one has yet found a case in which true world-class expertise was accomplished in less time. It seems that it takes the brain this long to assimilate all that it needs to know to achieve true mastery" (Gladwell 40).

So do you have what it takes to be an "outlier" in writing? Are you willing to put in 10,000 hours? When I met with my Composition I students earlier this fall, I told them that if they completed the course, they would be 1% of the way there (assuming three hours in class per week times 15 weeks equals 45 hours plus a minimum of 45 hours of preparation time plus at least 10 hours on the research paper). Obviously, 1% doesn't sound like much, and that number could discourage some potential writers, but if "true mastery" and "success" are your goals, then 10,000 hours might be only the beginning to a long and prosperous career.

Chapter 12
The Reading-Writing Connection

What Will You Read This Summer?

By the time you finish writing your final research paper this semester, or by the time you complete all your exams, probably the last thing you'll want to do is open a book and begin reading. Yet, reading is exactly what you should do if you want to become a better writer.

Reading makes you a better writer because you get to see how professional writers organize their thoughts and express their ideas. That's why you typically have a literature textbook for all your writing courses. This reading-writing connection actually made me a better writer way back in high school. Here's how it happened.

As a boy, I was a sports fanatic, and I devoured the daily sports pages for articles on my favorite players and teams. I read the pre-season forecasts, the feature stories on the players, the pre-game articles, the post-game summaries, and the end-of-season analysis. By the time I was a junior in high school and eligible to write for the student newspaper, I was all set.

Naturally, I volunteered to write the sports articles for the school teams,

and, quite honestly, the newspaper advisor didn't have to show me what to do. I had read thousands of these articles over the years, so all I had to do was gather my information and begin writing. When writing a game summary, for instance, I knew I had to include upfront the names of the two teams, the date and location of the game, and the final score. I found out later that journalists called this the "lead paragraph." So even though I didn't know the terminology for what I was doing, I had absorbed the technique through frequent reading.

Best-selling author Stephen King tells a similar story in his non-fiction book entitled *On Writing – A Memoir of the Craft*. When King was about six years old, he suffered through some health problems that kept him from attending school. Looking back on that first-grade year, King writes: "Most of that year I spent either in bed or housebound. I read my way through approximately six tons of comic books, progressed to Tom Swift and Dave Dawson (a heroic World War II pilot whose various planes were always 'prop-clawing for altitude') then moved on to Jack London's bloodcurdling animal tales. At some point I began to write my own stories" (27). Most authors could probably tell their own stories of how reading affected or influenced their writing.

Obviously, you can write your own stories without doing much reading, but you'll probably write much better stories if you're familiar with the ways words and sentences work together. If you want to write poetry, for instance, you should probably read poems by a variety of authors. If you want to write fiction, you should read short stories and novels. Early on in the process, your writing may sound like the authors you're reading, but, gradually, you'll start to develop your own tone and style.

So does that mean you need to read term papers in order to write a term paper of your own? Yes, you really should. In fact, most writing handbooks include sample term papers written by students for just that reason. You can read these papers and see how the various parts – the introduction, the thesis, the organizational pattern, the point of view, the evidence, and the conclusion – all work together to form a unified whole. Some teachers also hand out samples of student work, so you can get a better idea of how a particular assignment should be written.

Personally, I write fiction, and I like to use the summer months to read classic novels that I've never read before. One summer, for instance, I read *Les Misérables* by Victor Hugo. The next year, I read *The Illiad* by Homer. And this summer, I plan to read *Main Street* by Sinclair Lewis.

So even though you may not want to open a book this summer, why not give reading a try. Choose something fun, something you considered previously but didn't have time for during the hectic fall and spring semesters. Then, when you return to classes in the fall, believe it or not, you'll be a better writer.

Literary Lunches

I had lunch with Pulitzer Prize-winning novelist Richard Russo last spring. I ate a sandwich with poet Gary Soto during the summer. And I munched on pretzels with essayist Bill McKibben just the other day.

Okay, I admit, I didn't really share lunch with these authors. I ate my lunch while reading their works. My reading was "food for thought," you might say.

As a person who loves literature, I often ask others what books they've read lately. Too often, the response is, "Oh, I don't have time to read for pleasure." Naturally, I empathize with that response; no one has time to read these days with our hectic lifestyles. This is especially true at a college where students are overwhelmed with textbook readings, tests, and term-paper assignments, and faculty are constantly working on lesson plans and correcting those tests and term papers. Still, the question remains: What have you read lately?

As a freelance writer, I've also been to numerous writing workshops where the speakers typically talk about the importance of reading as a way of learning how to write. In fact, one person suggested that we all read for four hours every day, and, ideally, we should do it in the morning before we do anything else.

Four hours a day? That may be possible for successful authors, but what about those of us who have to work or attend school all day, go home to family responsibilities at night, and try to find time to read before we fall asleep? If only we had a half hour every once in a while, then, maybe we'd read more.

Fortunately, that extra half hour does exist in our schedules. I stumbled across the possibility many years ago, and I've been taking advantage of it ever since. I call it my "literary lunch hour."

When I discovered it, I was working as a high-school English teacher at a small Catholic school in Cohoes, New York. Through a quirk in the schedule, I found myself alone in the faculty lunchroom every day. So, rather than eat by myself, I began reading a book of old newspaper columns called *The Red Smith Reader*. I stayed with light sports reading for a month or so before I switched over to fiction. In fact, I read all of Herman Melville's *Moby Dick* in half-hour segments that year.

The following year, I didn't have to eat alone. The faculty lunchroom was busy every day during my lunch break. By then, however, I had found a pleasant respite from my busyness, and I wasn't ready to give it up completely. Thus, while I returned to sharing lunch with real rather than fictional characters most of the time, I still ate lunch with my literary friends at least once a week. I do the same thing to this day.

I found myself thinking about my literary lunches recently because at the beginning of each semester,

I always tell my students about the importance of reading. I highlight the fact that extensive reading will actually make students better writers. Most students are skeptical, of course, but when you read, you gradually absorb the techniques of great writers. You see how they draw you in, how they describe the scene, and how they move you from one idea or event to another. Naturally, the transformation from tentative writer to confident writer may take a while; however, the results will surprise both you and your teachers. So rather than bemoan the fact that you don't have time to read, why not visit the library today and invite your favorite author out to lunch.

Expand Your Vocabulary and Improve Your Writing

I remember the first time I looked up a word in the dictionary because I sincerely wanted to know the word's meaning. Previously, I looked up words only because a teacher made me or because I needed to fulfill some other academic task. In this particular case, however, a beautiful, young lady had said something about me, and I thought it was a compliment, but I wasn't sure.

At the time, I was a senior at Siena College, and I had just applied to serve in the Peace Corps. When I mentioned this to Beth – a junior and an adorable cheerleader for the basketball team – she made the following comment: "Jim, you will do really well in the Peace Corps because you have such empathy for people."

"Thank you," I replied, though, quite honestly, I didn't know the meaning of the word "empathy"; I had never heard it before. Fortunately, I was able to interpret her tone, her body language, and her surrounding words to correctly decipher her remark and respond to it. I suppose I could have admitted my ignorance and asked her to explain the word, but I was much too vain. So, when our cafeteria conversation ended, I returned to my dormitory to look up the word in the dictionary.

As I walked, I thought about the word "empathy." It sounded a bit like "sympathy": "sharing the feelings of another" (*The American Heritage College Dictionary* 1375). However, empathy sounded even more powerful, and my initial interpretation of this word proved to be true.

Empathy means "identification with and understanding of another's situation, feelings, and motives" (*The American Heritage College Dictionary* 450). When I read the definition, I felt a mixed surge of emotions. On one hand, I experienced the full joy of Beth's compliment, but on the other hand, I felt a certain responsibility to live up to her high expectations. Though I haven't seen or communicated with Beth in over 40 years, her comment stayed with me, and the experience has instilled in me a love for new words and a love for stimulating conversations with various people.

As a college student, you've probably been taught to use your dictionary to look up the unfamiliar words you encounter in your reading. That's great advice, but I would encourage you to go one step further. Rather than wait for these new words to come to you in your reading, seek out these words by talking to others who are new acquaintances on campus: your classmates, your teachers, and your advisers. If possible, try to move beyond greetings and small talk and into serious conversations about topics of common interest. Most likely, their backgrounds and their experiences are different from yours, and their comments and their stories will enlighten you in ways that books cannot. For while the written word has long-lasting power, the spoken word – especially a word spoken in a one-on-one conversation – may have a more immediate impact on your consciousness.

Understanding a word's meaning, however, is not the only benefit of learning new words. When you become familiar with a new word, an amazing process begins in your mind. That word doesn't just sit there and wait to be understood again and again. No, the word – like a young child – grows and develops and demands to be seen and heard. So one day, when you least expect it, that new word will show up in your own speaking or your own writing. Thus, you will become a better speaker and a better writer because you were willing to read new texts, to talk to new people, to look up unfamiliar words in the dictionary, and to allow those words to communicate the empathy you have for others.

You Might Be a Writer If . . .

A while ago, comedian Jeff Foxworthy became nationally famous for his series of one-liners that all began with the phrase "You might be a redneck if . . . ." Foxworthy – who later served as the host of the television show *Are You Smarter Than a Fifth Grader?* – actually had some great literary lines such as the following: "You might be a redneck if you stare at an orange juice container because it says 'concentrate,'" and "You might be a redneck if you think Sherlock Holmes is a housing project down in Biloxi."

Recently, as I was preparing to give a literary talk at a local bookstore, Foxworthy's key introductory phrase popped into my head with a bit of a twist, and I came up with some key phrases of my own. Read through this list, and see if perhaps you, too, might be a writer.

You might be a writer if you read a lot. As a writing instructor at a community college in upstate New York, students will sometimes ask me, "What can I do to improve my writing?" and I think my answer surprises them. I

tell them to "read as much as you can." At first, they don't see the connection, but I try to explain that reading allows them to subconsciously absorb the craft of writing. Then, to reinforce my point, I tell them about Stephen King. In his book entitled *On Writing*, King says, aspiring writers have to do only two things: "read a lot and write a lot" (145). King's first exposure to extensive reading occurred when he was about six years old. Since he was sick at home for most of that school year, King claims that he read "approximately six tons of comic books" (27), and, eventually, he began to write his own stories.

You might be a writer if you cry a lot. Do you cry at the end of sad movies? Do you weep at weddings? Do you get choked up when you see people cry? If so, you may be an extremely sensitive person who empathizes with others who are experiencing life's universal moments. At those special times, you may be recalling similar experiences or anticipating those moments in your own life. Socrates once said, "the unexamined life is not worth living" (Baggini) and when those tears hit you, you may be examining life's eternal truths. Usually at those moments, you can't find the words to express what's happening, but therein lies the beauty of writing. Those speechless moments usually stay with you for a long while, and with time and with meditation, you can eventually express your feeling and your emotions on paper.

You might be a writer if you can't sleep at night. Do you wake up in the middle of the night and find that you can't get back to sleep, even when you're physically exhausted, and you need rest desperately? Most likely, that happens because certain thoughts are banging around in your brain, and the noise won't let you sleep. When that occurs, you will always be tempted to roll over and try a new position, but generally, the banging doesn't stop. You will lie awake and play with the possibilities until you finally have to crawl out of bed to jot down whatever you have at that point. If only a few sentences appear, you can be back to sleep in ten minutes, but if the ideas come in paragraphs, you could be writing for hours.

You might be a writer if your mind wanders during the day. Depending on your job, you may have only a little wandering time during the workday. For example, if you're in an intense position that requires lots of human interaction, you may not have the opportunity to daydream. But if you're performing a mindless chore – like stuffing envelopes or cutting the grass – you may use that time to your advantage. Instead of cursing the task, you might imagine how a particular character could enliven that activity, or you might imagine a similar setting where characters and conflicts easily present themselves.

You might be a writer if you're somewhat shy and introverted. In his essay entitled "How to Write a Personal Letter," Garrison Keillor says, "We shy persons need to write a letter now and then, or else we'll dry up and blow away" (224). I, too, am basically a shy person, and I don't think well or process conversations thoroughly when I am in the midst of them. Thus, I have to replay the conversation in my mind, and, if appropriate, I write a short note to the person, or I might turn the entire experience into a poem or use the conversation in a work of fiction. If you struggle to speak with others, or if you lack the confidence to speak in a group, you may want to keep a diary or write in a journal, anything to help you at least record your thoughts for use at some point in the future.

You might be a writer if you wonder about and appreciate ordinary things. Some people pick up the Sunday newspaper and immediately begin reading the comics, the movie reviews, or the business articles. These people never ponder all the activity that goes into producing that massive work. Others, however, like former *60 Minutes* commentator Andy Rooney, take time to examine the things that most people take for granted. In fact, while Rooney sometimes commented on politics or controversial issues, most of his monologues focused on the truly mundane items of daily life like water, watches, and kitchen tools. Author Thornton Wilder also highlighted the mundane in his play *Our Town*. In Act Three, Wilder had Emily say good-bye to "clocks ticking . . . and Mama's sunflowers. And food and coffee. And new-ironed dresses and hot baths . . . and sleeping and waking up" (216).

You might be a writer if you have an opinion about important controversial issues. The opinion pages of most newspapers are filled with editorials and letters to the

Jim LaBate

editor. If you read these pages and care about the key issues in your community and throughout the world, you may be prompted to write a letter or an essay. Most likely, you won't write if you see your opinion expressed logically and coherently, but if your ideas are being ignored or misrepresented, you may decide to participate in this public forum.

You might be a writer if you have an opinion about unimportant, trivial topics like sports. Even if you don't care too much about the so-called "hot" issues, you might get worked up about an athletic team in your area, whether it is high school, college, or professional. In years past, these arguments about "who's number one" were often confined to verbal warfare at the office water cooler or at the local diner or watering hole. With the Internet, however, almost every fan can sit at a computer keyboard and participate. Most online sportswriters will allow you to post comments about their columns, and if you are a really dedicated fan, you can set up your own blog or web page.

You might be a writer if you buy blank cards instead of Hallmark greetings. The people who write for Hallmark do a wonderful job of expressing common sentiments for special occasions such as birthdays, anniversaries, and other milestones. However, sometimes, you may want to say something altogether different, or you may want to describe the unique relationship you have with one special person. When that moment occurs, you don't want your loved one to be distracted by a funny picture or cartoon, and you don't want your words to appear as an afterthought. Thus, you may have to buy a blank card and fill it with your own unique prose. Typically, too, those are the cards that get saved when all the rest are thrown away.

You might be a writer if you like to see your name in print. Let's face the truth; most of us want to be remembered, and when we attach our name to something we've written, we're

grabbing a small slice of immortality, especially if that composition is actually published. Publishing, however, also brings additional benefits: dialogue and encouragement. When your letter to the editor shows up in the newspaper or when your essay appears in print, readers will often let you know they saw it, and they may want to discuss the subject with you. Others will write back to confirm or contradict what you have said. In both cases, your writing has stirred a conversation, and you may be encouraged to write even more. Yes, the byline is nice, but the subsequent interaction is even better.

So are you a writer? I'm guessing you are. If you picked up this essay in the first place, you must be at least somewhat interested. If you read this entire article, you may have even identified with one of the above statements, and said, "Yes, that line fits me perfectly." So now, you need to simply take that interest and follow through on that particular characteristic or habit that will allow you to join the writing community. And even if you don't consider yourself a writer or don't relate to any of the lines listed above, I bet you're thinking that I'm wrong or that I left out something. If that's the case, why don't you send me an e-mail at jimlabate@hotmail.com.

Is Your Writing Readable?

If you've ever struggled to understand the directions in a computer manual, you know that not all writing is readable. But have you ever wondered about your own writing? Perhaps your readers can't understand what you've written. To make sure that your essays, your term papers, and your personal letters are understood by those who read them, you should know a little bit about readability statistics.

Readability statistics have been developed over the years to measure the reading level of a particular piece of writing. For example, a sixth-grade history book should be much easier to read than a college-level history book. So if you are writing a history book, you need to make sure that the level of your writing doesn't exceed the educational level of your intended readers. Basically, the readability level measures the education required to read the text easily. If your essay, for example, measures a "10" on the readability scale, that means anyone who has completed tenth grade should be able to understand the essay.

As an example, the readability for this essay should not exceed 12 because most of the readers for this particular essay are first-year college students, and grade 12 is the last year of school completed by most first-year college students. In fact, some writing professionals suggest that as a writer, you should never exceed 12 because at levels 13 and higher, your writing becomes less clear and more difficult to understand. Before you can lower your readability level, however, you need to know how the level is measured.

Various indexes measure readability, but the most basic one calculates the number of words per sentence and the number of long words used. (A long word, generally, is any word of three syllables or more.) So, if you use short sentences and short words, your readability level will be low, but if you use long words and long sentences, your readability level will be much higher. Many college students are tempted to use long words and long, complicated sentences to impress their teachers. You should try to resist that temptation.

Short Words Versus Long Words. According to Edward T. Thompson, the former editor of *The Reader's Digest*, words can be classified as first-degree, second-degree, and third-degree. He describes first-degree words as words that "immediately bring an image to your mind." He uses the word "book," for example, as a first-degree word that is easily understood and visualized. Second- and third-degree words, however, are a bit more complicated and "must be 'translated' through the first-degree word before you see the image." Second- and third-degree words related to the word "book" are words such as "volume" and "publication." These second- and third-degree words are usually longer and more specific, but if your readers are unfamiliar with those words, your readers may not fully understand what you've written.

Does that mean you should never pull out your thesaurus and try a new word? No, not at all. But make sure you use the precise word that says what you want it to say and will be understood by your readers. Don't choose a big word simply to show off your vocabulary and impress your readers.

Short Sentences Versus Long Sentences. When I sit in The Writing and Research Center and review an essay with a student, the student will sometimes ask, "Is that sentence too long?" Generally, my answer is "Yes," but not because there's a magic number of words for the ideal sentence. Instead, if you as a writer feel the sentence might be too long, your reader may also struggle with the sentence's length.

A while back, many English teachers were using sentence-combining exercises to encourage their students

to write longer sentences. This is a good strategy if students are writing too many short sentences, one right after another. Unfortunately, some students get carried away with this sentence-combining strategy, and they cram too many clauses into their sentences. When this occurs, readers often have to stop and re-read the sentence to make sure they understand it. That's not a good thing. You want to keep your readers moving forward.

Readability. To check the readability level of your writing, take the following steps. First, after you've written an essay using Microsoft Word, click on "File" at the top left of your computer screen. Then, click on "Options" near the bottom of that drop-down menu. Next, click on the "Proofing" tab on the screen that appears. At the bottom of that screen, you should see a box that reads "Show Readability Statistics." Click on that box, and a checkmark should appear indicating that you want to see your readability statistics. Finally, click on "OK" to return to your document. Once you've returned to your document, you can click on the "Review" tab at the top of the screen. Next, click on "Spelling and Grammar" on the drop-down menu. At that point, the computer will check the spelling and grammar for the entire document, and the "Readability Statistics" will appear at the end. The "Flesch-Kinciad Grade Level" at the bottom of that box will provide you with the readability level for that document.

The reading level for this essay, by the way, is 9.5, so it should be easily understood by anyone who has completed the first half of tenth grade. If after reviewing your essay, you discover that the reading level for your work is 12 or higher, you may want to consider revisions.

Pulitzer Examples

If I told you that the Capital District near Albany, New York, is one of the most fertile areas for American writers, you might view my comment with a bit of skepticism. After all, usually when people think of literary hot spots in this country, they think of major metropolitan areas such as New York City, Los Angeles, and Chicago before they think of upstate New York. However, in 2013, two Capital District natives won Pulitzer Prizes for their writing, and their success adds to five previous examples to back up my argument; naturally, as a writer, you, too, can use examples to make a point.

In 1980, Gilbert King graduated from Niskayuna High School, and Philip Kennicott completed eighth grade at nearby Burnt Hills-Ballston Lake High School. Thirty-three years later, they are both Pulitzer Prize winners. King won the general non-fiction prize for his book entitled *Devil in the Grove*, which is about a racial incident in Florida in 1949; Kennicott won the criticism prize for a series of essays he wrote for *The Washington Post*. Thus, they join a prestigious list of Capital District authors who have all won the Pulitzer Prize (Grondahl).

Another Capital District writer who won the Pulitzer for his newspaper work is Mark Mahoney, who won in 2009. Mahoney, who grew up south of the Capital District in Poughkeepsie, began working as a reporter for *The Post-Star* in Glens Falls at the northern edge of the Capital District in 1988. About a decade later, he began writing editorials in 1999, and a decade after that, he earned the Pulitzer in the editorial category (Patterson).

Novelist and Pulitzer Prize winner for fiction William Kennedy started out as a newspaper writer but later began writing novels. He grew up in Albany, graduated from Siena College, wrote for both *The Post-Star* in Glens Falls and the Albany *Times Union*, and also taught at the University at Albany. His novels focused primarily on the rich, political history of Albany, and while his first few novels did not garner a lot of recognition, his fourth novel, *Ironweed*, was a phenomenal success. Not only did the book win the 1984 Pulitzer Prize, but it was also later made into a movie with Hollywood stars Jack Nicholson and Meryl Streep in the leading roles ("William J. Kennedy – Biography").

Another writer with ties to the Capital District is Toni Morrison. Originally from Ohio, Morrison earned her master's degree from Cornell University in Ithaca. Before achieving literary fame, Morrison, like Kennedy, combined teaching and writing, and she, too, taught at the University of Albany. Though Morrison only worked at the University for a short time, during that time, she wrote a book called *Beloved*. This book also won the Pulitzer Prize for fiction in 1988 ("Toni Morrison").

At about that same time, Steven Millhauser began teaching English at Skidmore College in Saratoga. Born and educated in New York City, Millhauser is still teaching at Skidmore today. Though he maintains a rather low profile, Millhauser is well known in the literary world, and he has also won a Pulitzer Prize for fiction. He won the award in 1997 for his novel entitled *Martin Dressler: the Tale of an American Dreamer* (Potter).

Finally, the last member of this local Pulitzer Prize-winning fiction quartet is Richard Russo. Russo was born in Johnstown and grew up in Gloversville, two cities on the western edge of the extended Capital District. Like William Kennedy, Russo draws upon his community of origin for his early novels. His fictional setting for those novels is a town called Mohawk, but the characters and the conflicts Russo writes about come straight from the dying industrial towns with which

he is most familiar. In 2001, Russo published a novel called *Empire Falls*, and even though this novel takes place in Maine and Russo now lives in Maine, the theme of life in a dying mill town is reminiscent of his earlier works. And, yes, Russo's *Empire Falls* also won the Pulitzer Prize for fiction in 2002 (Routhier).

So what is the Pulitzer Prize, and why is it that authors with connections to the Capital District have won seven times in 30 years? The answer to the first question is easy.

Each year, Columbia University in New York City offers a prize of $10,000 in various categories such as journalism, letters, drama, and music. Obviously, King, Kennicott, and Mahoney won for their non-fiction, and Kennedy, Morrison, Millhauser, and Russo won for their novels, work which the Pulitzer Prize committee describes as "distinguished fiction by an American author, preferably dealing with American life" ("Book Submission Guidelines and Requirements").

And why is it that authors with connections to the Capital District have won so often? If this were a cause-and-effect essay, I would definitely have to provide you with an answer to that second question. However, since this is an example essay, I only need to provide you with the names and stories of Capital District writers who have achieved literary success to support my main idea that this is a fertile area for American writers. Obviously, I don't know why the writers from this area are thriving, but if you have a theory or an idea, I'd love to hear from you; please send your thoughts to jimlabate@hotmail.com.

Chapter 13
Miscellaneous

Avoid Logical Fallacies in Your Thinking and in Your Writing

Have you ever heard a young child say to his or her parent or teacher, "It's not fair"? Of course you have. This cry is common among frustrated children, and perhaps you've even used that phrase yourself when you felt wronged or unfairly punished. While this cry may be justified at times, the young child, or adult, using it may be guilty of using a logical fallacy.

A logical fallacy is a paradox, a phrase that sounds contradictory at first but upon reflection makes perfect sense. The contradiction occurs because "logical" sounds positive, and "fallacy" sounds negative. Overall, however, the fallacy is negative; the user has simply used a logical form to make the argument appear more reasonable. Let's look at some common examples.

One of the most common complaints I hear in The Writing and Research Center is that a teacher grades too harshly. Since I don't want to encourage such discussions, I try to change the subject, but the complainer wants to convince me, so he'll add a phrase like, "Seriously, she did the same thing to

my girlfriend last semester and to my brother last year." Thus, the argument sounds logical: "This teacher graded my papers, my girlfriend's papers, and my brother's papers too harshly; therefore, she is a teacher who grades everyone's papers too harshly." In reality, however, the argument is a fallacy called a "hasty generalization."

A hasty generalization is a conclusion based on too few examples. Most full-time teachers have 20-30 students in a class. Thus, just because three students – out of 100 or 150 – feel a particular teacher grades too harshly does not necessarily mean the charge is true. If a much larger number of students complained about the teacher, or if student evaluations over the years had generally made that same observation, then the criticism might have to be taken more seriously. But if only three students feel this way over a period of three semesters, then the argument – even though it sounds logical – is a fallacy.

Another common complaint goes something like this: "This teacher gives too much homework. I have a three-year-old child at home, and I have a full-time job; I can't be expected to do all this school work." Do you see the fallacy present here? A student who complains this way is guilty of using a "non sequitur" or an irrelevant argument.

The phrase "non sequitur" comes from Latin and means "does not follow." In other words, the two statements are not connected at all. Just because a student's personal life is busy and complicated doesn't mean that the student should be exempt from course requirements. Thus, if in your writing, you try to connect points or arguments that are unrelated, you are guilty of using the logical fallacy called a non sequitur.

Finally, I often see arguments like the following in student essays: "The politician's plan to balance the budget won't work because he cheats on his wife." This type of fallacy is similar to the non sequitur because the ability to balance a budget isn't quite the same as the ability to maintain a healthy marriage. However, this type of fallacy is more precisely referred to as an "argument to the person."

The argument to the person is sometimes called an "ad hominem" attack from the Latin phrase meaning "to the man." Unfortunately, many political debates are full of this type of argument; the candidates simply criticize each other rather than the important issues of the day. In other words, the argument criticizes the man rather than the budget the man has put forward.

Some people resort to logical fallacies in their thinking or their writing because these people are so personally involved in an issue that they're not thinking clearly or because they haven't taken the time to dig up any reliable evidence. Are there other logical fallacies besides the three mentioned here? Yes, numerous logical fallacies exist, and advertisers often use them to persuade you to buy a particular product or service. As a serious academic writer, though, you shouldn't use logical fallacies because most readers will see through your flimsy arguments and will, as a result, refuse to take your writing seriously. Here's one more example of a non sequitur.

I live in a suburban community that requires us to keep our cars in our driveways rather than in the streets during snowstorms, so the road crews can come through and plow easily. Last winter, as I looked out our front door before going to bed, I noticed the snow falling lightly on my car which was parked in the street. Feeling sleepy and lazy, I left my car in the street and went to bed thinking, "It's not going to snow that much." By the next morning, of course, we had ten inches of snow, and I found a fifty-dollar parking ticket on my windshield. In my anger and my frustration, I committed a logical fallacy of my own when I said to my wife, "That's not fair."

Finding Time to Write

Most writing instructors will tell you that if you want to become a better writer, you must write on a daily basis. You might record your activities every day in a diary, for instance, or you might reflect upon those activities in a journal. However, knowing what to write or how to write isn't typically the real struggle. Instead, most people struggle with finding time to write. Fortunately, some successful writers have shared their secrets to finding time to write, and you may be able to duplicate their methods.

Writing Early in the Morning. For many people, writing early in the morning is the best and most productive time to write. Yes, you may have to get up earlier than normal to find time to write, but if you don't write in the morning, the normal activities and interruptions of the day may prevent you from writing later on. British novelist Anthony Trollope worked in a London post office in the 19th century, but he wrote every morning before he went to work (Scanlan). In fact, he was such a disciplined writer that he used to write for three hours

every day, and his goal was 250 words every fifteen minutes (Trollope 168).

Writing on the Way to Work or School. If you ride the bus in the morning or car pool with someone, you may be able to use your travel time to get some writing done. Current American author Scott Turow, who writes legal thrillers, had to find time to write early in his career, so he wrote while he rode a commuter train into Chicago. He admits that "it was sometimes no more than a paragraph a day, but it kept the candle burning," and he wrote a good portion of his first novel, *Présuméd Innocent*, on that train (Scanlan).

Writing During the Day. Daytime writing may be difficult for most people, but American novelist Anne Tyler found her time to write while her children were in school. If the children left for school at 8:00 a.m., Tyler made sure she was in her study and writing by 8:05, and she was methodical about it: "As I close the door on the kids, I go up to my room – like one of Pavlov's dogs. Otherwise, I'll get sidetracked" (Michaels). Similarly, if you are a full-time student, you may want to write during the breaks between classes, and if you are a full-time worker, you may want to write during a portion of your lunch hour.

Writing at Night. While I wouldn't describe myself as a "successful" author, I am one of those authors who writes mostly at night. The task is not easy, however, because after a day at work and after an evening meal, I am committed to or tempted by many other activities: household chores, church meetings, television, reading, or even a game of checkers. Thus, I have to discipline myself to write, and I usually find myself at the keyboard when everyone else in the house has already gone to sleep. In fact, our younger daughter, Katrina, who is now almost 30, says she has fond early memories of falling to sleep to the sound of my typing.

Writing in the Middle of the Night. Personally, this sounds like the most difficult time to write, but this is the time that worked for author Richard Selzer. Selzer didn't begin writing until he reached the age of 40; he had worked exclusively as a surgeon until that time. Once he knew he had that passion to write, however, he eliminated certain activities from his life, and he found a time and a place that worked for him: "Every night at one o'clock in the morning, I got up and went down to the kitchen for two hours. While the rest of the world was asleep and all the light in the universe shone upon one page, I wrote my heart out" (Selzer). He continued as both surgeon and writer for the next 18 years before he retired from surgery to write exclusively. At that point, he says, "I left my beloved workbench in the operating room and became what I am now, a writer" (Selzer).

So do you really want to become a better writer? Of course you do. All you have to do now is commit yourself to the task and, like the authors mentioned above, find a time and a place that works for you.

The Greatest Commencement Speech of All Time

When people discuss great speeches, they often refer to Abraham Lincoln's Gettysburg Address delivered on November 19, 1863, in Gettysburg, Pennsylvania. This two-minute oration included only 272 words and was not a commencement but a eulogy to the men who had given their lives in one of the turning-point battles of the Civil War. The speech is memorable because of its brevity and because of its emotional power.

Lincoln praises "those who gave their lives that that nation might live" . . . , and he encourages "the living . . . to be dedicated here to the unfinished work . . . that this nation, under God, shall have a new birth of freedom – and . . . shall not perish from the earth." In terms of brevity and power, however, another well-known speech may well be considered the greatest commencement speech of all time.

This particular commencement speech was delivered approximately 1,830 years prior to Lincoln's address, on a mountaintop in Galilee. The speaker – Jesus Christ – is often referred to as the greatest teacher of all time, and His speech, naturally, includes His final directions to His closest students. His "Great Commission" to these 11 disciples includes only 61 words at the end of the Gospel of Matthew (*NIV Study Bible*: Matthew 28:18-20), yet His three primary statements have served as a general outline for every graduation speech since.

"All authority in heaven and on earth has been given to me" (verse 18). As the Son of God, Jesus has access to all wisdom and all authority. His followers, of course, knew this, but Jesus was reminding them of His authority and exhorting them to pay attention.

Like any good commencement speaker, Christ was establishing His credibility. He wanted His apostles to know that this address was more than a simple farewell. These final directions were a timeless exhortation intended not only for His listeners but also for future Bible readers worldwide.

"Therefore go and make disciples of all nations, baptizing them in the name of the Father and of the Son and of the Holy Spirit and teaching them to obey everything I have commanded you" (verses 19-20). This is Christ's call to action. He didn't want His followers to simply absorb the truth of His teachings. Instead, He wanted His followers to share the truth, to help make other disciples who would multiply the effect of His teachings.

All subsequent commencement speakers offer that same basic advice. Whether their words echo through an amphitheater in Greece, a tiny village in Africa, or a gymnasium in upstate New York, the call to action for all graduates is essentially the same: "Take your knowledge and share it with others."

"And surely I am with you always, to the very end of the age" (verse 20). This is a reminder from Jesus that He will not leave His disciples nor will He forsake them. Even though Jesus is about to ascend into heaven, and even though these disciples must descend from the mountaintop, both Jesus and His disciples will all still be together in Spirit (*NIV Study Bible*).

All commencement speakers – whether they are valedictorians, salutatorians, college presidents, faculty members, or invited dignitaries – offer a version of that same wisdom. The new graduates may feel timid and insecure, and they may feel they are solitary figures who are unprepared for the tasks ahead of them. Fortunately, that's not the case. Graduating seniors should go boldly into their professions because they are ready and capable, and they move on as the next wave of educated individuals who will build upon the work of those who preceded them.

On that mountaintop in Galilee almost 2,000 years ago, Jesus knew His graduates were ready too. He knew that the three years they had spent together would bind them and strengthen them. He knew, too, that from that day forward, when His graduates, or any graduates for that matter, faced a difficult situation, they would probably ask themselves the same question that graduates everywhere ask today: "What would my teacher do?"

Where You Choose to Sit in Your First College Class Says a Lot About You

Almost 50 years ago, I was a college freshman during the fall of 1969, shortly after the United States put a man on the moon and right after music lovers in the Northeast celebrated Woodstock. Though I was a pretty good student in high school, I was still somewhat immature and, quite honestly, more interested in athletics than academics. Thus, when I walked into my first college class, I immediately made my first college mistake; I sat in the absolute worst seat in the entire classroom: the last seat in the last row, right next to the windows.

At the time, I think I convinced myself that I wanted to sit in the back, so I could clearly see everything that was going on and fully absorb the academic college experience. If I'm really honest with myself, though, I think I can finally admit that I wasn't feeling too sure about my abilities. I didn't want to sit up front because that meant I'd have to be prepared for class, paying attention to the professor, and willing to answer questions or participate in discussions. As a lifelong doodler, daydreamer, and procrastinator, I didn't think I could handle all the pressure.

Today, after a long career as a teacher, I now know that my choice of a seat said a lot about me. That choice demonstrated my uncertainty, my lack of confidence, and my unwillingness to take a chance. If you are about to enter a college classroom for the first time, where you choose to sit will also say a lot about you.

While exceptions do exist, of course, generally, if you sit in the back of the classroom or on the edges near the wall or windows, you are telling your teacher that you don't really want to be a full participant in the class activities. You are content to sit on the sideline, almost like a substitute in an athletic contest; you're willing to watch, but you don't really want to play the game. Naturally, experienced teachers know this, and they may call on you anyway, despite your attempt to hide in plain sight.

In fact, the ancient Greek writer Homer chronicled a somewhat similar situation in *The Iliad*. In his story about the siege of Troy, he explained how the military leaders at that time would often place the youngest and least experienced soldiers in the center of a formation, surrounded by the older and more experienced fighters. The leaders did this because they feared that if the unseasoned soldiers were on the edge of the formation, they would run at the first sign of danger, but if they were on the inside, they would be more likely to stay and fight (155). Unfortunately, if you sit on the edge or at the rear of the classroom, you, too, may be tempted to give up and leave when the work appears too difficult or overwhelming.

If you choose to sit in the front or in the center of the classroom, you are saying something else altogether, and you may encounter a much more positive experience. Veteran teachers refer to those front and center seats as the "Action Zone" of a classroom. If you sit in those seats, you are essentially telling your teacher that you are ready, eager, and excited to begin an intellectual adventure.

In addition, you will be surrounded by like-minded students, and you will probably get caught up in their enthusiasm and exuberance for learning. As a result, you may find yourself in a study group with some of those students, and you are more likely to remember what was discussed in class if you participated in the discussion.

So, is the typical college classroom really like an ancient battlefield where you have to fight for your survival? No, not really. Instead, the classroom is more like a concert hall where your favorite musician or band is playing, and the seats are available on a first-come, first-served basis. Under those circumstances, wouldn't you try to get a good seat up front, where you could see and hear everything and participate fully? Of course, you would. So why not approach your first college class in that same manner and find yourself a good seat in the action zone.

Where You Choose to Sit During Your First College Class Says a Lot About You.

I am terrified.	When will this class be over?	I hope he doesn't call on me.	Dear Chris, I miss you already.	I'm not sure I can do this.
What a waste of time!	I should have taken this course online.	I have to get a better seat next time.	When is the first football game?	I wish I were still at the beach.
Who is that beauty in the front row?	I love taking notes.	Call on me; I'm right here.	Law school or medical school?	I love sitting near the window.
I should have eaten breakfast.	Look out world. Here I come!	This is going to be awesome.	I am so psyched to begin.	Can I major in doodling?
I wish I were still in high school.	I am ready; let's go!	I can't wait to get started.	I love learning.	I need a seat in back next time.

"Seating Chart" by Professor Jim LaBate – Copyright © 2017

A Planning Sheet for Your Writing Assignment

Student _____ Course _____ Instructor _____

Description of Assignment _____

Thesis – What's the main idea you want to express? Try to summarize your main idea in one sentence, and use that sentence at the end of your first paragraph.

_____

Which of the following will be the major structure of your paper? Check one.

_____ Narration – Telling a story, usually in chronological order
_____ Description – Showing how someone or something appeals to the five senses
_____ Comparison and Contrast – Pointing out similarities and differences
_____ Examples – Describing people or things with common characteristics
_____ Definition – Explaining the meaning of a word or phrase
_____ Division and Classification – Separating the parts from a whole
_____ Process Analysis – Explaining how to do something or how something works
_____ Cause and Effect – Showing connections among various events
_____ Persuasion – Trying to convince someone to do something or to believe something

Outline of Main Points
1. _____
2. _____
3. _____
4. _____
5. _____

Introductory and Concluding Devices – Mark one of the following with an "I" for your Introduction and one with a "C" for your Conclusion, and make a brief note about both.

_____ A question _____
_____ A joke or story _____
_____ A quotation or bit of dialogue _____
_____ A detailed description _____
_____ A comparison _____
_____ A vivid example _____
_____ A startling statement or statistic or an unusual fact _____
_____ A definition _____
_____ An allusion _____
_____ A summary _____
_____ A call to action _____

You may want to write a few introductions and conclusions, so you can choose the most effective.

Angelina's Story

I was invited into a student's home today. Unfortunately, the home was much different from what I remembered from a previous visit years earlier, when this girl was so much younger – and so much happier.

The first time I visited Angelina's home, she was about eight years old. She and her older brother lived with their parents in a humble but well kept neighborhood of two-family flats. I was there on a Saturday morning, and Angelina's dad cooked pancakes for all of us. As he cooked, he told funny stories about his youth; meanwhile, his wife and his children laughed in both amazement and adoration.

"You really did that to your friends, Dad?" Angelina asked.

"This next story's even better," he replied and began again.

About ten years have passed since that first visit. I wasn't sure I wanted to go to that rented set of rooms again. I knew it would be darker, lonelier. I could see it in Angelina's eyes. Yet, she asked me to come. She asked for my help.

Again, it was a Saturday morning; again about 10:00. This time, though, the kitchen was empty, and the sink was full. Angelina's mom and brother were still sleeping: one exhausted from too much work; the other hung over from not enough. Dad was gone – long gone.

"He left about four years ago," Angelina explained. "They argued constantly; he couldn't stay. I miss his pancakes – and his stories."

Now, Angelina tells stories of her own. She doesn't have her father's flair or his energy or his humor. Her life changed too much when he left. Her stories are darker, sadder, and so much more powerful than his – unfortunately.

When Angelina finished her story, she looked to me for advice. I offered what I could: kind words, encouragement, small constructive criticism. "So sad," I thought as I left. Then, I went into another student's home.

Most teachers stand in front of their classroom and speak. They lecture, they question, they probe, they prompt, they quiz, and they correct. Not I.

I merely listen. I watch. I sniff. I feel. I laugh. I mourn. I am touched by their lives. I am silent until the end. Then, and only then, do I speak – slowly, softly, and carefully.

No, I do not have a typical classroom. I sit in The Writing and Research Center – near the dictionary and the thesaurus – and I wait. My students come to me, and their essays take me to their neighborhoods and into their homes. I am a writing specialist. I read student essays. I read their lives. And I am richer for it.

Works Cited

ABKCO Music vs. Harrisongs Music. No. 71, Civ. 602. U.S. Dist. Ct. for the Southern Dist. of NY., 19 Feb. 1981, *LexisNexis*, www.lexisnexis.com/en-us/gateway.page.

ABKCO Music vs. Harrisongs Music. Nos. 82-7421, 82-7461, Nos. 505, 600. U.S. Ct. of Appeals for the Second Circuit, 24 Nov. 1982, *LexisNexis*, www.lexisnexis.com/en-us/gateway.page.

"About APA Style." *American Psychological Association,* 2017, www.apastyle.org/about-apa-style.aspx.

"Are Notes Compatible with MLA Style?" *The MLA Style Center,* 29 Feb. 2016, style.mla. org/2016/02/29/using-notes-in-mla-style/.

Ashe, Arthur. "Send Your Children to the Libraries." Funk et al., 1997, pp. 286-89.

Atwood, Margaret. "Pornography." Neuleib, et al., pp. 20-26.

Baggini, Julian. "Wisdom's Folly." *The Guardian,* 12 May 2005, www.theguardian.com/ theguardian/2005/may/12/features11.g24.

Baker, James T. "How Do We Find the Student in a World of Academic Gymnasts and Worker Ants?" Muller and Wiener, 2003, pp. 316-19.

Baker, Russell. *Growing Up*. Plume, 1982.

Bella. Dir. Alejandro Monteverde. Performances by Eduardo Verástegui, Tammy Blanchard, and Manny Perez. Metanoia Films, 2006.

Bettelheim, Bruno. "The Holocaust." *The Bedford Reader.* 6th ed., edited by X.J. Kennedy, et al., Bedford, 1997, pp. 434-37.

"Book Submission Guidelines and Requirements." *The Pulitzer Prizes*, 2016, www.pulitzer.org/page/books-submission-guidelines-and-requirements.

Brian's Song. Directed by Buzz Kulik. Performances by James Caan, Billy Dee Williams, and Jack Warden, Screen Gems Television, 1971.

Bull Durham. Dir. Ron Shelton. Performances by Kevin Costner, Susan Sarandon, and Tim Robbins, Metro Goldwyn Mayer, 1988.

Caesar, Julius. "I came, I saw, I conquered." *English Club,* 15 June 2015, www.englishclub.com/ref/esl/ Quotes/War/I_came_I_saw_I_conquered._2631.htm.

Castro, Janice. "Spanglish." Muller and Wiener, 2003, pp. 259-61.

Cather, Willa. "On the Art of Fiction." *The Borzoi: Being a Sort of Record of Five Years of Publishing, 1920,* edited by Alfred A. Knopf, Alfred A. Knopf Publishing, 1920, pp. 7-8.

Catton, Bruce. "Grant and Lee: A Study in Contrasts." McCuen and Winkler, pp. 535-38.

Chapman, Gary. *The 5 Love Languages: The Secret to Love that Lasts.* Northfield, 2015.

Charlton, James, editor. *The Writer's Quotation Book: A Literary Companion.* Penguin, 1981.

Cofer, Judith Ortiz. "More Room." Funk, et al., 2000, pp. 54-57.

Deford, Frank. *Alex: The Life of a Child.* Viking Press, 1983.

Dickinson, Emily. "Because I Could Not Stop for Death." *The Complete Poems of Emily Dickinson,* edited by Thomas H. Johnson, Little, Brown, 1960, p. 350.

Elbow, Peter. *Writing Without Teachers.* Oxford University Press, 1998.

"Empathy." *The American Heritage College Dictionary.* 3rd ed., Houghton Mifflin, 1993.

Ericsson, K. Anders, et al. "The Role of Deliberate Practice in the Acquisition of Expert Performance." *Psychological Review,* vol. 100, no. 3, 1993, pp. 363-406, *PsychArticles,* eds.a.ebsco host.com/ehost/search/advanced?sid=d2223599-c1ed-4421-bc27-5284c2daf557%40session mgr4009&vid=0&hid=4202.

The Fugitive. Directed by Andrew Davis. Performances by Harrison Ford, Tommy Lee Jones, and Sela Ward, Warner Brothers, 1993.

Finding Forrester. Directed by Gus Van Sant. Performances by Sean Connery and Rob Brown, Columbia Pictures, 2000.

Foxworthy, Jeff. "You Might Be a Redneck If . . . ." *Fort Ogden,* 22 Jan. 2012, www.fortogden.com/foredneck.html.

Frost, Robert. "Stopping by Woods on a Snowy Evening." *The Poetry of Robert Frost: The Collected Poems,* edited by Edward Connery Lathem, Henry Holt, 1979, pp. 224-25.

Funk, Robert, et al., editors. *The Simon and Schuster Short Prose Reader.* Prentice Hall, 1997.

---. *The Simon and Schuster Short Prose Reader.* 2nd ed., Prentice Hall, 2000.

Gladwell, Malcolm. *Outliers: The Story of Success.* Little Brown, 2008.

Gomez, Rogelio R. "Foul Shots." Funk, et al., 1997, pp. 367-69.

Goodman, Ellen. "The Tapestry of Friendship." Muller and Wiener, 2003, pp. 238-39.

Grondahl, Paul. "Pulitzer Winners Have Local Roots." *Times Union* [Albany, NY], 17 Apr. 2013, www.timesunion.com/local/article/Pulitzer-winners-have-local-roots-4439885.php.

Hacker, Diana, and Nancy Sommers. *The Bedford Handbook.* 8th ed., Bedford/St. Martin's, 2010.

Halberstam, David. *October 1964.* Fawcett Columbine, 1995.

Haley, Alex. "Thank You." Funk, et al., 1997, pp. 352-56.

Hansen, Brian. "Combating Plagiarism." *CQ Researcher,* vol. 13, no. 32, 19 Sept. 2003, pp. 773-96. *CQ Researcher,* http://library.cqpress.com/cqresearcher/getpdf.php?id=cqresrre2003091900.

Harris, Robert. "Anti-Plagiarism Strategies for Research Papers." *Virtual Salt*, 18 May 2015, www.virtualsalt.com/antiplag.htm.

Heat-Moon, William Least. "Wind." Funk, et al., 2000, pp. 34-35.

Heilbroner, Robert. "Don't Let Stereotypes Warp Your Judgments." Neuleib, et al., pp. 110-13.

Hemingway, Ernest. "Camping Out." Muller and Wiener, 2009, pp. 196-99.

Highet, Gilbert. "Kitsch." McCuen and Winkler, pp. 471-78.

Homer. *The Iliad.* Translated by Robert Fagles, Penguin, 1990.

Howe, Neil, and William Strauss. *Millennials Rising: The Next Great Generation.* Vintage, 2000.

Hudson Valley Community College Catalog 2013-2014. Hudson Valley Community College, 2015.

Jordan, Suzanne Britt. "Fun, Oh Boy. Fun. You Could Die from It." Muller and Wiener, 2003, pp. 266-67.

Keillor, Garrison. "How to Write a Personal Letter." Funk, et al., 1997, pp. 224-27.

Kennedy, John F. "Inaugural Address of President John F. Kennedy: Washington, D.C. January 20, 1961." *John F. Kennedy Presidential Library and Museum,* 15 June 2016, www.jfklibrary.org/Research/Research-Aids/Ready-Reference/JFK-Quotations/Inaugural-Address.aspx.

Kennedy, William. "HVCC READS." Hudson Valley Community College, Troy, NY, 28 Mar. 2007.

King, Karen L. *What Is Gnosticism?* Belknap Press of Harvard UP, 2003.

King, Martin Luther, Jr. "I Have a Dream." Muller and Wiener, 2003, pp. 506-09.

King, Stephen. *On Writing – A Memoir on the Craft.* Schribner, 2000.

Kübler-Ross, Elisabeth. *On Death and Dying.* Scribner Classics, 1997.

Lamott, Anne. *Bird by Bird.* Anchor Books, 1994.

Lantos, John. "Life and Death in Neonatal Intensive Care." Muller and Wiener, 2003, pp. 350-55.

Lathrop, Ann, and Kathleen Foss. *Student Cheating and Plagiarism in the Internet Era.* Libraries Unlimited, 2000.

Lincoln, Abraham. "Gettysburg Address." *Abraham Lincoln Online,* 2017, www.abrahamlincolnonline. org/lincoln/speeches/gettysburg.htm.

Lopate, Philip. "A Nonsmoker with a Smoker." *Against Joie de Vivre: Personal Essays.* Bison, 2008, pp. 70-74.

Maimon, Elaine P., et al. *The New McGraw-Hill Handbook.* McGraw-Hill, 2007.

---. *The New McGraw-Hill Handbook.* 2nd ed., McGraw-Hill, 2009.

Mallon, Thomas. *Stolen Words: Forays into the Origins and Ravages of Plagiarism.* Ticknor and Fields, 1989.

Mangano, Joseph J. *Living Legacy: How 1964 Changed America.* University Press of America, 1994.

"Martin Moynihan; Longtime '*TU*' Writer." *Times Union* [Albany, NY], 3 June 1993, albarchive.merlinone.net/mweb/wmsql.wm.request?oneimage&imageid=5679025.

Masters, Edgar Lee. "Silence." Miller, et al., pp. 248-49.

McCormick, Patrick. "Cheaters Never Win." *U.S. Catholic,* vol. 69, no. 7, July 2004, *Academic One File,* 17 Feb. 2007, http://eds.b.ebscohost.com/eds/pdfviewer/pdfviewer?vid=7&sid=701f71b0-0c06-4 99d-94cc-9f8c1c01a650%40sessionmgr102.

McCuen, Jo Ray and Anthony C. Winkler, editors. *Readings for Writers.* 9th ed., Harcourt Brace, 1998.

Michaels, Marguerite. "Anne Tyler, Writer 8:05 to 3:30." *The New York Times* on the
    Web, 8 May 1977, www.google.com/search?hl=en&q=%E2%80%9CAnne+Tyler%2C+
    Writer+8%3A05+to+3%3A30.%E2%80%9D+&btnG=Google+Search.

Miller, James E. Jr., et al., editors. *Question and Form in Literature*. Scott Foresman, 1979.

MLA Handbook. 8th ed., Modern Language Association of America, 2016.

"MLA Formatting and Style Guide." *Purdue University Writing Lab*, 2017,
    owl.english.purdue.edu/owl/resource/747/01/.

Muller, Gilbert H., and Harvey S. Wiener, editors. *The Short Prose Reader*. 10th ed., McGraw-Hill, 2003.

---. *The Short Prose Reader*. 12th ed., McGraw-Hill, 2009.

Namath, Joe with Dick Schaap. *I Can't Wait Until Tomorrow ('Cause I Get Better-Looking
    Every Day)*. Random House, 1969.

Naylor, Gloria. "Mommy, What Does 'Nigger' Mean?" Funk, et al., 1997, pp. 108-11.

Neuleib, Janice, et al., editors. *The Mercury Reader: A Custom Publication (Hudson Valley
    Community College)*, Vol 2. Pearson, 2001.

The NIV Study Bible (The New International Version). General editor Kenneth Barber, Zondervan, 1985.

Orwell, George. *Animal Farm*. New American Library, 1952.

"Outlier." *The American Heritage College Dictionary*. 3rd ed., Houghton Mifflin, 1993.

Patterson, Adam. "Putting the 'Star' in *Post-Star*." *All Points North*, 2010, www.apnmag.com
    /spring 2010/staff%20stories%20HERE/APATT/patterson pulitzer.php.

"Plagiarism." *The Newbury House Dictionary*. Heinle & Heinle, 1999.

"Plagiarism." *The Oxford English Dictionary*. 2nd ed., Vol. 11, Clarendon Press, 1989. 20 vols.

Plagiarism Policy: Hudson Valley Community College. Hudson Valley Community College, 2005.

Poe, Edgar Allan. "The Purloined Letter." *The Complete Tales and Poems of Edgar Allan Poe*.
    Vintage Books, 1975, pp. 208-22.

Potter, Russell A. "Steven Millhauser." *Rhode Island College*, 2006.
    www.ric.edu/faculty/rpotter/millhauser.htm.

Roberts, Roxanne. "The Grieving Never Ends." McCuen and Winkler, pp. 151-57.

Routhier, Ray. "For Pulitzer Prize-Winning Portland Author Richard Russo, the Story Starts at
    Home." *The Portland Press Herald* [Maine], 21 Feb. 2016, www.pressherald.com
    /2016/02/21/for-pulitzer-prize-winning-portland-author-richard-russo-the-story-starts-at-home/.

Sandberg, Carl. "Chicago." *Carl Sandburg: Selected Poems*. Gramercy Books, 1992, pp. 17-18.

Scanlan, Chip. "Time Is on Our Side; Write to the Beat of Your Circadian Rhythms." *Poynteronline*,
    30 May 2007, www.poynter.org/dg.lts/id.52/aid.123845/column.htm.

Seabrook, John. "Feel No Pain." *New Yorker*, 22 July 1996, pp. 32-35. *Academic Search Complete*,
    19 May 2015, eds.a.ebscohost.com/ehost/search/advanced?sid=e8ed9266-0e45-4e9b-a299-c
    6f102d255b5%40sessionmgr4009&vid=0&hid=4202.

Selzer, Richard. "Doctor-Writer Disconnect." *Fathom: The Source for Online Learning,* 2002, www.fathom.com/feature/2093/.

Shakespeare, William. "Et tu, Brutus." *Julius Caesar* (III, i, 77). Washington Square Press, 1977.

---. "To be or not to be." *Hamlet* (III, i, 64). Washington Square Press, 1977.

---. "To thine own self be true." *Hamlet* (I, iii, 82). Washington Square Press, 1977.

Silverstein, Shel. *The Giving Tree.* Harper Collins, 1964.

Smith, Dinitia. "Novelist Says She Read Copied Books Several Times." *The New York Times,* 27 Apr. 2006 (late ed. - final): p. 16. *LexisNexis,* www.lexisnexis.com/en-us/gateway.page.

Solomon. "Proverbs 25." *The NIV (New International Version) Study Bible.* Zondervan, 1985.

Soto, Gary. "The Jacket." Neulieb, et al., pp. 255-58.

Speed, Directed by Jan de Bont. Performances by Keanu Reeves, Dennis Hopper, and Sandra Bullock, Twentieth Century Fox, 1994.

Staples, Brent. "'Just Walk on By': A Black Man Ponders His Power to Alter Public Space." Funk, et al., 2000, pp. 75-78.

Steinbeck, John, and Robert J. DeMott. *Working Days: The Journals of the Grapes of Wrath, 1938-1941.* Viking, 1989.

Steinberg, Sybil. "Richard Selzer: The Surgeon/Writer Reflects on Youth in the Depression and His Two Careers." *Publishers Weekly,* 10 Aug. 1992, pp. 48-49, *Literature Resource Center,* go.galegroup.com/ps/?&u=hvcc&p=LitRC&v=2.1&authCount=1.

Strauss, Robert. "The Bright Side of a Wet Summer." *The New York Times*, 19 Oct. 2003, p. 4. New York State Newspapers, search.proquest.com/docview/432544095/fulltext /9CF69505024542B3PQ/1?accountid=6155.

"Sympathy." *The American Heritage College Dictionary.* 3rd ed., Houghton Mifflin, 1993.

Thompson, Edward T. "How To Write Clearly." *Harmonize,* www.harmonize.com/probe /BulletinEditors/BE-Manual/Write cl.htm.

"Toni Morrison." *African American Literature Book Club*, 2016, aalbc.com/authors /author.php?author_name=Toni+Morrison.

Trollope, Anthony. "250 Words Every Quarter of an Hour." *Great Writing: A Reader for Writers,* edited by Harvey S. Wiener and Nora Eisenberg, McGraw-Hill, 1987, pp. 168-69.

Troyka, Lynn Quitman. *Simon & Schuster Handbook for Writers.* 7th ed., Pearson/Prentice Hall, 2005.

Troyka, Lynn Quitman, and Douglas Hesse. *Simon & Schuster Handbook for Writers.* Pearson/Prentice-Hall, 2007.

Turque, B., and N. Joseph. "Not in His Own Words." *Newsweek,* 19 Nov. 1990, p. 61. *LexisNexis,* www.lexisnexis.com/en-us/gateway.page.

Viorst, Judith. "Friends, Good Friends, and Such Good Friends." Funk, et al., 2000, pp. 143-47.

Vonnegut, Kurt, J. "How to Write with Style." Muller and Wiener, 2003, pp. 20-23.

Wechsler, Alan. "UAlbany Teacher Leaves Quietly; Albany Professor Who Set Off Plagiarism Dispute Retires, Moves to Colorado." *The Times Union* [Albany, NY], 23 May 2002, p. B1, *LexisNexis*, www.lexisnexis.com/en-us/gateway.page.

"When the Words Aren't Yours, Say So." *The Recorder Online* [Amsterdam, NY], 13 Dec. 2006, 18 Feb. 2006.

White, E. B. *Here Is New York*. Harper, 1949.

---. "Once More to the Lake." *Patterns for College Writing,* 12th ed., edited by Laurie G. Kirszner and Stephen R. Mandell. Bedford/St. Martin's, 2012, pp. 194-99.

Wiener, Jon. *Historians in Trouble*. The New Press, 2005.

Wilder, Thornton. *Our Town.* Miller, et al., 1979, pp. 182-217.

"William J. Kennedy – Biography." *New York State Writers Institute,* www.albany.edu/writers-inst/wjkennedybio.html#.V21sEvkrKig.

The Wizard of Oz. Directed by Victor Fleming. Performances by Judy Garland, Frank Morgan, Ray Bolger, Bert Lahr, and Jack Haley, Metro-Goldwyn-Mayer, 1939.

Woodlief, Wayne. "Op-Ed; Time Heals Biden's Self-Inflicted Wound." *The Boston Herald,* 26 Jan. 2007, p. 19, *LexisNexis*, www.lexisnexis.com/en-us/gateway.page.

X, Malcolm. "Prison Studies." Muller and Wiener (2009), pp. 74-77.

Zinsser, William. "College Pressures." Neuleib, et al., pp. 308-16.

---. "*Simplicity.*" Muller and Wiener, 2009, pp. 30-33.

The Author . . .

Since January of 2000, Jim LaBate has worked as a writing specialist in The Writing and Research Center at Hudson Valley Community College in Troy, New York.

Originally from Amsterdam, New York, Jim graduated from Saint Mary's Institute and Bishop Scully High School. He earned his bachelor's degree in English from Siena College in Loudonville, New York, and his master's degree, also in English, from The College of Saint Rose in Albany, New York.

Jim has spent his entire career as either a teacher or a writer. He taught physical education as a Peace Corps Volunteer in Golfito, Costa Rica, for two years. He taught high-school English for ten years (one year at Vincentian Institute in Albany, New York, and nine years at Keveny Memorial Academy in Cohoes, New York). Then, he worked for ten years as a writer for Newkirk Products in Albany, New York.

Jim lives in Clifton Park, New York, with his wife, Barbara; they have two daughters: Maria and Katrina.

Previous Works

Let's Go, Gaels – This novella tells the story of one week in the life of a 12-year-old boy. The story takes place in a Catholic school in upstate New York in 1964. As the week begins, the narrator is thinking about a speech he has to give in English class on Friday, a big basketball game on Saturday, and a trip to the movies on Saturday night. During the week, however, something happens that changes his life – and his outlook on life – forever. The event moves him further away from his innocent boyhood and closer to his eventual maturity as a man.

Mickey Mantle Day in Amsterdam – This novella is also about growing up. This particular story focuses on baseball and on baseball's biggest name in the 1950s and the 1960s. The story takes place during the summer of 1963 when Mantle is on the disabled list, recovering from a broken foot. When his car breaks down near the "Rug City," the 12-year-old narrator and his dad stop to help, and Mantle's Amsterdam adventure begins. By the time it ends, 24 hours later, both the narrator and the reader have learned a valuable lesson.

Things I Threw in the River: The Story of One Man's Life – In this novel, the first-person narrator lives near the Mohawk River in upstate New York during the 1950s, '60s, '70s, and '80s. He tells a series of related stories about what he threw into the river and why. The first story concerns an incident that occurs when the narrator is four years old, and the final story occurs in 1988 when he is 37. That final story is the most dramatic of all, takes up 50% of the novel, and is based on a real incident.

My Teacher's Password – Tom Sullivan is a 21-year-old college student, and he's in love with his creative writing professor – as well he should be. Margaret Cavellari is hot! She looks like a cross between Catherine Zeta-Jones and Penelope Cruz. Okay, so no one is really that hot, but Margaret is close. In addition, she's kind. She's funny. She's interesting. And she's a great teacher. So when Tom accidentally discovers her computer password, what will he do? Will he read her e-mail? Will he look at her pictures and her word-processing files? Will he go into her gradebook? Naturally, Tom Sullivan is curious. But is he also stupid? Of course he is. Read all about Tom's computer adventures in this contemporary novel.

Order Form

Please send to the following address:

Name _____

Address _____

City _____ State_____ Zip _____

Let's Go, Gaels	$5.95 x _____	copies = _____
Mickey Mantle Day in Amsterdam	$7.95 x _____	copies = _____
Things I Threw in the River	$9.95 x _____	copies = _____
My Teacher's Password	$9.95 x _____	copies = _____
Writing Is Hard	$19.95 x _____	copies = _____
Postage	$3.00 x _____	copies = _____
		Subtotal _____

Add appropriate sales tax.   _____

                                                    Total   _____

Please enclose a check for your order and mail to:

Mohawk River Press

P.O. Box 4095
Clifton Park, New York 12065-0850
518-383-2254
www.MohawkRiverPress.com

Made in the USA
Middletown, DE
31 August 2018